Chinese Hand Analysis

A practical guidebook for
physical, psychological and spiritual
diagnosis through hand analysis
focusing on the fundamental metaphysical teachings
of the Wu-Hsing method practised within
Chen Yen Esoteric Buddhism

Esoteric Master Ching Kang Szu
Head of the Chinese Wu Hsing traditions, photographed before his temple, circa 1912 by D.C. Graham. Reproduced by courtesy and permission of the Smithsonian Institute, Washington, D.C.

Chinese Hand Analysis

Shifu Terence Dukes

AQUARIAN

THE AQUARIAN PRESS
Wellingborough, Northamptonshire

UK edition first published 1988
First published in the USA by Samuel Weiser Inc. 1987

British Library Cataloguing in Publication Data

Dukes, Terence
Chinese hand analysis.
1. Palmistry
I. Title
133.6   BF921

ISBN 0-85030-745-7

*The Aquarian Press is part of the Thorsons Publishing Group,
Wellingborough, Northamptonshire, NN8 2RQ, England*

Printed in Great Britain by St Edmundsbury Press,
Bury St Edmunds, Suffolk.

To my parents
Catherine and John Dukes
for their love and devotion
to their strangest son

Contents

About the Author

Shifu Terence Dukes is President of the Cheirological Society of Britain where he also conducts seminars in the art of hand analysis. From a very early age, he was exposed to esoteric teachings of many kinds. Probably his most important influence was the Shingon Acarya Fa Tao Meng (Hotomo), a remarkable Master of Chinese mystical Buddhism. Terence Dukes has studied with Buddhist teachers from Japan, Korea, Thailand, Ceylon and Tibet, and is an Adept in the art of Kempo, natural medicine, cheirology, and Shingon ritual. He has taught at both Cambridge and Oxford Universities, and is the founder of the Kongoryuji Temple in Norfolk, and the Hakurenji Temple in London. His teaching places great importance on coinciding the mystical and the mundane within day-to-day life. Dukes shows clearly that spiritual studies are not 'out of this world', but part of it and aid all levels of life equally. He has a talent for making the often complicated principles of Shingon tradition accessible to students of all levels. He is the author of *No Nonsense Hand Reading, A Sourcebook of Shingon Buddhism in the Chinese Esoteric Tradition,* and *Teachings of Shingon Buddhism.*

Acknowledgments

I would like to express my appreciation and gratitude to all those members of the Cheirological Society who have helped me in my work, whether by contributing prints for our national files, or teaching students, raising funds, submitting research or books, and all the other little tasks which usually pass unnoticed. My thanks to you all.

I would also like to thank Maggie Dobson, Dylan Warren-Davis, and Priscilla Sherlock (nee Osband) for their work with the Society, and Ruth Cigman, who helped me make this a better book.

Preface

This work began when I was eight years old and first encountered divination in the form of teachings imparted me by my maternal grandmother, Edith Martha Engeham. Since then my studies and researches have taken me into the teachings of China, Tibet, India, Japan and the ancient Middle East. All of these countries have or had traditions relevant to hand analysis—some more consistent than others. During my travels and researches I took every opportunity to study with those deemed masters in arts which I considered relevant to my studies—the tale of those studies would warrant a book of their own. Finally I entered training in the esoteric Buddhist school and for many years since have maintained those studies.

Because of my earlier study of divinity in several forms and traditions, I came to realize some of the underlying but not necessarily unifying principles common to all those cultures which sought to eclipse and experience the integration of macrocosm and microcosm. Through my experience of Chinese Buddhism I came also to realize the significance of the metacosm. Since becoming a lecturer of the Cheirological Society, I have found myself constantly in the company of many who wish to perfect and project the noble art of cheirology.

In this work, some of my notes are presented for the edification of those students who seriously wish to master the art and its philosophy. I have included all that I feel relevant and of use to students, and I feel that every topic contained here needs to be fully understood by those who wish more than average skills. A great many themes are merely touched upon, but I have outlined the principles so readers should be able to enlarge upon them without much difficulty.

During my life I have been fortunate to have had contact from a very early age with those who have ventured beyond the usual limits of knowledge, and I have been able to observe and study such teachers in many different countries. Each showed me a little stone of the Great Wall of Wisdom.

In any study of the ancient esteemed masters it becomes obvious that all of those who were considered above average based their studies on or around some form of esoteric or spiritual teaching. These days it is difficult to find a teacher who really understands and has experienced such doctrines. Despite my own contacts with many European teachers it was not until I had studied Buddhism that I came to fully appreciate the implications of cheirological philosophy and practice. By becoming a disciple of one who had mastered the Chinese *Wu Hsing* method, and who could actually communicate it clearly, I was placed on a path that I have never since stopped treading. There is much to learn and time is swift, so all we students must make best use of our energies and reserve them for the real study of inner life itself. If through cheirology you come to understand a little of this life, you can give immeasurable aid to yourself and others.

In the fields of medical and psychological diagnosis much more has to be researched and discovered by us, as the available literature in English covers only very specialized areas, and also lacks firm spiritual basis. The limitations of such approaches are immense, for the criteria of analysis used are such that their holistic significance is totally obscured. In all my studies I have not yet encountered a theme of study which has not already been dealt with in our school at least 400 years ago and often earlier. We have still much to discover in the past treatises, let alone future speculations. If we cannot yet understand ourselves, how can we hope to understand others? Such simple truths are easily overlooked by those of specialized studies but should never be forgotten by students of Wu Hsing traditions. In this work I have tried to avoid specialized terms as much as possible, for I believe, as did Kant, that one must exhaust the old terms before commencing the new. However, some have been unavoidable purely for reasons of total accuracy, so I must beg forgiveness for them as and when they occur. I have written the practical sections of this work in the Wu Hsing tradition without reference to any other text or book whatsoever. However, I list works which I have studied over the years and which have developed my concepts and presentations a little. Many of the Taoist works mentioned, although ancient, contribute very little to proper cheirology (though some are very popular in modern China). They can safely be ignored by serious researchers.

I have presented in this work the ancient Chinese system within which I trained, in a modern and Occidental language form, adding experiences and modifications of my own which were developed solely from those ancient teachings, and which have proved accurate and reliable over a number of years. The result is a non-theistic system of hand analysis based on Oriental principles and symbols quite readily applicable to modern life situations and thought. It deals with methods of health, psychological and vocational analysis which can be understood and acted upon by anyone.

Shifu T. Dukes
Kongoryuji Temple
Norfolk, England

PART ONE

Jumen Hsueh

Entering the Gates of Study

CHAPTER 1

An Introduction to Cheirology and the Prophetic Arts

In our modern, so-called "enlightened" times the prophetic arts are generally regarded as being the preoccupation of those not quite right in the head. The general attitude seems to be that those who do practice such arts need only a lack of intelligence and a gullible customer to make their art successful. The prophetic arts tend to get short shrift. But what about those who prophecy with contemporary social sanctions and acceptance?—the weather forecaster, medical doctors, political journalists and financial advisers to name a few. You may say, "but these people work from known facts,"—but what is fact to one is fiction to another. Facts are generally only opinions held by the majority and not universal truths. It is obvious that those who place more importance on spiritual facts do not necessarily hold a similar reverence for mundane values—they may be totally uninterested in them. In most cases, modern lifestyles appear to have made the need for prophecy less urgent or relevant. However, this appearance does not correspond to reality. If we think of the role the ancient seers played in society, we can observe that they acted as diagnosticians, psychotherapists, investment consultants, marriage brokers, medical practitioners, advisers and family friends. All of these functions have now become the realm of specialist practitioners.

There are still areas of the world where the correctly trained seer is considered indispensable to both the mundane and spiritual life—India, Tibet, Malaysia and Africa are a few examples. In these countries, the importance of acknowledging the influences of metaphysical forces has never been eclipsed by the development of modern, over-specialized sciences. Rather, the seer occupies an official, if not state-appointed, position. Many consider these countries "backward" from a materialistic point of view, but Western scholars and academics still spend many years studying their spiritual doctrines. We can truly say that more hours have been put into the research of Oriental spiritual culture than into Occidental technology! Westerners have been fascinated by Oriental beliefs and practices. Every significant religion we have studied comes from the mid or far Eastern lands.

The "one who really sees" (seer) and "the one who calms with speech" (sooth-sayer) have and fulfill a position vitally important to modern day life, whether they now take the role of a Secretary of State, international diplomat, psychiatrist or investment tycoon. Much of our civilization has been built upon the concepts which were created indirectly by "oracles" (those who can listen to the spirit).

These oracles, both Greek and Etruscan, were practitioners of the art of listening to and understanding the speech of the infinite powers. Oracles were held in great respect in all ancient civilizations, and were usually part of the ruling court—they were consulted on all matters of state. The ancient Greeks wrote down many of the more famous pronouncements of the oracles, and recorded the gradual growth in power of these practitioners. The Greeks called the art of prophecy by the overall name of *Mantike*, and distinguished between prophecy that used techniques (*Technos Mantike*) and prophecy that did not (*Atechnos Mantike*). This latter method was considered more pure and accurate. Technos Mantike referred to the techniques of prediction which used intermediary objects—such as bones or animal sacrifice. Atechnos meant the art of prophecy that relied upon nothing but the perceptive skill of the practitioner

Many of our modern problems have been created by ignoring or attempting to invalidate these sources of knowledge. It is important for modern humanity to attain self-understanding—thus we will be able to free ourselves from environmental stress or dependence. Only with freedom from such self-destruction can we truly be masters of our own lives and freely aid others in need. This compassionate attitude is the only true reason for commencing study and it is the only attitude through which we can attain mastery of hand analysis itself.

FATE AND THE MODERN IMAGE

Some people believe that we each have an inescapable fate ordained by deity and that to interfere with such fate is morally and ethically wrong. In Chinese Buddhism such a viewpoint is termed *determinist*. This viewpoint, although sincerely held, ignores many basic facts about cheirology itself and reveals a degree of unfamiliarity with its practice. *Interference* I understand as meaning prediction of future events in the life of the subject. Many cheirologists refuse to indulge in, nor do they accept the validity of, the predictive aspects of cheirology. This is as it should be; each of us must rest within that level to which we are most suited, and if that does not include an acceptance of the possibility of prediction so much the better. In cheirology, experience is the key factor, and if we deny the ability to judge the outcome of a particular condition, then that ability must be denied to us. Medical doctors do not deny predictive abilities—they call it prognosis. Do determinists visit doctors? I expect they do.

But, let us return again to this idea of fate itself: Could it not be that it is the fate of a subject to actually learn of it him- or herself? Biblical sources describe mantic consultation as a common feature of ancient days and, although condemning certain forms of practice, accept its validity as an art. We must reach the conclusion that *mantika*, or prophecy, is a valid art in its own right, but that only certain persons were permitted to use it. Such persons were invariably the "holy ones" of a particular religious denomination and were presumably upright, serious and responsible. In European tradition, we often find the opposite in the form of the palmist. It is not surprising that the negative biblical quotations would be invoked against such people. Unfortunately, much of the modern image of cheirology still lies surrounded by the image of the palmist and everything that the term evokes in the mind. Contemporary society does not equate a scientist with an alchemist nor a doctor with a "leech man." It seems, at least to me, unreasonable to do so in the case of a modern cheirologist. I'm afraid we need a much better and wider public image.

THE MORALITY OF CHEIROLOGY

Cheirology has as its context universal symbolism, and therefore can be embraced by persons of all ages, creeds or race. There is something within it for everyone. The emphasis within the traditional Chinese school is that of embracing all other viewpoints and thus developing within oneself the state of universal being. Such a person cannot be bound by any particular frame of reference nor claimed by any special creed as its own, for the universal being encompasses all creations of humanity or cosmos and finds a resting place amid all equally. The more dogmatic or exclusive one is, the more difficult it is to fully understand both the method and the technique of cheirology. Embracing the study can and should be a remedy to elitism or sectarian viewpoints.

Continual practice of cheirology will bring greater understanding of how the elements manifest within the life of yourself and others. It provides a valuable starting point for an explanation of disharmony in human life patterns. We can see therefore that the understanding of cheirology is simultaneously both self and others transmutative.

This concept of self-transmutation is not new, nor is it particularly Oriental. Many European religious systems have as their goal a special kind of self-transmutation; indeed the Roman Catholic Mass includes a form of it.

Differences do, however, exist in the manner in which we describe or define this self-transmutation, but the most important aspect we consider here is the actual experience of such transmutation in the lives of those we aid via our practice of cheirology. If we can free others of useless and self-imposed restrictions, we are giving them access to a fuller and freer understanding of life itself.

HEURISM AND ONTOLOGICAL PROCESSES

The word *heurism* stems from the same root as Archimedes' *eureka* (I have found it!). It describes a particular attitude towards study. Heuristic study is self-programmed and assessed. It is a program of advancement in which tests or examinations are seen only as guides to self-evaluation. A student should understand what he or she knows. Apart from actually living full time with the teacher, it is impossible for another person to completely assess the student's talents. Heuristic study stresses self-responsibility and encourages independence, for both qualities are vital to the potential teacher or student. By encouraging prior consideration of one's course of study, heurism helps develop the calm clear-mindedness attained by the masters.

Heurism also gets rid of the emotional or psychological dependence which so easily develops in those willing to immerse themselves totally within a structured, rigid system of education. The motive of heurism is similar in nature to that of meditation: it is intended to develop independent, self-experienced insight into one's real nature. Heuristic studies are not opposed to the rigid educational systems. They take most effect within these, for by re-orientating a student's attitude towards self-evaluation, they grant him or her freedom, along with responsibility, from the system itself—and release the student from useless social demands and evaluations.

Heurism is not an excuse for slackness nor is it a means of evading achievements when followed properly, although weak-willed students can sabotage its good effects as effectively as they can other systems. The onus is primarily on the student's motivation. Heurism is a very ancient and very modern concept. Ancient races based their knowledge on direct experience; the best modern scientists also do this. A course designed to encourage students to follow the guidelines suggested by a tutor continually develops the participants' awareness of the object of study and the subject experiencing such awareness.

The ancient Oriental Buddhists distinguished very carefully between apparent and ultimate reality, and showed most clearly that much of our understanding arose from taking the apparent for the real. That which is ultimately real is beyond predication, existing only as a concept to those who have not attained its experience. When we set about approaching this experience, the catalyst that enables us to realize it is, in fact, our own mind. In order to progress we must come to know this mind very well, not just its obvious or unthought of aspects, but also its very essence. Ontology— the study of the nature of being—is thus inseparable from individual progress. It is assumed throughout the initial phases of research that we actually understand what we experience; such an assumption is foolish, to say the least. Experience can often be "experienceless" in nature if we do not understand who or what experiences it.

The Buddhist monk Sangharakshita has a masterful taxonomy for non-experience. He describes two manifestations of this as alienated awareness and integrated awareness. Alienated awareness is awareness without genuine experience of awareness. Integrated awareness involves this experience of awareness. True heurism leads to autonomous and integrated awareness of the subject matter in hand. Pseudo-heurism leads nowhere.

All too often a field of study can be incompletely understood. Such partial mastery can be at best self-deceptive and at worst dangerous. The yoga student who identifies consciousness with the body is already divorced from yoga. The martial arts practitioner who mistakenly believes techniques are effective realizes they are not when he is about to be killed by an assailant, and his students will probably fare the same. The cheirologist who gives clients mistaken, ill-timed or incomplete guidance has already increased suffering. Incomplete self-understanding continually modifies or inhibits its possessor and misleads its recipients. At every level we should never rest content with the praise or approval of others. Nor should we praise ourselves. Heuristic attitude, by invalidating the environment, causation, and the effect of self-deception, serves as a cautionary method of attaining real experience and understanding of others. Only from such beginnings can we begin genuine study.

CHAPTER 2

The Development and Nature of Chinese Divination

In most systems of hand analysis, each palmar marking is given one special meaning, or area, of import. Because of this, hand analysts have had to memorize the features of many hundreds of possible combinations of lines. Those who have persevered in this task often find markings in the hand which defy explanation and therefore have to ignore their implications in hand analysis. This "textbook" memorization of hundreds of facts creates an attitude towards interpreting hands that precludes harmonious development. While it is necessary to memorize certain fundamental structures, the Chinese Wu Hsing method utilizes principle (*Li*) rather than features. When the principle is understood, it is possible to analyze cheirologically any formation present within the palm and to deduce its causal factors. The concept of principle is unknown in European hand analysis, and consequently those aspects of study developed directly from an understanding of *Li* are unknown and unknowable by ordinary researchers.

The study and adoption of the principles of the Buddhist method require that we conceive palmar lines as simultaneous manifestations or reflections of physical, psychological, and spiritual energies. By diagnosing these energies via their concomitant manifestations, we can understand their quality and import within the actions of body, mind and spirit. At its highest level this understanding is termed *Chih*.

Chih and Li must always be developed equally, for they are co-dependent and inseparable. When you are able to see and recognize a palmar formation, Li permits you to realize its significance. Chih enables you to know, understand, and articulate that significance in an appropriate manner. Both Li and Chih are capable of varying descriptive explanations according to the circumstances or situations from which they are considered. However, the consistent meaning of Li within Wu Hsing method is that described as graduated materiality (at the mundane level), or as macro-microcosmic integration (at the holistic level). Implicit in the concept of Li is the possibility of experiencing a greater and freer viewpoint of existence at all levels. Implicit in the concept of Chih is the ability of a student to

Figure 1. Shakyamuni Buddha, the Indian founder of Buddhism and all its subsequent cultural arts.

overcome limitations of all forms and to attain transcendental understanding of all mind/body experiences. Only through such development can one come to truly know others.

As the Chinese nation nurtured Buddhist teachings, the native words Li and Chih came to be replaced by other, more Buddhistic terms. Li became *Fa*—the teachings of enlightenment—and Chih became *Pan Jo*—transcendental wisdom. These latter terms have specifically Buddhist spiritual overtones, but as hand analysis was utilized among the general populace, the native terminology was equally adhered to. Li and Chih became the common property of Buddhists and Shamans alike. With the use of Chen Yen integrative and esoteric Buddhism, Li and Fa, and Chih and Pan Jo became synonymous, along with many other adopted linguistic terms.

Within the esoteric temples, the art of hand analysis became a metaphor for spiritual evolution, each feature of analysis forming paradigms of Buddha consciousness and spiritual development. In a manner similar in nature to European alchemy, the mastery of self-understanding through an intermediary art was considered as valid as direct doctrinal immersion. Such teachings are essentially tantric in essence, and indeed it was directly through Tantric Buddhism that the Wu Hsing technique of explication was developed, refined and taught in many different manners.

Within China the art of hand analysis developed initially from earlier traditions developed within the Indian Vedic religion and was modified by Buddhist thought. Native Chinese methods of physiognomy (Jen Hsiang) also included a primitive form of palmar analysis. When these two streams of teaching were integrated within the early esoteric schools, cheirology as we now understand it developed rapidly. On the whole such traditions were kept secret and not divulged to the general enquirer. This was a wise move prompted more by spiritual aspiration than anything else. The monk mystics had seen that the ordinary folk farmers were very superstitious and would have appropriated the core of cheirological data, creating traditions unrelated to spiritual development. This proved the case with later Taoistic versions of hand analysis. What we popularly call Taoism was, more often than not, a folk religion far removed from the philosophy of Lao Tzu and his contemporaries—but the later Taoist attitudes certainly influenced the attitudes of Chinese shamans and caused them to adopt or adapt holistic attitudes in both the study and practice of their arts.

The refusal to separate a human being from the environment, or one part of the body from other parts, was a teaching common to both exoteric Taoism and esoteric Buddhism within China. In palmar medical diagnosis (Shou Chen-Tuan), this unification is most evident. The inter-reflection of each action within the human body is indeed similar in nature to the interaction taking place within the heavens. For Taoists the two were integral; each caused the other. Omens or celestial occurrences were seen as portents of earthly events and in fact many of the disasters which did occur in China were presaged by such phenomena as solar eclipses, meteoric storms or

Figure 2. The Buddha, shown here in his Chinese form of "all fulfilling wisdom," flanked by his emanated bodies taking the form of a Chinese sage and a Japanese pilgrim.

comets. Even European history records the appearance of Haley's Comet a the time of the Norman invasion of England. Chinese astrology (Hsien Hsing or Hsing Hsiang) was in fact developed from omenic art. Its native development gave it a form quite distinct from the Indian form, and Chinese astrology still remains socially, rather than personally, orientated in present times. It is a study designed for state ministers rather than the common folk.

The astrological data used tangentially within Wu Hsing cheirology are developed and influenced from the Indian form, only marginally including native Chinese concepts. Likewise, the system of elemental classification utilized stems from the Indian esoteric systems (Pancatattva Tantra) developed at the Buddhist University of Nalanda in Northern India. There is also evidence to show that in the eighth century A.D. masters from southern India and Ceylon gave new impetus to the esoteric, philosophical structure in China. The period from 500 B.C., which included the beginnings of Buddhism, saw the teachings of people like Pythagoras who instructed the mystically orientated athletes and boxers of the early Olympic Games in a similar set of doctrines. Some 1,000 years later, within China, Tantric Buddhism produced a system which also included esoteric physical arts of movement and unarmed combat. At least one of the historical Buddha's immediate disciples became interested in Buddhism solely through awareness of the physical bearing and movements of a Buddhist monk; physiognomy was a very ancient practice in Indian life.

In China all methods of analyzing physical forms were known generally as *Hsiang*. Specialized studies of particular parts of the body were

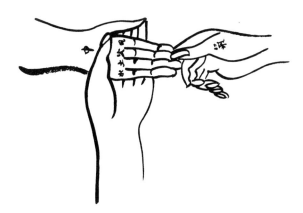

Figure 3. Feeling the energy in the finger phalanges. An illustration from an ancient Chinese text, circa 18th century A.D. Manuscript in the library of Kongoryuji Temple, Norfolk, England.

described by a prefix attached to this term. Thus hand analysis became Shou Hsiang (Shou equals hands); facial analysis became Jen Hsiang (Jen equals person). Modern day Japanese mystics still use these terms to describe arts which they first brought from the Chinese mainland in the 7th century A.D., even though the term *Hsiang* has now ceased to convey its original meaning in contemporary speech. The Chinese prognosticators (*Wu*) were deemed so only because they had mastered various forms of Hsiang, which they practiced among the general populace.

Buddhist masters of Shou Hsiang were usually medical doctors and practiced their art primarily within the religious environment. Thus, in general, Chinese natives were used to seeing the *Wu* rather than the monk when they wished to know their future. Monks would be consulted for effective medical treatment or diagnosis. Although the events and features of Chines history later changed many of these roles, Shou Hsiang remained firmly in the hands of esoteric Buddhists while Jen Hsiang and other arts became common property of all inhabitants of China.

This is not to say that Shou Hsiang was unknown among non-Buddhist. Shamans, Wu and Taoists did possess forms of their own, but this was not an art rooted in spiritual experience as it was with the Buddhists. It was instead merely an extension of the Taoist descriptions of change projected on to the hands. Thus we find hands being made to fit the I-Ching trigrams rather than the reverse in the Taoist textbooks.

Esoteric Buddhism put great stress on hands in general—one third of its traditional studies were of ritual hand gestures (Yin). Certain positions and poses were related to different levels of consciousness and not, as in the case of Taoists, stars, divinities or nature spirits. The extension of this object of study resulted in the birth of the Buddhist meditational boxing (Chuan-Fa). The art of the hands produced paintings of *Man-To-Lo* (Mandalas) by means of which the teachings were conveyed and preserved in symbolic shape by chromatic form. We can observe consequently that within certain forms of Chinese tradition the human hand was regarded as a very special source of knowledge. In the medieval Chinese text entitled *The Golden Lotus*, which forms a saga of the events in the life of a noble family, a prognosticator (named Wu) refers continually to physiognomical features in his diagnosis of the family's illnesses and fortunes.

CHAPTER 3

Wu Hsing Cheirology

Hands as a whole represent a matrix for personal development, a usually unrecognized yet potential paradigm of the experience and discoveries available to the individual. This unrecognized and potential condition has been described in many religious systems and philosophies as a *plenum void*. The "blank" hand represents the matriarchal divinity, a womb awaiting to produce. Lines represent the patriarchal divinity, clarifying, ordering and expressing the realized potential. As any spiritual system based on duality cannot ignore its own constituent polarities, so likewise does hand analysis acknowledge, encompass and express such polarities. These take form in the analysis of shape and structure, known as *cheirognomy*, and the analysis of lineal assessment, known as *cheiromancy*. The former is the seed, the latter the fruit. It is interesting to note that in the various spiritual systems that were based on female, or goddess, worship cheiromancy was most popular. In patriarchal systems, cheirognomy was prominent.

LEVELS OF STUDY

The art and craft of Wu Hsing (five elements) cheirology has four major fields of activity. These can be classified according to their original Greek and Chinese equivalent nomenclature (more is said of these origins later). The primary classification is as follows:

Mantic (Hsiang): This is the general study of hands with a view to developing from this study a prognostic awareness of the patterns and events of everyday life. The mantic method also covers "inspired" prophecies loosely centered on hand analysis—the realm of "palmistry," as commonly understood.

Personal (Chih): The study of hands with a view to understanding and evaluating the nature of human character and consciousness.

Therapeutic (Yi): The study of hands and their morphological patterns with a view to utilizing such studies as diagnostic techniques. This classification also includes therapies applied to or originating from the hands.

Metaphysical (Li): The study of hands in order to determine something of the structure and order of the metaphysical principles perceived within human existence.

Each of these general orientations to study can be subdivided into studies which specialize in hand lines, form, or combinations of both. From these combinations, twelve patterns emerge (each area having three forms). The third and fourth methods must, of necessity, include related studies or arts of a non-cheirological nature. Each of these areas is important to those who wish to fully understand the art of cheirology.

In any serious consideration of cheirological analysis, several levels of understanding become evident. Certainly within the Wu Hsing method, these levels are pre-eminent. (In the European versions these levels do not appear to be recognized or appreciated correctly.) We can distinguish these levels quite easily by considering the import drawn from any one specific feature of cheirology. When, for example, we consider any element line found in the palm, the following points can be observed concerning it:

- We can attribute import to the line's presence or absence in the hand.

- We can attribute import to the direction or orientation of the line within the hand.

- We can attribute import to special markings, deviations, endings and commencement area of the line.

These three factors are found in the better forms of hand analysis going under the name of "palmistry." However, in Wu Hsing, additional features may be found such as:

- Implications of the element balance of the hand as relating to the line's appearance and termination.

- Consideration of the precise depth and nature of the line irrespective of direction.

- Accurate correlations between health balance and imbalance, and cause and effect of illness.

- A quantitative assessment of the line's import in relation to other connected lines.

- A qualitative assessment of the line's import related to a multi-dimensional conception of being.

• The relationship of the line to specific value or chronological patterns such as season, celestial rhythm, and physical metabolism.

• Explanations as to why the particular line is there both in terms of the subject in question and in metaphysical terms.

• Explanations as to why specific deviations, patterns and markings should occur.

• A practical method of evaluating mental and symbolic paradigmatic experiences vial lineal manifestation.

There are several more features which could be mentioned but it is apparent that ordinary palmistry can only concern itself superficially with what is in the palm, whereas our cheirology teaches the source and fundamental meanings of such manifestations.

WU HSING TAXONOMY AND SYMBOLISM

It can be seen that the Wu Hsing description of the four aspects within hand analysis gives a much clearer view of what is to be achieved within the study. Such clarity is essential at the onset of research and discovery in order to channel one's energy into paths which are useful and formative. Popular palmistry, lacking a specific taxonomy, has meandered into too many areas and dissipated much of its import by doing so. Each of the four aspects outlined may become special areas of study and practice and it is necessary eventually to traverse each of them in order to achieve a balanced and harmonious understanding of cheirology.

Table 1. The Three Stages of Study

Stage One Four Fields	Stage Two Three Periods	Stage Three Four Imports
Cheiromorphognomy	Analysis, Diagnosis, Prognosis	of Mind, Body, Emotion, Spirit
Cheiromorphomancy	Analysis, Diagnosis, Prognosis	of Mind, Body, Emotion, Spirit
Cheirogrammeognomy	Analysis, Diagnosis, Prognosis	of Mind, Body, Emotion, Spirit
Cheirogrammeomancy	Analysis, Diagnosis, Prognosis	of Mind, Body, Emotion, Spirit

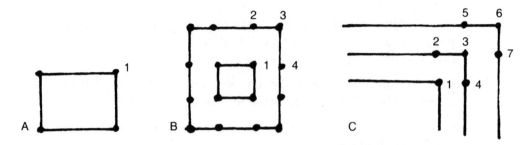

Figure 4. The three stages of study shown as a mandala: a) shows Stage One, representing the four fields of cheirological analysis; b) represents Stage Two, developed to include the three periods, making each corner a miniature replica of the original pattern; c) here we see Stage Three, wherein the four imports are added so that each corner is replicating the original form, and creating an extra border.

Figure 5. The Mantolo, or mandala. This represents the four approaches to reality utilized in cheirology and esoteric Buddhism. The pagoda of five shapes, representing the elements, is positioned in the four directions. Each shape ties with a square, representing its range of cause and effect. The intermediary squares between each pagoda describe different qualities and forms of interacting energies. The Chinese characters represent the relationships between the three time periods: Brilliant Light (wisdom), Mind, and Absence of Ego. Everything represented in an artistic mandala is also represented in the human hands.

The name "cheirology" is an umbrella term of Greek origin referring to four sub-studies. These are known in Chinese as the Shi T'ien (Four Fields) of investigation. In Classical Greek these would be termed as follows:

Cheiromorphognomy: The study and science of interpreting hand shape and form. The Chinese equivalent is Shou Hsing Chih.

Cheiromorphomancy: The actual interpretation of hand shape in order to determine prognostic import (Shou Hsing Hsiang).

Cheirogrammeognomy: The study of the lineal formations found on the palmar surface (Shou Hsien Chih).

Cheirogrammeomancy: The interpretation of lineal formations in order to determine prognostic import (Shou Hsien Hsiang).

We can subdivide each of the above into three areas of inquiry known in Chinese as San Hou (the Three Periods).

1. Analysis of past trends or conditions (Hsien Chen)

2. Diagnosis of the present condition (Tsai Chen)

3. Prognosis derived from consideration of 1 and 2 (Lai Chen)

The final level of understanding relates to the particular field of import we are to consider in relation to the two preceding stages. Known as Shi Tung (the Four Imports), this generally covers the following:

Mind: Psychological condition and personal level (Hsin).

Body: Physiological condition and quality (Shen).

Emotion: Orientations stemming from mind and body (I).

Spirit: Metaphysical influences or balances common to all levels (Chi).

Thus each of the Four Fields that form cheirology contains 36 aspects. Looking at Table 1 we can see that the total number of aspects for each of the Four Fields is 36; and the total number of all possible aspects is thus 144. In the esoteric Wu Hsing tradition these stages are represented symbolically by a mandala (a picture or set of artistic and spiritual symbols). These stages are shown in figure 4. Mandala in Chinese is known as Mantolo. Figure 5 is one example of the Mantolo.

This artistic format is very important to recognize, for within Chen Yen Buddhism the Mantolo became the sole method of preserving teachings. In

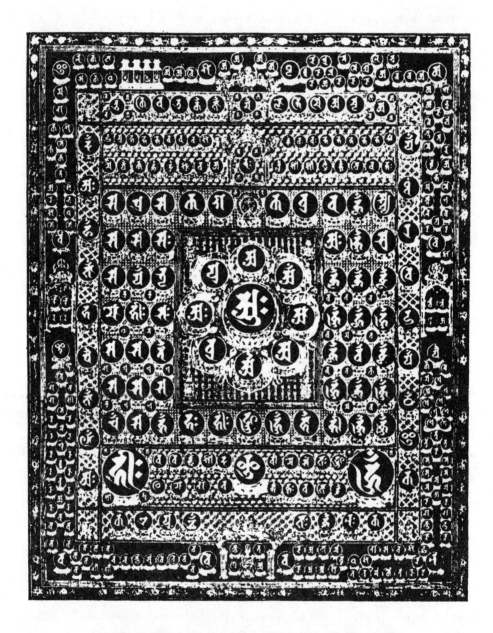

真言宗金剛雷電派

Figure 6. An esoteric mandala of the Shingon Sect. This one describes the various powers and Buddha knowledge as they manifest in human experience. From the author's collection.

the Wu Hsing school, the Mantolo were passed from teacher to pupil over each generation. It was by studying their structure that the student became familiar with the spiritual meanings inherent within cheirology (see figure 6). Without this spiritual understanding, progress is not possible. One further symbol is used in Chen Yen Buddhism and in effect represents the integration of all five elements. This is the To-Pa (Stupa) shown in figure 7. Each of the special geometrical shapes attributed to the elements is shown as a complete design. The To-Pa also represents the body of a Buddha—that is, an enlightened being who has achieved mastery over the elements at all levels. The To-Pa became a common graveyard symbol for Chen Yen adherents, and gave birth to an artistically refined architectural form—the Pagoda—which is known throughout the world. The next time you see a picture of a Pagoda pause to reflect that you are observing a direct result of esoteric symbology and that the shape you see is one form of the Buddha, the elements, and the human hand.

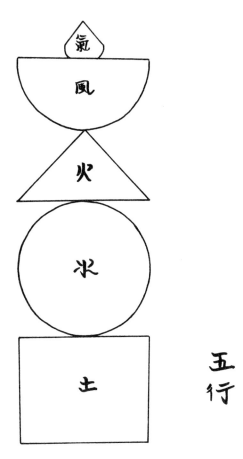

Figure 7. The To-Pa.

Both the Pagoda and Mantolo are exoteric representations of esoteric principles, which are based on structure and trans-symbolism. Complementary symbols are used to describe the gradual refinement of consciousness until it approaches or realizes transcendental wisdom. Thus the concept of gradual attainment is suggested, as opposed to the "sudden" enlightenment found in Southern Chinese Zen (Ch'an) meditation. This suggestion is related to what is known as the "Principle of Graduated Materiality," which is based on the idea that the elements possess a diminishing solidarity and thus show metaphorically the advance from solid ignorance to vacuous wisdom.

CHAPTER 4

Elements and the Principle of Graduated Materiality

Since the dawn of human self-consciousness, we have used various tools or methods of understanding. One of these was the tool of natural association; that is, allying an unknown with a known and seeking to find some connective factor through which greater understanding could be gained. Nature itself became the first known "slide rule." The seasons, the material elements, etc., were all related to human situations, events, or temperaments. From this co-relation magic and religion developed. Astrology gave birth to astronomy, alchemy to chemistry, and what was originally recognized through faith and sensitivity became subject to newly created "laws" based upon the principle of reproducibility.

Certain subjects resisted this new mode of ascertaining validity—for example, occultism and certain types of philosophy and healing. Proponents of these arts, as indeed teachers of the original arts from which the later sciences developed, considered the reproducibility criterion itself as invalid.

The development of "scientific" criteria was admirable, for it gave a needed emphasis to criticism and development. It forced the sham practitioner out of business and made accessible to many people certain fundamental facts of life. However, and unfortunately, most science began and ended with material substances. Its first and basic dialectic sprang from a material grammar which, although it appealed to the intellect, did not enrich the spirit of the research worker. Instead it seemed to bind him even more closely to the rules he was inventing in order to explain or demonstrate his discoveries. The "esoteric" originators (as they were later termed) of the arts from which the sciences sprang explained that the material criterion was in fact only one of many, and the esotericist, in holistic appreciation, described differing levels of equal validity, all of which could be experienced.

With the formation of such teachings an enrichment of language was necessary, both to elucidate the processes or stages being described and to hide the process itself from "outsiders." Remember that many of the original and later sciences were considered evil by the early churches and governments. Since many of these enriched language forms were based on natural rhythms, an approximation was conceived to reflect natural synchronicities or phenomena. The elements were among these, as were the seasons. Each was used by Orient and Occident alike. Although many of these enriched languages later developed sophisticated language forms, many also relied solely on oral transmission of the symbolism involved—linguistic or otherwise. This successfully prevented the development of arts (such as philosophy, theology, etc.), which were dependent upon literal study instead of living experience. It made certain that the direct personal element was never separated from what was being studied.

The understanding attained by those who devoted the greater part of their lives to the practice and experience of such arts was later termed "mystical" by some academics. These mystical understandings were not directly communicable, or able to be appreciated in the by now usual manner of classroom, book, or other media. In fact, those natural wisdoms precluded the type of environment later generated by scientists and academics. We find in history that most of our greatest exponents of the so-called mystical sciences lived simple, natural lives in the countryside. Not only religious mystics but also the originators of early sciences, political figures, philosophers and doctors of medicine all thrived when attuned to unspoiled naturals rhythms and energies.

OLD HANDS AND NEW HANDS

Ancient humanity used both symbol and paradigm to explain and interpret the world. Our hands serve us more than any other limb. It is the instrument of our minds, the executor of our thoughts. It is not surprising that sooner or later careful attention should have been turned to its symbolism. Perhaps because the hand naturally divides itself into two parts—fingers and palm—those religious systems which concerned themselves with theism and a singular divinity missed its dualistic suggestions. Such systems did not, in general, come to recognize the value of the hand as a source of spiritual edification. Their concern was with a universe of a singular, omnipotent deity or emanation. Consequently the value of individuated sources in that emanation could not be appreciated fully, nor could the concept of pantheism and its inevitable concomitant anthropomorphism be accepted or recognized. Those spiritual systems which did accept or teach both multiple manifestation and reflection or presence of deities also produced an environment conducive to the development of cheirology or related arts as spiritual Docetics reflecting the "source." Reflection occurred continuously, whether recognized or not. Those with perception benefited

from their understanding of it. Both Chinese and ancient Greek folk medicine utilized the principle of reflection in medical diagnosis, seeing the
action or condition of one part of the body in another. At a higher level of
manifestation they saw the course of history reflected in the stars and the
stars reflected in the body. Once this primary connection had been made,
evolutionary concepts could begin.

One of the most significant of these concepts was that termed by cheirologists *Graduated Materiality*. This refers to a fundamental view of existence
which sees all things a representing various degrees of interconnection
between the five elements: earth, water, fire, air and ether. These elements
serve to describe processes of being which manifest in multiple and variable
patterns, at many different levels of existence. The recognition of such patterns within the hands and the capacity to interpret them constitutes the
basis of cheirology.

THE PRINCIPLE OF GRADUATED MATERIALITY

In studying the principle of graduated materiality, we can realize that over
the ages, mankind has always sought to explain the internal and external
environment by means of symbols. One pre-eminent symbolism was that
of the elements. These were projected into different areas of experience
and, by working from a basic premise of five main manifestations, certain
correspondences were noted between natural and human phenomena.
Both Taoists and alchemists used this principle. The medieval alchemists
developed their system of balances under the title of "The Doctrine of Signatures." The Chinese Taoist joined the Indian energies of fire and air
together terming them *Yang*. Water and earth were termed *Yin* energy.
What applies to yang also applies to fire and air elements, etc. When reading Chinese texts you should bear this in mind. The four elements are in
fact much clearer methods of understanding the forces of human consciousness. This important principle of reflection developed in both Orient
and Occident equally, and this trait—seeing one situation within another—
was the characteristic of many a great sage. For example, to many, the skies
especially reflected human endeavor. Planets were reflections of thoughts.
Astrology was developed from this. In all early cultures, astrolatry (the worship of stars as deities) preceded astrology. In the same way, physiolatry
(the worship of parts of the body as deities) came before physiognomy. In
fact, it is a recognizable trait that the ancients worshipped before seeking
to understand. Understanding brought the development of the principle
of reflection.

Proper cheirology did not develop from astrology, as is commonly
believed, though later it often adopted astrological symbols (i.e., planets).

Historically, even these symbols did not have a constant value to astrolatrists themselves. Many ancients believed in the planets as important gods; others saw them only as minor emanations of mundane deities. Their import varied widely from culture to culture.

The theistic pantheons necessary for cheirology to commence had already existed *prior* to the systemization of astrology. Indeed there are, in both India and China, cave carvings of hands and palms bearing distinct lineal patterns which pre-date any astrological chart or reference work. In trying to discover the beginnings of cheirology we should not turn to astrology or any other extra-terrestrial source. Instead we should look at the ever present human faculty of inquiry and comparison. Because two are common to all races of humanity, we can discern many rational environments which could have produced the attitude conducive to an inter-relational study. China, India, Persia, Egypt and the Middle East all retained factors necessary to, or supportive of, its study within their spiritual systems.

In Buddhism we would turn to the later tantric movement rather than the Theravada Sect; in Hinduism to the Samkhya or Dvaita rather than the Advaita Yogas; in Christianity to the Gnostics rather than the European Papal Catholics; in Judaism, to the post-12th century Kabbalah rather than the Orthodox Torah, Targums or Talmud. As long as we accept manifestation as a principle of life—irrespective of whether we call that manifestation by a name—so will arts such as cheirology develop and spiritually enrich the lives of those who study them. Reflecting the cosmic principle into body and mind enables each to understand more about the other, and to perceive the significance of the connection between them. In China the nature of this connection was generally conceived by Taoists as dualistic—a connection of an active nature (*Yang*) and passive nature (*Yin*). Many aspects of each type were considered together with their interconnection. Certain acts, events, emotions and other phenomena were at home within a specific polarity. Others were not. Thus the effect of one being in, or of, its antagonist was potentially destructive and undermining. Only if and when this was recognized could steps be taken to remedy the situation.

All progression is seen as a result of attaining a balance between these polarities at all levels of existence. How we do so depends on the method used to approach and understand them. Our form of cheirological philosophy developed from the school know in China as the *Wu Hsing* (five elements). This doctrine of esoteric Buddhist physiognomy utilized the elements and their paradigms as a primary and spiritual architectonical source. It elucidates a quadripartite elemental nature and effect of energy within the body and mind. Some other forms of a reflective nature can be seen in action with homeopathy, Buddhist yoga, health diagnosis, Gnostic Christianity, and Greek or Roman theology. Each of these selects a specific area of activity to work within in order to discover and interpret the balance of energy within their boundaries. To cheirologists, the area of reflection used is the human hand. This forms the "mirror" of existence through which we perceive and understand our real nature. Any school of any art which does not accommodate this principle of reflection is imbalanced and inaccurate. The inter-reflective principle extends into every area of human endeavor and experience. Philosophy, religion, medicine, dietetics, movement meditation, healing, construction and metaphysics are among some of them.

When we observe hands we must be aware that each function we can see represented in them possesses an inner and an outer aspect. Each line representing an outer manifestation of consciousness also has a line reflecting an inner manifestation. Each line representing an organ of the body has its reflection describing either another organ involved in its activity or the inner function of that same organ. When you learn the value of correspondences, reflections can be fully understood; in fact the whole art of cheirology is but a study of particular reflections hermeneutically stated and presented within the limits of mind, body and communication.

The Five Levels of Cheirology

Cheirology mainly concerns itself with five different aspects of human life, which we term the Five Levels. These describe the most immediately relevant and cogent aspects of our experience with which we are involved in day to day life. Each of these five levels represents an important facet of our being, and a level that cannot be ignored or otherwise misused without rapid repercussions within that or another of the levels. The five levels also represent the ascent of humanity from primary stages of evolution to that of divinelike wisdom. They are as follows:

Physical	=	Earth
Emotional	=	Water
Creative	=	Fire
Intellectual	=	Air
Spiritual	=	Ether

Each of these aspects can form a special focus of cheirological study and analysis, and illuminates particular parts of our nature:

Physical	Physical condition and quality
	Disease and infectious predisposition
	Organic or postural malfunction
Emotional	Ability to share and experience with others
	Creative and artistic appreciation
	The development of the personal ideal

Creative	Vocational or professional aptitudes Mechanical or organizational abilities Personal drive and leadership qualities
Intellectual	Development of personal knowledge and education Linguistic or communicative techniques The ability to develop panoramic understanding
Spiritual	The inner development of practicable wisdom and compassion Understanding of human and natural energies The ability to transcend human consciousness

In Chinese cheirology each of these aspects serves as a common denominator of the whole. From any one of these all others may be determined providing you understand the interpretive key to be employed.

The five elements serve to represent the boundaries of the cheirologist's understanding of both the world and his or her relationship to it. In fact, within cheirology, every single process or outcome of experience can be enclosed within the elemental descriptive reference. By becoming increasingly familiar with the multi-level manifestations of this reference you will both deepen and broaden your personal understanding of the five levels and absorb their significance into your personal experience of human activity.

THE ELEMENTS AS SYMBOLS OF EXPERIENCE

It does not seem strange that a basic method of describing a common principle, that of graduated materiality, should find a home within the elements of fire, water, earth, air and ether. These seemingly simple substances came to be the foundation for many later and much more complicated symbolisms. Indeed, even consciousness itself was graduated according to the intensity or quality indicated by the principle of which the elements were a reflection.

We can approach these differing energies and principles from many manners and levels. Each energy is unique to ourselves and only has real significance in terms of our own consciousness. We may find that this consciousness is insufficient, but we can then develop it as a result of this discovery. Discovery is in fact a foundation for evolution. Mindful awareness is the foundation for discovery; a pattern arises thus:

Awareness → Discovery → Change → Evolution → Perfect Integration

This pattern can be expressed elementally in the following order

Water → Air → Fire → Earth → Ether

When we become familiar with the qualities represented by the elements, the pattern or structure of gradual transformation can be recognized.

The Tree of Knowledge in the Garden of Eden—with its roots, trunk, branches and leaves—could also be used as a symbol of this evolution. We can see that it is vital to have access to the hermeneutic as well as the grammar and language used. Knowing an alphabet does not enable us to create Shakespeare. Knowing language does not guarantee we can communicate. Because we can see that the most effective use of language only provides a linguistic approximation to our own experience, we can be aware that mutual communication alters with each person, situation and time. The most real terms of description take this into account, and provide simultaneous and multi-level understanding.

The Taoist system of philosophy projected its understanding of elements into cheirology and devised a system not unlike the Buddhist one. However, the Taoist elements are rather different. Recent research suggests that these were not representative of natural elements at all, but instead clever paradigms of a chronological nature devised to explicate different understandings of the time and nature of change itself. Chinese mystical Buddhism (Chen-Yen) used elements in much the same manner as the Indian Vedic teachings and thus a direct and physical (material) relationship between the body and its representative energies was emphasized. Some followers of the Tao did develop their personal experiences and thoughts along lines very similar to the esoteric Buddhists. Historically, it is sometimes very difficult to decide whether an esoteric Taoist was more Buddhistic or vice versa. Both however were Chinese, and that is an important common denominator, for both Buddhist and Taoist esotericists invariably used their knowledge in ways of *practical* importance—a distinctive feature of all Chinese teachers. Chen Yen teachers saw all experience as reflections of these five elements, and used their symbolism of ascending materiality to explain certain physical phenomena. For some it was Feng Shui (geomancy), for others Shu-Hsiang (cheirology). The latter art took the hand and explained it in terms of the five elements. Perhaps the fact that we have five fingers prompted this. Certainly the hand was viewed as a perfect representation of the five energy forms.

Interpretation became a matter of balancing the inner vision of the perfectly balanced and harmoniously lineated hand with the actual one observed. From this comparison deviances could be noted and conclusions drawn as to the nature of the subject. Explaining this deviation was always articulated in terms of the paradigmatic qualities of the elements themselves. It is very important to recognize this. If the hands were balanced, so was the body, the speech, and the consciousness of the subject. In this event, the Taoists and Confucians said that the owner of such hands was beloved by the gods or ancestors. Disease also would be non-existent in a perfect hand. Diagnosis of disease thus required familiarity with spiritual, psychological and physical energy in the manner of Chinese traditional and holistic medicine.

Because of the principle (Li) of transmutative levels, it also became possible to interpret a hand from its energy flow rather than its physical attributes, and the "psychic" element (as we would call it today) became accepted. The interpretation would differ depending on the level of paradigmatic and hermeneutical ability of the analyst. From observed hand patterns, a Taoist analyst may be able to tell that you have rebuilt your home, a Chen-Yen Buddhist that your grandmother's spirit was watching over you, and a Buddhist-cum-Taoist that your liver was overworking! The well-trained cheirologist could tell you all three and more, for such training implies trans-level understanding and not just prognostic ability.

Observing the multi-level and interacting strata of the hand, you can come to recognize your individual pattern of activity within the world and hopefully see where this pattern can be clarified and improved upon. Self-communication is a basic and implicit factor of cheirology. You cannot analyze another if your own consciousness is unclear. It is also important that you actually be able to communicate your understanding in a manner that your clients can both understand and see to be relevant. If you cannot, you have no business telling him or her anything! If a subject cannot understand the nature of change or its relevance to individual transformation, he or she will not appreciate anything you say, except perhaps at its lowest level.

What the scientist Buckminster Fuller calls "synergism" is highly significant to cheirological analysis, for by viewing cheirological phenomena in a synergetic manner we understand the present as an inseparable part of the transition to the future from the past. The present is a term describing only the experience of transit between moments of consciousness. The hand represents the manner in which we are able to appreciate and understand this transit. Cheirology is thus clearly seen as a *dynamic* practice, and one impossible to penetrate except by constant practice and study of life *as it is lived*, here and now. It can never truly be a study of material enclosed in old books written in bygone days, though from studying these we can come to appreciate our present more fully.

Esoteric Buddhist teaching relates every feature of the hand to particular manifestations and modes of consciousness and places these into the wide perspective of human spiritual emancipation. Although this perspective is sometimes difficult to comprehend fully (we do not always have the ability to plumb the cosmic mind), simple metaphorical descriptions enable us to relate the whole to the one and to understand at least more than we did. *Any* movement out of mental or spiritual inertia is creative.

Ancient Chinese religious pictures often depict three animals connected to each other, each biting the other's rear. They are the cock, the snake, and the pig. They depict the three vices common to us and through which we prolong personal suffering. They describe greed, ignorance and hatred respectively. Their opposites—non-attachment, wisdom, and compassion—are the qualities of a Buddha or enlightened being.

In cheirological terms the qualities represented by the animals are related to the finger digits. The proximal phalanges (those nearest the palm) relate to *greed*, the mid-phalanges to *hatred*, the nail phalanges to *ignorance*. We can see in this portrayal a description of a transformative process:

Greed is the most mundane. It can be physical or emotional, but it always relates to immediate and personal experience itself.

Hatred can take place at many levels. Though a purely mental phenomenon, it has direct physical manifestations. It is dynamic and repetitive in nature, and is also self-perpetuating.

Ignorance is related to the top (nail) phalanges—those furthest from the body of the palm. They represent the processes—physical or mental—that are most subtle in nature and closest, in terms of graduated materiality, to the air or ether element.

In temporal terms greed represents the past as it impinges on the present. Hatred represents the present as it impinges on the future. Ignorance represents a quality maintaining the previous two. It could be seen as a super-mundane time, and is related to karmic pattern. Ignorance is a most refined and active factor of human consciousness.

Within the British Cheirological Society, hand shape analysis is based upon the elemental description. Indeed all hand features are classified according to the elements. In our traditional system these elements can also be elevated: they become descriptions of those dimensions of experience discovered by radical alchemists and esotericists of Orient and Occident:

    Earth = Matter/Systematization
    Fire = Time/Evaluation
    Water = Energy/Communication
    Air   = Space/Consciousness

The elements are foundations of physical being. They state the foundations of conscious self-experience. If we relate the elements to their natural counterparts, interesting developments appear:

Earth and water are complementary
Fire and air are complementary
Earth and air are antagonistic
Fire and water are antagonistic

When we observe a hand in which fire and water predominate—either by lineation or morphological formation—we know there is emotional or sexual imbalance. If we then use their esoteric qualities we can see that the subject's use of timing and energy are likely to be out of key. This can of course be physical, emotional or mental, depending upon the level of self-communication attained by the subject.

In a hand with earth and air predominant the subject's understanding of matter—constituent factors—and spatial awareness is likely to be confused. At one level this may produce a clumsy person or, at an academic level, a person who is a square peg in a round, intellectual, hole. He is immersed in the wrong subject unless, through a subject like philosophy, he succeeds in integrating these elements.

In terms of illness, fire and water predominance would suggest metabolic (time) and neural (energy) dysfunction, as well as emotionally based disorders. At the lineation level, fire and water would evidence such illness.

By being constantly aware that all symbols used in cheirology are multi-dimensional in nature, we can begin to see that a hand pattern tells us many different things according to the level at which we approach analysis. Old fashioned "palmists" recognize no difference of elemental level, while we recognize five. The examples above demonstrate these levels in action. Ruling a subject's spiritual aspiration, intellectual orientation and method, executive style, communicative patterns, and physical status, the five levels are indispensable to any serious analytical application. In the Wu Hsing school, this principle of multi-level manifestation is termed "Graduated Materiality," and is the most important ontological method developed within cheirological science.

There are many ways of understanding the principles embodied as elements and seeing how they affect us. Every aspect of life can be interpreted using the four cornerstones of the elements as a key to give some structure or coherence to confusing life experiences. The more we use the elemental symbolism, both as archetypes and as real experience, the more we come to understand them in a manner which is not predominantly conceptual or philosophic, but intuitive. The more we interpret those areas of life with which we come into contact using them, the more we begin, albeit unconsciously, to redefine our own nature and mode of consciousness. Most of our Occidental lifestyle is excessively fire element orientated. Culture, religion and relationships all evidence an overload of fire. We find therefore that that which comes under its rulership is most readily understood and usable to us. This facility extends even into our study of hands. We will find it easier to recognize fire shapes than others, and even may be consciously attracted to attributes of the fire element. This tendency has to be noted, not because it is in itself incorrect, but more because (in our terms) it is only ¼ complete.

ELEMENTAL ARCHETYPES

Cheirology uses groupings of traits—elemental traits—to describe "typical" personality types and characteristics. These groupings are referred to as the elemental archetypes. Each of us has, to some degree or another, an insight into our nature—our individual "fate" depends very much on the degree of personal self-understanding that we each possess. On a daily basis, we modify our actions and decisions in the light of this understanding; for instance, we decline to take on certain responsibilities because we know that we simply could not handle them. To a greater or lesser degree, each of us can see a pattern of strengths and weaknesses within ourselves.

This type of understanding gives us a pattern of human nature. We meet others that have patterns and limitations similar to our own—and as the variety of possible experiences available to us is fairly limited, we can form groupings of "personality types" based on general strengths and weaknesses. Such groupings fall into broad patterns and serve to describe, in a generalized manner, the mass of humanity. But such groupings—in our case, by their elemental nature—serve very well our purposes of analysis and study and will help the student of cheirology to understand the relationship of the elements to human nature. Let's take a look at these archetypes and survey some of their major characteristics.

The Earth Archetype

While others are eager to rush away seeking fame and fortune, the owners of an earth hand are not. The latter understand the merits of conservation, reliability and stability, and always endeavor to achieve these within daily life. They are solid, secure and rhythmic in their use of time and energy expenditure, often preferring vocations which demand clarity, simplicity of outlook and craftmanship. They are natural menders of broken objects and often have collections of unusual bits and pieces. Naturalness is their keynote and the simple, rustic style of life greatly appeals to them. Earth people are quiet, not always by choice—invariably they tend to mistrust the art of talking itself. They prefer actions to words. The earth type is a natural outdoor type and is greatly attracted to the countryside. In relationships, earth types may be rather quiet and uninviting, but they will care for their children carefully and delight in teaching them new things. Quite naturally earth prefers vocations connected with the country or earth in some way: growing, gardening, herbalism, natural foods, cooking, mining and trades connected to these, building, antique collecting. Precious stones also attract.

Earth people are strong and resistant to illness. They live quietly and long, usually free from the stress-illness which characterize the other elemental types. The intestines and liver are often weak spots with them—but usually from excessive food consumption rather than organic malfunction. In matters of love, the earth type tends to mistrust superficiality and outward beauty and settles for a person who is perhaps plain but secure—the boy or girl "next door." The tendency is towards fully trusting one's partner and relating in a clear and simple manner.

Earth types should cultivate the arts of healing via herbalism; they are especially suited for it. They should also develop an active interest in reading and conversation (which they often find difficult). By practicing communication with others they will often overcome their innate reticence. Writing should also occupy a place in their works—it poses difficulties for the typical earth type but should be regarded more as a therapeutic exercise than an attempt to become a great author. Pure earth types are often gifted with natural intuition and can predict the weather, use herbs or dowse for water. These talents should be developed and actively encouraged if present.

The Water Archetype

This is a receptive type whose deep awareness and vivid impressions often create a hyper-sensitive nature. Water tends to be quiet and calm. They are sympathetic and care about others and are often drawn into vocations requiring understanding of others. They are characterized by a love of animals, people and life in general, and they often feel for others as much as for themselves. Because they are very receptive to the influence of color and sound, they are often artistic or musical, and many are good cooks. Other people make deep impressions upon them; subsequently their troubles in life often stem from other people. Emotional entanglements or confusion are things water people should avoid. Water types often run small, personal businesses very successfully, especially buying or selling. Slim and feminine in outlook, they are often good dancers, and excel in fashion and design of all forms. They are often very magnetic to others. Many are highly psychic and excel in occult studies, providing a reliable teacher is obtained. In health their circulatory system, joints and skin tend to be the weaker areas. Water types are often attracted to smaller, fatter persons than themselves. Reliability and security is what they both seek and need. They like to travel, and in youth will set off for distant shores in search of some adventure. When married they develop great understanding and affection for partner and children (water is highly fertile), but are classic victims of the "seven year itch." Their clothes are carefully chosen and close fitting. Women like to use perfume and men scented lotions, for both have a keen sense of smell. Water has a non-discriminative empathy towards all, and tends to maintain ties with friends. They accept their own and others' vices or virtues easily. As they grow older they tend to put on weight but get "plump" rather than fat. Long hair is especially favored by young water types. The sea, excitement, mystery and sympathy are all emotive words to male and female water element types.

The Fire Archetype

When this element predominates within the hand it indicates an intense inner energy which is continually seeking expression and activity. Fire can warm or burn; thus a fire type shows a tendency towards extremities of action, feeling and word. At its highest development the fire type can recreate, rebuild, and enlighten others. Low level development results in destructive and explosive emotions and thoughts. Fire types require the continual fuel of activity and spirit around them. Thus every owner of such a hand should endeavor to cultivate both an active hobby and a challenging career. Boredom or dullness are two qualities which fire types cannot stand and, if forced to endure them by unalterable circumstance, they may become frustrated and irritable. This inner tension often draws them towards rich foods or drinks and they are especially prone to the illnesses of excess.

Fire people are drawn to warm countries and people. They are generous (often too much so), exhibitionistic and fond of group activities. One often finds them in sport clubs or professions connected with industry, engineering, arms manufacture; in fact any profession where the elements (or tools) of danger are present. In relationships, the ideal fire type tends to favor those of a very dark or very fair complexion and invariably marries young and produces children. Fire is the most fertile of the elemental types. Ideally the fire person has a strong and fit body but tends to become fatter in old age. Often circulatory problems develop in later life. Fire types are at their best in the summer months and enjoy their holidays immensely. Being rather bold and outspoken they are usually respected and (at times) feared by their contemporaries. They are better suited for positions of leadership rather than service. The rebellious streak in all of them needs to be channeled into constructive use. If this is wisely done in youth, a contented old age will be attained. Because of their intense energy the fire person will attract others—great care should be taken in the choice of friends—for the fire person can be led towards good or bad pursuits equally. Adequate rest and a healthy, moderate, and balanced diet are advised for all types.

The Air Archetype

This type is characterized by mental elasticity, inventiveness and thirst for new horizons. Air people are inventive, original and witty, delighting in the subtleties of thought, feeling and inference. The air person is usually thinner than most people and has finer hair and skin. Air types are sensitive, refined and usually intelligent. Principle is more important than action and friends will include people of greatly varying cultures, talents, intellects and circumstances. The more serious air types tend toward professions like law, science and medicine; the less serious towards entertainment, design and art in all forms. Music appeals to them, as do bright colors and electric gadgets. The main fault with air is that it tends to disperse too widely—their energies should be channeled only into one or two endeavors. Air likes to rebel and be outrageous; often air children are very noisy. During holidays they are drawn to the hot zones, the mysterious or the inspiring. Air tends to be unconventional in relationships, often resenting and resisting marriage. Air is attracted by intelligence and originality in the partner. Good looks take second place to shared intellectual ideologies. Air has either a very good or very bad memory and often weak eyes. They are attracted to unusual hobbies and pets. In their negative aspect, air types cam be deceptive and misleading. Great care should be taken in youth to develop an appreciation of social and moral ethics. Air is often attracted to sports which require skill and timing—tennis, squash and racing are favorites. Air is the principle of intellect, truth and freedom, so one expects to find a predominance of air types wherever these values are considered important—politics, university or travel often obsess air for some years before they finally settle down. Marriage often comes late as there is so much for them to learn or achieve. But since marriage is usually based upon idealistic qualities, they make good partners so long as they are honest with each other and share equally all the tasks and trials of life. Air excels in communication and writing, and the air type often makes a severe critic. Extremism and tension should be avoided and great care taken to have plenty of rest and fresh food. In old age the air type retires with many memories and a life full of experience.

PART TWO

Shou Hsing Chih
The Study of Hand Shape

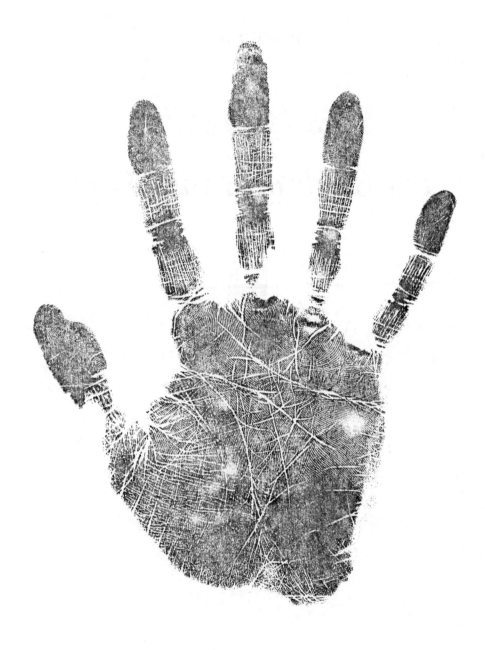

Master Print One

CHAPTER 5

The Basics

We will begin our study of cheirology with the shape of the hand. The palm and fingers will be considered both independently and together. As a simplification, it may be said that the palm reveals more about the physical being, whereas the fingers show the mental nature. The fingers—furthest from the body—express the quality of experience, and impressions from the world.

ACTIVE AND PASSIVE HANDS

Having come so far, a student will be able to realize that the symbolism of hand analysis is very ancient and full of tradition. We now come to the practice of utilizing those ancient principles in contemporary life. This is begun by observing both hands, noting their shape, size and formation carefully and comparing one with the other. The left hand of a right-handed person represents the passive aspects of the subject's consciousness. The right hand indicates the active and present mode of consciousness. The opposite is true for a left-handed person. Both hands must be observed equally and any differences noted carefully.

The relationship of passive and active hands is like that of seed and flower. The passive hand represents the complete matrix of a person's sources. In cheirological taxonomy this is referred to as the family hand. The family symbol represents the source influences of the individual temperament, aspirations and fulfillments. In contrast the active, "father" hand represents cognitively manifest qualities derived from that source.

Each hand has its correspondent source and manifestation, and it is from an evaluation of the progression from one to the other that we come to understand the nature and quality of individual consciousness:

> *Passive hand digits* describe latent conceptual structures potentially accessible to the subject.

> *Passive hand palmar features* describe inherited physiological factors from which the subject has developed.

Active hand digits describe the present patterns and objects of the subject's consciousness.

Active hand palms describe the present condition of the subject's physiological homeostasis.

Everything connected to, or stemming from a subject's physical patterns, psychological patterns, habits, tastes, and individual preferences manifests in a symbolic representative form within the active hand. Every inherited sources of such traits, at all levels, is found within the passive hand.

BASIC PALMAR SHAPES AND TYPES

Each of the elements has a distinctive palmar shape attributed to it. These are considered separately from the element ruling the whole hand itself. Normally you don't need to attach special significance to the palmar shape alone—nor indeed to any other unit found in the hand itself—but you must clearly identify a palmar shape as this will reveal a distinctive pattern of development that will affect the balance of the hand as a whole.

The energy of the elements creates basic palmar patterns, and we can see that any distinctive (predominating) attribute invariably occurs at the expense of another. When one element is strong, its opposite is weak. There are limits to the predominance of any given feature in a hand, and shape shows both those limitations and their concomitants. Compensatory developments, due to predominance of one or other of the elements, automatically come into action when imbalance occurs. The hand will always attempt to adjust itself to any one growing feature by adapting its shape, gesture, or line patterns.

The predominating element of hands creates distinct patterns of natural movements peculiar to each element:

Earth hands create simple rhythmic or minimal movements.

Water hands move in circular, expansive patterns.

Fire hands use direct and angular poses, often pointing with the fingers.

Air hands describe curving or semicircular patterns.

Let's look at an example of how the elements manifest in the shape of the hand. If we take the earth square of the To-Pa as the basis of the palmar shape, the next form upwards is that of water. Water palms are distinguished by their narrowness—they are roughly ¼ less wide than an earth

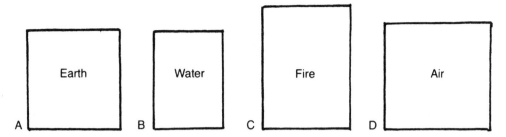

Figure 8. The elemental palmar shapes: a) the square palm represents the earth element; b) the narrow oblong represents the water element; c) the large oblong palm represents the fire element; and the d) the large square palm represents the air element.

palm. They have an oblong shape. Next up in elemental progression is fire. Fire palms are oblong and of larger size than earth. They have a softer skin and are more lean looking. Air palms are square in shape and have fine skin. They are the largest sized palms. The element shape of the palm describes the level and type of physical energy present within the subject's body. Figure 8 shows us the elemental palmar shapes.

The majority of palms are either square or rectangular in shape. This is because the root energies of the body are based upon the earth element. The earth—its food (minerals, vitamins, etc.)—is essential to life. Also, at another level, the square shape describes the ability to experience the karmic forces of time, space, matter and energy. When palms deviate from this normal shape, imbalanced patterns of consciousness are suggested.

Uncommon Palmar Shapes

Figure 9 on page 42 shows some uncommon palmar shapes. With a palm of a circular shape (a rare form), the receptivity of earth element has vastly increased, so much so that earth is failing to perform its function as a base or stabilizer to the physical being. This shape is often being found in genetic illness—all the extremes of personality are emerging as a result of the "corners" of the mind being eroded. The ability to judge, to initiate or execute suffers restriction. Everything is reaching an excess of uncontrolled activity, and mental deterioriation of some form is foreshadowed.

When the palm is triangular two major types are discernible: pointing upwards and pointing downwards. The former erodes the fire and air elements with the result that impressions and physical drives are accentuated. Such development often reduces the fingers in size and is common in imbeciles. With the latter the opposite occurs: the earth and water quadrants are inhibited that an excessively mental approach to experience is formed. The subject can become out of touch with his or her body. This shape is

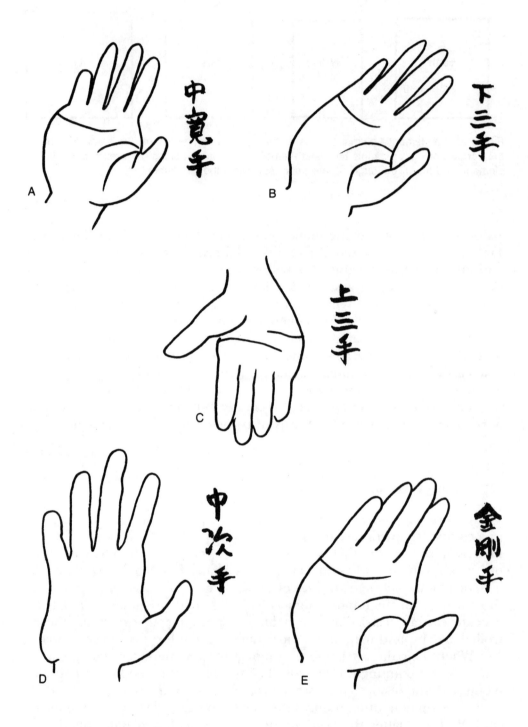

Figure 9. Some unusual palmar shapes: a) circular; b) downward triangle; c) upward triangle; d) hourglass; and e) diamond.

often found associated with digestive illness, or other functions dealing with earth factors. Fire in general is not complementary to earth, and so it commonly shows some form of tension or apprehension.

In traditional cheirology, the crescent is never found as a basis palmar shape. It would be so unusual that it would be considered a deformity. Such a deformity could only represent a particular type of elemental disharmony. It is not considered as a viable illustration of fundamental importance. There are other, composite shapes which should be noted; for example, the hourglass, in which the midsection looks pinched inwards (hence the name). This shape reveals insufficiency in translating physical impulse—often the pain threshold of such palms is extremely high. It is as if the neural impulse does not get through. There is also a lack of coordination between body and thought: clumsiness or physical insufficiency. When the opposite shape (the diamond) is seen it reveals too great a preoccupational with method and order. Such palms tend to create situations around them, which prove difficult for others to deal with. The diamond shape produces a rare insufficiency between basic physical interaction and perceptual awareness. These produce the "difficult" person, prone to argument and contention. Their discriminative, translative impulses prove hard to control.

FINGERS AND PALM SHAPES COMBINED

By relating the length of fingers to that of the palm, we can deduce the balance of physical and mental activity present in the hand examined. Basically, fingers are either longer or shorter than the palm. We use the middle finger as the "ruler" by means of which we judge length. If the hand has

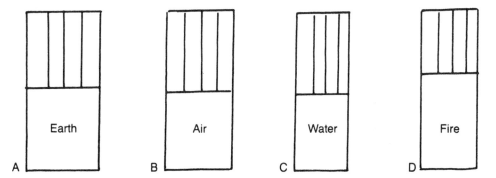

Figure 10. The four archetypal element rulerships are determined by the relationship of fingers to palm: a) short fingers and a square palm indicate earth; b) long fingers and a square palm, air; c) long fingers and an oblong narrow palm represent water: and d) short fingers and an oblong palm represent fire.

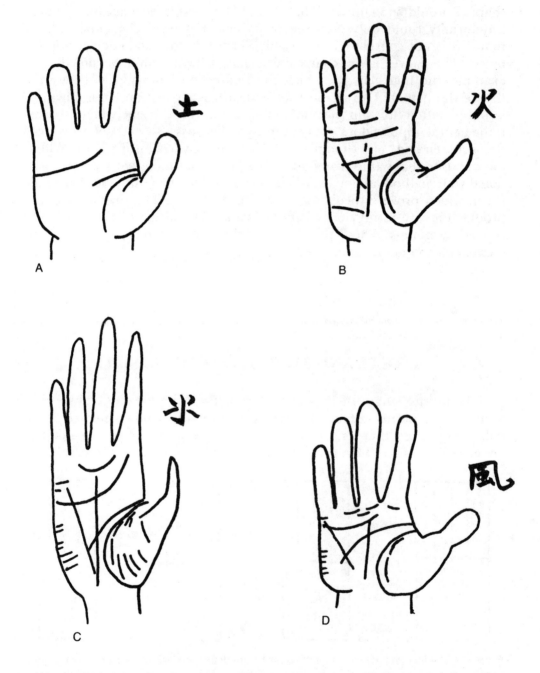

Figure 11. The four elemental handshapes and their Chinese idiograms: a) earth, b) air, c) water, and d) fire.

fingers that are longer than the palm it shows that thoughts preoccupy the mind and that the motivation of the subject is conceptual. If fingers are shorter it shows that physical or material activities are predominant and that feelings motivate the subject. In combination, the length of fingers and the shape of the palms give us four archetypal element rulerships that symbolize the particular integration of physical and mental motivations held by the subject. These combinations are shown in their geometric simplicity in figure 10 on page 43.

Relating fingers and palm areas gives us the overall element as shown in figure 11. But we must also observe other factors—i.e., skin texture may show the manner of expressing this overall palmar element. It is quite common to see a fire shape possess an air skin or vice versa.

Now let's look at an actual example of determining the elemental qualities by looking at a live hand. The hand in Master Print One is of the fire element, the palm being longer than the fingers. This is, in the west, by far the most common handshape.

CHAPTER 6

Quadrant Analysis of the Palm

The hand is divided into four areas termed *quadrants*, which will show you the elemental balance of the palm. Quadrant analysis is the first important stage of cheiromorphognomic analytical technique. When analyzing hands, you must decide the order of predominance of these elements, as this reveals the various strengths and weaknesses in the consciousness of the subject. Note especially differences between left and right hands to determine which is developed and which is repressed, remembering that the right-handed person has the right hand *active*. It is thus used to indicate his or her *present condition*. The left hand shows past conditions and formative influences fulfilling *passive* functions. In a left-handed person this is reversed, i.e., left is active and right is passive.

The quadrants are delineated in two successive stages, each stage determining two areas. You can practice initially on the outline of a hand—trace around the outline of a hand on a piece of paper. The quadranture is determined as follows:

Take a point at the apex of the middle finger and a point at the center of the wrist end of the palm. Draw a line connecting the two. This may not necessarily be upright, depending on the palm. The thumb side represents conscious activities (A); the other side represents unconscious activities (B).

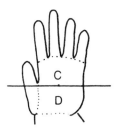

Divide the palm across its middle, excluding the finger area. The top of the palm is taken to be the base of the middle finger. The bottom of the palm is at the wrist point used for the longitudinal line. Draw a line at right angles to the upright. This may not be horizontal as shown here. (The thumb area is excluded in quadrant analysis.) Area C represents active cognition. Area D represents passive cognition.

Now you have the four elemental quadrants of this hand. The elements, and their Chinese terms, are as follows: Fire (Huo); Earth (Ti); Air (Feng); Water (Shui). Fire and air are masculine, active and public in import (yang). Earth and water are feminine, passive and private in import (yin).

The four-part division is notated as here indicated. The different numbers show the elements in their order of size or predominance. In this example the order is water, earth, air, fire. Predominance of a quadrant is decided mainly by its total surface area. The letter *R* shows this is the right hand.

This method gives you the four elemental areas of the palm:

> The fire quadrant is conscious and active
> The air quadrant is conscious and passive
> The earth quadrant is unconscious and active
> The water quadrant is unconscious and passive

When we have outlined the quadrants in this manner we have a visual, symbolic presentation of the various mental and physical factors that serve to make up an individual's personality and nature.

We can discern whether active or passive mental actions predominate in a hand by noting the order of area size in the quadrants. The larger areas represent the fund of functions most readily used by the subject. The smallest areas represent those functions or qualities that the subject finds difficult or awkward to put into practice. They also show the areas in which the individual is most insecure.

As we study cheirology, we become more familiar with the aspects of human activity represented by the elements, and that these aspects manifest in several levels of activity and significance. The elements describe activities of mind and body equally. If the active elements predominate in a palm, we see that the subject is an active person, in both attitude and action. The reverse is true if the passive elements predominate. Later on in this book we will learn more about the specific features of the various predominances in specific elements. For now it is important that you practice making print outlines and determining the order of elemental predominance within a palm. Much of the later and advanced forms of analysis depend on you making the quadrant analysis accurately. You should regard them as the foundation stone of self-understanding.

If you make a mistake in the early stages as you progress in the analytical techniques, you will realize that there is something wrong. The self corrective feature of cheirology—which contains so much cross-checking and comparison—will not permit you to unconsciously make a long lasting error. However, it may be a little while before you realize the error you have made! If you make sure this first stage is correct, you will save yourself a great deal of later revisions and amendments.

Each person we study is thus a combination of various strong and weak points. By determining the predominant order of the elemental representations of these strong and weak points, we can get to understand them better. The quadrant order describes how those forces within us and represented by the elements interact between themselves to produce our particular consciousness and personality. As in the Chinese system, the elements are related equally to physical organs and processes. They can also be used to reveal inherent physical weaknesses.

In determining the elemental order, we use area size as the guideline. The largest area is numbered 1, the second largest is number 2, and so on until we reach the fourth and smallest area. In your analysis, you should express this order in a small diagram of four boxes next to the imprint, as we have done on page 48. The order of numbers from one to four signifies the descending order of element predominance within the subject's hand.

The quadrant order of the active hand represents the pattern of consciousness the individual has created in order to deal with the world. The quadrant order of the passive hand shows the inherited influences of the family or early social environment. It also describes the particular manner in which the memory of early times functions. It can therefore be of great use in psychological diagnosis.

Each of us is a living representation of the past and the present. We are equally a summary of our own past as we are a creation of our conscious present. It's obvious then that any analysis has to consider both past and present equally. In cheirology this consideration is accounted for by studying both the active and passive hands. We trace present psychological orientation by examining the lines of both hands. This enables us to follow the inception of an idea of motivation (from the passive hand) and to see its resultant conscious effect or form (in the active hand). (We will go into this in more depth in Part Three of this work.) By noting the quadrant order of right and left hands one can discern progressive alterations which may take place in attitudes and consciousness from childhood up to the present time. The degree of difference between each hand reveals the underlying motivation stemming from both family life or environment and the present relationship with the external world at large.

If you trace an outline of Master Print One onto another piece of paper, and subject this outline to quadrant delineation as shown on page 47, you will see that the areas that predominate are those of air, earth, water and fire, in that order. This order symbolically describes how the subject views himself. This also symbolizes how other see him as well. Even at this early stage of analysis, we can see that the quadrant order alternates between active and passive elements. Such a progression we know to be antagonistic. In order to understand the nature and significance of such antagonistic elements, we need to consider the significance of the order of the elements themselves. When this is understood the areas of meaning in the order observed within this hand will be a little clearer.

ELEMENTAL BALANCE

As we have already discussed, the basic cheiromorphognomical structure of elements in the hand is assessed from two points: the overall hand shape element, and the order of prominence within the quadrants. The latter is determined by the relative sizes of the areas. An ordering of 1, 2, 3, 4 is thus determined. In dealing with this ordering we should remember the following points:

The first element describes the conscious attitude the subject most readily utilizes in dealing with the world. It is this attitude others would identify the subject as really *being*, irrespective of his or her public image (see third element below). This element symbolizes the subject's basic impetus and tactic for understanding the interaction between self and experience.

The second element describes the nature of those forces inherent within the subject which make him or her feel least capable or most vulnerable. It is usually repressed or ignored by the subject's conscious mind.

The third element describes the public or professional face. It is how the subject likes or wishes to be recognized or acknowledged by others.

The fourth element describes the ultimate, integrative goal of the subject's consciousness. It is often used to describe life goals or motivations within cheirology but is usually inaccessible to the subject's ordinary and conceptual consciousness. In this element lies the cause and resolve of all the subject's problems. It describes the pattern of positive action needed by the subject to realize his or her inner potential.

In determining the active persona we need to consider the first and third elements. In determining the inner life we use the second and fourth elements. Table 2 shows us the psychological characteristics for each element. In all cases we must not overlook the correspondences to these elements in terms of physical archetype, chronological sense, color and form, degree of materiality, and method of understanding. Each is vitally important. You

Table 2. Quadrant Ordering: Psychological Characteristics (Positive and Negative Aspects)

Quadrant	1st Element Basic Temperament	2nd Element Inner Challenges	3rd Element Public Images	4th Element Higher Aspirations
Fire	+ Energetic, enthusiastic, active, expansive, continuous. − Impatient, destructive, unfeeling, cruel, unaware.	Fears restriction, apprehensive of the future, weak willed.	+ Creative energy, leadership, management capability. − Dominative attitudes, dislike of criticism, argumentative.	Freedom from or of responsibility, security, positions of power.
Air	+ Studious, intense, truth seeking, open-minded, intelligent. − Deceptive, fickle, dissipative, plagiaristic, dull.	Dislike of superiors, political extremes, ultra independent.	+ Skill in argument and teaching, theoretical talent. − Erratic behavior, over-talkative, demanding.	Fame and recognition, achieving one's ideals, harmony, truth.
Water	+ Sensitive, intuitive, compassionate, self-effacing. − Depressive, immoral, unbalanced, vindictive.	Hyper-sensitivity, emotional coldness, intolerance.	+ Sales, public relations, sensuality, projection. − Egocentricity, emotional possessiveness, over-sentimentality.	Peace, home security, children, free expression.
Earth	+ Reliable, ordered, tolerant, constructive. − Unaware, materialistic, domineering, cautious.	Lack of care in planning, wastefulness, misuse of things.	+ Reliability, soberness, judgment and experience. − Dislike of change, unadaptability, material avarice, love of solitude.	Success in career, justice, continuity and tradition.

should continually build up your own table of correspondences in your practice. Nor should the male/female element balance be overlooked. Ideally the elements would be in correspondence with the subject's astrological elements. The astrological elements are as follows:

> Fire   = Leo, Aries, Sagittarius.
> Air   = Aquarius, Gemini, Libra.
> Water = Pisces, Cancer, Scorpio.
> Earth = Taurus, Virgo, Capricorn.

Western students took these elements (and astrology itself) from Oriental mystical tradition. Various countries show different rulers. The Occidental continents tend to fire or air; the Oriental to water or earth. In all cases the elements ruling the fingers maintain the same interpretive meaning and area of activity as those of the palm. Some Westerners have especially "Orientally" balanced hands and vice versa. As your familiarity with correspondences grows, the precision with which you can judge the ideal environment of a subject also develops.

EXAMPLES OF QUADRANT ANALYSIS

Let's look at several examples of elemental diagnosis based on quadrant analysis. Before we go further into the specifics of cheiromorphognomy, it's essential that you be able to analyze the quadrants, for this is the first thing you will do after looking at the overall shape of the hand. Here we are using the method described on page 47, which is the notation method. We are numbering the quadrants based on the size or predominance of the elements. The illustrations show the large and small areas. Many cheirologists use the box system to note their findings, as shown on page 48.

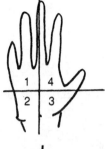

Here we have a hand predominated in the air, water, earth and fire order. This makes the subject thoughtful, sensitive, comfort loving, but lacking confidence.

In this hand the governing order is fire, air, earth, then water. This makes the subject energetic, independent, persistent and security conscious. Both dominants are in the active sections of the hand.

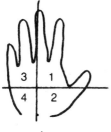

Here the order is fire, earth, air and water. The conscious side of the hand is strong. This combination makes the subject energetic, inhibited in understanding of others, and lacking imagination in daily life.

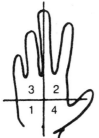

In this order the imagination is strong. Fire being second predisposes to communication difficulties within professional life. Earth here gives an ultimate wish and love for home comfort, air a tendency to gossip.

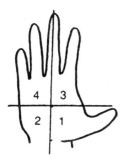

When the lower elements occupy the two primary orders, a strong interest in physical activities is indicated. The combination here produces a sober but imaginative person who, although lacking deep understanding, is lively and materially orientated.

Cross Correlation of Quadrants in Both Hands

The next step in quadrant analysis is to compare the hands, keeping in mind what you have learned of active and passive hands. The individual in our study is right-handed, which means this hand is active and will describe his present condition.

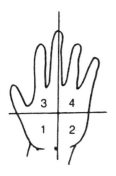

This is an imaginative and physically orientated quadrant balance predisposing towards sport, communication and creative arts. Common to dancers, yogins and athletes or those who write on such themes. As a passive hand it suggests simple and strong family connections, fully of tactile expression and good food. The tendency is to want to work hard for that which is attained and to appreciate things which have taken time to mature. A strong and emotional translation of life's experiences and a tendency to go quietly along one's own chosen path irrespective of others.

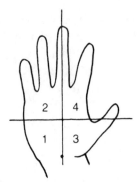

This balance shows a charging of the earth and air elements. The subject now has accentuated his thoughtful and security orientations. This usually occurs when the lack of confidence has brought disappointment in life. Air as a pure force is inhibited. Earth has been accentuated. The basic insecurity still predominates (as the 4th element), and this new order leads the subject away from physical expressions and towards simple introversion and/or pure artistic pursuits. This has now become a quieter hand and more moody in temperament.

CHAPTER 7

The Palmar Mounts

The term *mount* usually describes the small area lying at the base of each digit and within the area of the palm. Mounts represent the highest area of the palm itself. The term also refers to other areas situated at various points around the palmar surface (see figure 12 on page 57). In both ancient and modern popular palmistry, each of the mounts was named after a particular planet and, in common with astrology, the qualities associated with that planet became ascribed to the mount areas of the palm. Palmistry also ascribes these same planets to the fingers.

In ancient Rome and Greece, the divinities represented by the planets were often transient beings. They occasionally came down to our planet and involved themselves in various dramas and human encounters. Thus the ancients had a view of their gods quite unlike the Judeo-Christian traditions. To the ancient Romans and Greeks, the gods were living, breathing personalities and it was possible to encounter them in daily life—Greek myths are filled with stories of such encounters. Consequently, most people were completely familiar with the personalities expressed by each particular divinity—they became a form of "shorthand" used to describe character traits. Popular palmistry utilized this common shorthand and included it into its descriptive terminology. It thus became what is perhaps Europe's first form of characterology.

The symbolism of the mounts is relatively simple, compared, say, to the subtle levels of the fingers—which we shall discuss in the next chapter. Mounts possess only one zone each. Due to this lack of descriptive potential, the specific markings on the mounts have become more significant than the mounts themselves. Palmistry thus has a very sparse and simplified presentation of the mounts. Their influence, however, is by no means diminished by such sparsity. Even nowadays we speak of people possessing qualities that are jovial (Jove is the Roman form of the Greek Jupiter), mercurial (Mercury), saturnine (Saturn), and so on. Modern day people identify themselves with these ancient divinities and are perhaps unaware of many of their qualities and attributes. For this reason, the correspondences used in palmistry are really appropriate, for they do not immediately convey a set of characteristics and qualities to us. Despite this, the human qualities embodied in many of these descriptions are very much in evidence. Human nature changes very little over the ages—the gods may pass away, but their nature still lies buried within us. Table 3 outlines some of the human attributes ascribed to the planets and correlates them with the elements utilized in Chinese cheirology.

Table 3 presents the distinctive meanings of the planets. Even though the deities/planets represented here are in Roman form, the human arche-

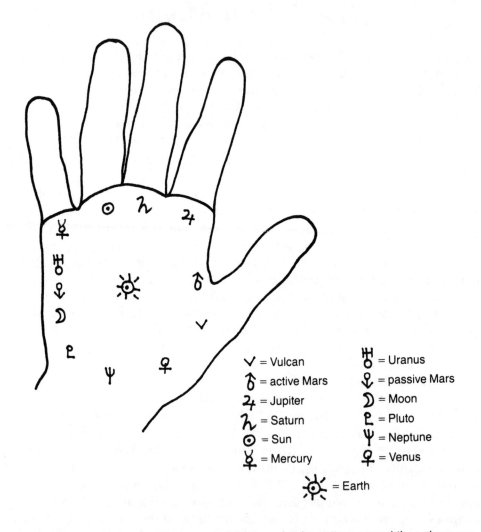

∨ = Vulcan	⛢ = Uranus
♂ = active Mars	♀ = passive Mars
♃ = Jupiter	☽ = Moon
♄ = Saturn	♇ = Pluto
☉ = Sun	♆ = Neptune
☿ = Mercury	♀ = Venus
☀ = Earth	

Figure 12. The palmar mounts. The mounts fall into a circular pattern around the palmar surface delineating the planetary symbols of the cosmos, and months of the year. Because twelve months are shown, we know this arrangement (from the European view) is post-Chaldean in origin. In pure Chinese tradition, the equivalent of the planet Mercury is omitted.

Table 3. Distinctive Meanings of the Planets

Planet	Element	Key Attribute	Yang Traits	Yin Traits
Jupiter	Water	Originality and independence	Expansion Benevolence Spiritual identity Idealism	Despotism Eccentricty Indulgence Lack of confidence
Moon	Water	Non-structural awareness	Sensitivity Receptivity Malleability Prophecy	Mental imbalance Physical degeneration Moodiness Emotional insecurity Lack of awareness
Venus	Earth	Pleasure and beauty	Friendliness Warmth Kindness and care Music Love of refined qualities	Snobbishness Misunderstanding Immorality Over-emotionalism Avarice
Mars	Fire	Growth, destruction and resistance	Decisiveness Power and spirit Leadership Organization Initiative	Cruelty Destructiveness Fear of responsibility Cowardliness Dissipation
Mercury	Air	Communication and hermeneutics	Medicine Speech Teaching Fertility	Lying Deceit Immorality Self-doubt Irresponsibility
Sol (Apollo)	Fire	Harmony	Inspiration Order and plan Beauty Balance in color and form	Egotism Unawareness Dissipation Excitability

Table 3. Distinctive Meanings of the Planets (*continued*)

Planet	Element	Key Attribute	Yang Traits	Yin Traits
Uranus	—	Transchronology	Genius Revelation Transmutation	Reversal and change Erraticness
Saturn	Earth	Order, tradition and continuity	Diligence Care Study Reliability	Irresponsibility Dogmatism Coldness Anachronisms
Neptune	Water	Transdimensional experience	Dreams and images Intuition	Self-deceit Irresponsibility Destruction
Pluto	Water	karma of mind, body, speech	Hidden influences	The Nemesis
Vulcan	Earth	Celestial Karma	Unknowable	Unknowable

Table 4. Comparative National Deities Reflected in Cheirological Terminology

Roman	Greek	Egyptian	Indian*	Chaldean	Japanese Buddhas
Jupiter	Zeus	Nut	Brahma	Marduk	Fukujoju
Mars	Ares	Horus	Agni	Nergal	Amida
Sol	Helios	Ra	Surya	—	Dainichi
Venus	Aphrodite	Hathor	Lalita	Ishtar	Kwannon
Luna	Selene	Isis	Chandra	—	Hosho
Saturn	Kronos	Anubis	Yama	Ninib	Ashuku
Mercury	Hermes	Thoth	Hanuman	Nebo	Yakushi

*The earliest Chinese utilized only 5 planets, as did the Chaldeans. It was only as Indian Buddhism came into China, bringing with it Indian astronomical information, that an impetus towards explorative astronomy developed.

types they used to represent are found in other countries under different names (see Table 4). Despite often vast geographical distances, the qualities ascribed to these deities are often remarkably similar in meaning and import. Because of this trait, it is possible to interpret the hands of Orientals using the Occidental values given above quite accurately, and vice versa in the Oriental systems. Some of the archetypal human qualities credited to the planets need to undergo modification and up-dating in order to insure their relevance within our contemporary world. It is to the credit of the ancient founders of cheirology that many of their pristine interpretations still retain a fair degree of accuracy and need but little modification. In most cases reassessment is necessary, not because the original attributes are incorrect, but because modern fields of interest, and the modern discovery of newer planets, change the balance and interaction between them. Their significance thus alters, rather than changes their fundamental meaning. Details of the macrocosmic values of the planets are highly relevant in cheirognomical research, but practically speaking, concise human microcosmic interpretations are also needed. Armed with a knowledge of both criteria, one's cheirological perception is deepened.

INTERPRETING THE MOUNTS THROUGH THE PRINCIPLE OF GRADUATED MATERIALITY

We first have to consider the principle of graduated materiality applied solely to the palmar surface. We then come to understand that a transposition of the qualities attributed to the palm and fingers as a whole can equally be applied to the palm alone. The proximal base of the palm and wrist corresponds to an earth function, and ascends through the various elements to terminate in air. It is this air element which signifies the area covered by the mounts (and also fingers). Mountains are higher than the plains, so it is not so unexpected that they should be ruled by air. As each finger represents a manifestation of consciousness of a special individuated type, mounts represent the formative ground which transmits those manifestations into higher and non-physical consciousness, commencing from the mundane physical (earth) impetus generated initially within the lower palmar area. (See figure 13 on page 60.)

We can discern two distinct functions of mounts: one is to translate the fundamental earth energies into a cognizant (air) form or structure amenable to articulation. The other is to maintain a balance between consciousness which is expressed and that which is "earthed" when an overload takes place. In the former case, mounts assume a larger area but are flatter

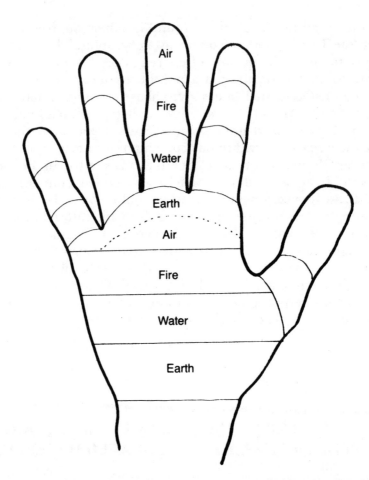

Figure 13. Elemental graduation in the palmar surface. The hand viewed in this manner represents the spiritual journey toward that which is most high. From the plains, across the rivers, through the flames and winds up into the mountains.

and less prominent. In the latter case, mounts are smaller in area and higher.

Any mount which rises (upwards, away from the palmar surface) reveals a surfeit of energy peculiar to that mount. Thus particular talents or skills attributed to a mount can be seen to be a manifestation of energy imbalance in some form or another. This is a natural phenomenon. We cannot be skilled in one thing without being less skilled in others. Acknowledged genius is rarely holistic; it is specialist. This is also seen in quadrant analysis where the enlargement of any one quadrant can only take place by decreasing the area and energy of another. Mounts thus represent specific influences or orientations which individual temperament selects to develop or bypass according to former experience and understanding.

All the finger based mounts have the same elemental implications, that is, they all describe the beginning of the air element functions. Because of this we can see that a potentially simultaneous mental development in all air aspects is possible. Considered in relation to the fingers alone, mounts describe an earth level of the air element.

This brings us to those mounts which lie lower than the finger based ones. Following the principle of graduated materiality we can understand that mounts which are situated lower than the air level do not consciously perform hermeneutical functions. Instead they are concerned with specific and personal balancings of physical, genetic, or karmic energies within consciousness. They act as a filter between those impulses unconsciously activated (be they metabolic or physical) in the palm, and those consciously created and orientated towards specific objectives. The unconscious impulse is described by the palm and the conscious orientation is described by the digits.

We can observe one obvious correlation with these elemental levels in the case of what are termed the mounts of Mars (see figure 12). In popular occidental palmistry the two areas ascribed to that planet, termed active and passive, lie in the fire level of translation (see figure 13). The mounts of Moon, Neptune, Pluto, Vulcan and Venus all lie within the levels of earth and water activity.

• • •

Popular palmistic works ascribe great significance to mounts. Modern students will often find them either totally absent or lacking any significant prominence. The emphasis on mounts probably stems from the fact that palmists invariably read the hands of those who could afford their fees (i.e., the upper classes) and these persons were not used to physical labor. Their hands would, more often than not, be plump, smooth and representative of a well-fed body! It is not surprising that later palmists represented them as so-called normal features more common to gentry than peasants. This error was not made in Oriental systems. Apparent absence of mounts is more the norm in present times and has little negative significance.

METAPHYSICAL INFLUENCES OF THE PALMAR MOUNTS

From the metaphysical qualities of mount energies, students can glean much knowledge if they apply themselves assiduously. It is important to recognize that each mount and its ruler represent an energic principle necessary for complete consciousness. The human, personalized implications of mount planets (as found within astrology) have some value in elucidating human nature. The implications of their cosmic nature, as given here, are generally unknown.

Neptune, standing at a midpoint between consciousness and unconsciousness, should be considered as an area indicating the development of experiences to be realized during life, a karmic point of initiation.

Moon falls in the unconscious and passive area of the palm. It governs the intuitive response of the metabolic and emotional forces inherited from genetic format and prior spiritual influences. An amorphous, loosely structured and symbolic, energy form.

Venus falls within the conscious but passive area of the palm. Being itself ruled by earth specifically, it governs domestic and emotional stability, receptivity and fecundity. Venus was Goddess of the forests, springs, love and sexuality. In fact, Guardian-ess of a Garden of Eden.

Pluto (and Neptune) are rulers of the unknown—forces not directly necessary to human consciousness and ones that can only be understood via dream or revelation.

Vulcan, an as yet undiscovered planet, rules the prevailing ethos of a period of humanity's destiny. For practical purposes it has no special significance.

Mars directs vital energy. The positive area (+) governs energy translated into personal intiative and also sexual fertility. The negative (−) governs that same energy used for repair and maintenance of the physical body.

Sol, the Sun, also occurs in two forms. Sol at its finger base represents the personal deity or genius with which one can communicate and exhibit. Its centrality represents the summit of supreme Wisdom accessible to all humanity. In theistic religions it has been termed the All Seeing Eye. The sigil for the earth ⊕ is often placed here.

Saturn represents individual timing, both metabolic and chronological. It directs the moment at which karmic traits initiate their activity and thus has a kindred rulership of fate or destiny.

Jupiter describes the personal ideal or summit of understanding conceived of by its possessor as being accessible and anthropomorphic in form.

Mercury governs the individual pattern in which a subject receives and passes on those structures of mind, speech or body which he or she is capable of understanding and experiencing.

Each mount area itself can be considered as a vortex of energy whirling and passing on waves of energy in a different form from which they were

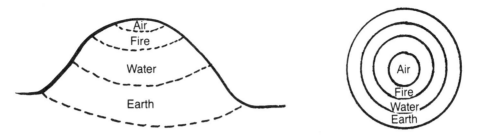

Figure 14. Elemental graduation of the mounts. The general element of a mount indicates a primal function and field. This clarifies its potential translative capabilities. The actual physical height and skin quality of the mount describe the personal communication the subject has with that energy, and at what level he or she allows it to develop, harmonize and balance consciousness.

received. Mounts of all areas possess boundaries of elemental influence, thus a high mount reveals air activity predominant. This shows that an appreciation of the non-material aspects of that mount's qualities are present. Height reveals air quality, lineation reveals fire and water quality, the basic size of the mount describes its earth qualities. (See figure 14.)

DIGITAL MOUNT LINEATION (Shan Hsien)

Mount areas describe the potential energy specific to the individual's consciousness—the markings upon the mounts are indications of specific modes and patterns of that consciousness. Energy flow within the palms is characterized by its lineal forms. All forms upon the specific mounts describe balances inherent in the fundamental perceptual modes of the individual.

When we consider mounts as significators of imbalanced energies—that is, as personalized features—the lineal forms upon each mount serve to identify the particular traits and orientations used by the subject. Practically speaking it is useful to consider each mount as a "mini palm" and divide it into quadrants, as shown in figure 15 on page 64. Lines which occur upon a mount therefore reveal energy flows connecting the quadripartite manifestation of each element peculiar to the digit below which the mount is found.

The general laws of elemental compatibility apply here. Lines connecting complementary element quadrants are beneficial. Those connecting antagonistic ones are not. We can summarize this by saying that all mount lines running *vertically* (parallel) signify hyperactive energies peculiar to the

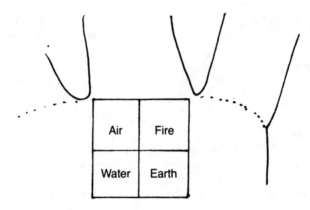

Figure 15. Quadranture of the mounts (right hand).

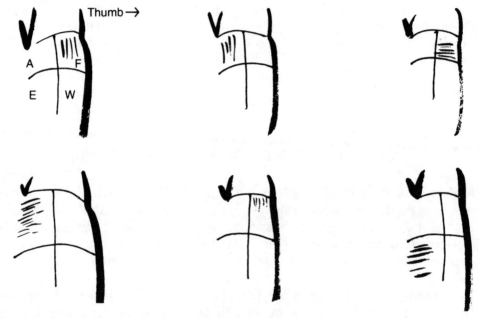

Figure 16. Some examples of lines on the quadrants of the water mount.

Figure 17. The true cross.

element of the mount as a whole. Lines which run *horizontally* signify hypoactive energies. If these lines are high (fire and air quadrant) they describe consciously directed hypoactivity; if low (earth and water) they describe unconscious inhibition. Such lines are often indicative of predisposition to illness (See figure 16.)

Diagonal lines connect directly antagonistic elemental modes and are invariably descriptive of active imbalances in the subject's ability. Of the diagonals, those found running towards the thumb side of a mount are more prominent within a subject's consciousness, being often motivations adopted in order to achieve specific goals. Those running to the little finger side describe purely intellectual or conceptual motivations influencing the manner in which the subject creates, understands or translates concepts.

The cross—a sign often given in European palmistry as an indication of impending doom—therefore signifies a strong unification of all quadrants. This is a hyperactive formation and describes an intensification of the mount's energy usage. It is thus often seen as a sign of extremism. The analyst should especially note if the cross is formed by two diagonal lines (a true cross) as shown in figure 17, or if by one vertical and one diagonal line (an incidental cross), shown in figure 18. This latter cross only signifies the combined meanings of the vertical and diagonal lines. The various quadrantal areas described by incidental crosses indicate that the particular sub-element usage of a mount is clearly defined within a subject's conscious-

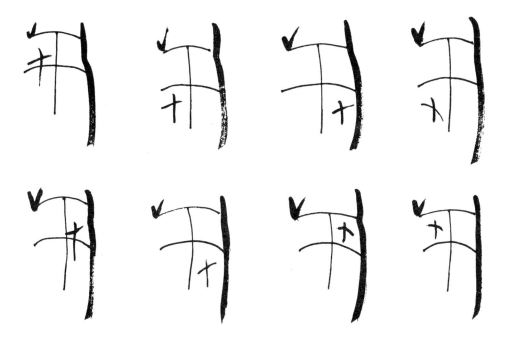

Figure 18. Some examples of the incidental cross.

ness. Those quadrant elements *not* bearing markings or lines are those in which the subject's intuitive faculty is most strong.

THE MOUNTS IN CHINESE TRADITION

In Chinese cheirology the significance of mounts is diminished, as they are regarded as translation areas in which stimuli from the palmar area cross over into the realm of mentality (represented by the digits). Mounts are thus like "roundabouts" (a traffic circle, or rotary) from which one can exit at any point. Where the energy of the palm eventually flows determines the significance of the mount area. Mounts are thus neutral in themselves and take on meanings according to their digits. It is from the digit that one understands the mount and not vice versa.

Those familiar with European astrology will see that the elements ascribed to the planets of mounts are not always the same as in astrology. This is due I think to the astrologers in the Occident losing touch with their original sources of information, i.e., the Far Eastern teachings, and subsequent generations merely repeating the preceding without much serious or individual thought as to the meaning of elemental significances. Unfortunately this is all too common in modern times.

Looking back at figure 12 on page 56, we can see that when elements are translated into palmar zones of influences and those zones are ascribed planetary names, it is necessary to include all the more recently discovered planets in order to present a set of symbols adequate to describe contemporary attitudes and psychological make-up. This is only because ancient European astrological tradition, for all its wisdoms, lacks a sufficient system of description. In practical terms, and bearing in mind the revised elemental rulership of these planets, one may regard specific markings as representing characteristics of interruption between palmar mind and digital mind—i.e., the individual manner of translating these two energy flows is shown by the presence of distinctive lineation.

CHAPTER 8

The Fingers

As we have seen, the palm reveals more about the fundamental pattern of the physical being, whether inherited or consciously developed. The fingers, however, represent the individually developed and non-physical characteristics of consciousness. The fingers symbolize and describe five specific channels of consciousness through which humanity interprets its experiences. Fingers modify elemental significance according to individual orientation. Finger phalanges reveal fifteen major aspects of these channels, all of which are united by a common source or "energizer." This latter is represented by the palm. The functions of consciousness may be understood at three important levels:

> the *exoteric*, dealing with what could be termed a psychology of the individual;
>
> the *esoteric*, dealing with the personal and private functions;
>
> and the integrative or *transcendental*, dealing with spiritual realization.

By inspecting the digits, the nature of the three major levels and fifteen sub-divisions can be recognized easily. Specific individual and exoteric functions are shown by each individual finger. The esoteric function and quality are seen by holistic examination and comparison of the hand with the body. The transcendental function is best perceived by special forms of meditation and by developed intuition.

When the energy of consciousness is active and functioning freely, the digit representing it stands straight and free of its neighbors. When the quality of consciousness is high, the structure of the skin, nail, and joints are of a fine appearance, and balanced in regard to elemental length, tip, shape, nail shape and skin texture. Inhibition or unoriginality causes the finger to hug others. Lack of quality is shown by shortness in length, coarse skin or nail texture, or imbalance in its basic form, element and function to the other digits.

Finger height must also be taken into consideration. Long fingers show that energy is subject to a greater flow coincident with physical being. Thus a slowing down in temporal understanding, analysis, or experience is revealed. Short fingers have less coincidence with the physical being and their energies are effulged rapidly. They subsequently become more exposed to non-physical influences. A speeding up of temporal awareness is revealed. Figure 19 shows average finger heights.

The same principles hold true for the large and small hands in general. Large hands or long fingers tend toward hesitancy or deliberation. We find that occupations or professions requiring care, precision, or long range decisions, contain a higher incidence of larger or longer hands. We find two polarities of a temporal nature within the hand. The first occurs in the region of the mount called Neptune. This is concerned with physical (metabolic) time. The other occurs in the fingertips (particularly that of earth), and deals with conscious time. Here five distinct chronological experiences are present, each symbolized by the elements of each specific finger itself (see figure 20).

In Chinese tradition it is said that energy flows through the hand from the body outwards via the fingertips (the opposite occurs in the pre-natal condition). Thus when we walk, our fingers point downwards to earth, the energy of consciousness. We then receive energy through the feet and pass it back through the hand. This cycle (circle) duplicates the cycle of the seasons and planets, and varies in intensity during the seasons. There are vari-

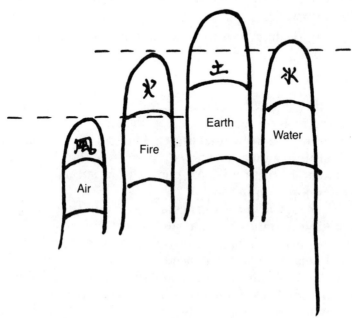

Figure 19. Average finger heights.

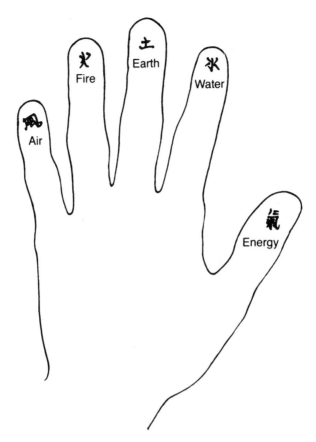

Figure 20. Finger elements.

ous kinds of energy envisaged in this process, and in cheirology we classify them into the elements. These can be understood as both indicating different kinds of energy and as different functions of the same energy.

DIGITAL VARIATIONS
AS MANIFESTATIONS OF PERSONALITY

Armed with what we know to this point, we may now begin to outline key variations of finger quality in relation to human personality. The thumb will be considered independent of this study. We will look at four aspects of the finger: the overall length, width and height; the direction of the finger; how the finger is set into the palm (called the setting); and finally, whether there are any knots, whorls, or other deviations in the finger. When seen together, these four aspects will begin to tell us something about the individual.

Length, Width, Height

In general terms fingers which are longer than the palm (as in water and air hands) show a slower and careful mode of thought. They indicate a deliberative attitude of mind—means is often more important that the ends. Fingers shorter than the palm (as in the fire and earth hands) show a quicker, more instinctive manner of thinking, and an ability to conceive a wider viewpoint. Long fingers are more subjective; short fingers are more objective. Bear this in mind when examining hand outlines and prints.

Each of the fingers represent a specific area and function of consciousness. Therefore, the longer and larger a finger, the more its element predominates in that person's consciousness. The wider or more fully formed a finger, the more refined its elemental quantity is present. The higher a finger—i.e., upwards from the palm surface—the higher the quality or sensitivity of that element has been developed. To give some examples: a fire finger being long, wide, but low shows a tendency to seek excitement and is associated with an attitude of foolhardiness. A fire finger short, narrow, but high reveals the energy channeled into art forms requiring fine timing and movement—ballet, skilled sports, etc. Every finger has its high and low manifestations. These must be balanced with the order of elements shown in the palm and the quality of the hands as a whole.

It is natural, therefore, that the finger representing the earth element and quality should be longest in the hand, and the finger representing the air (the least solid) should be shortest. We can deduce from this that most individuality is revealed via the fire and water elements.

Direction

Ideally, all fingers should be straight. If a finger leans towards another, it reveals that the element seeks fulfillment through another element. In your interpretation you must combine the qualities of the two elements in order to describe that person's consciousness. Fire and air blend well, earth and water blend well. Fire and water do not, nor do air and earth. Fingers which lean away from the hand, i.e., the air or water fingers, demonstrate the wish of their owners to be free from the formative structures of their mental environment. In a right-handed person, such a lean present in the left hand would suggest family pressures; in the right hand, professional or business pressures. The reverse is true for left-handed persons. The angle and lean positions of fingers may also alter from month to month, though there is a root position they return to by habit. Fingers curling in towards the palm show an acquisitive nature, as if the mind is grounding itself (earth) instead of expressing its energies. Figure 21 shows some variations on digital direction and what each symbolizes. Familiarize yourself with these, so you can learn how to read and combine various interpretations.

Wide spacing of all fingers shows an extroverted, active temperament

Digits curving into earth show acquisitiveness in thoughts or towards objects

When air digit is held close, speech or communication is inhibited or cautious.

When water leans to earth, a respect for orthodox standards is strong.

If earth and fire separate widely, security and activity exist independently of environment

The in-turned mental phalange of the water finger shows observance of orthodox views.

When water separates widely, subject shows freedom to feel, think and believe.

Turned out is shows a liking for material security and orthodox tastes in housing, diet, possessions.

All digits held curled over reveals a wish to remain anonymous and keep tight control over thoughts.

Here the opinions are highly independent and original. Material levels are conventional.

Figure 21. Some common digital directions.

Setting

In a normal hand the finger digits leave the palm at a more or less even level. The middle finger should be highest on the palm, followed by the index, ring and little fingers. This setting gives a graceful curve at the top edge of the palm. However, if we consider the various shapes of palm possible, we can see that the setting of fingers will deviate from this form considerably (see figure 22). The significance of this variable finger setting is best understood in elemental terms. Some common elemental formations would be:

Air element formation: This is the most common arc setting. Earth is highest, fire and water equal heights, and air lowest. This gives prominence to order and method, balanced by artistic and individual qualities.

Earth element formation: A straight line setting. Earth is effectively lowered with the result as described previously. This setting indicates a love of materiality, action, and an inability to relax.

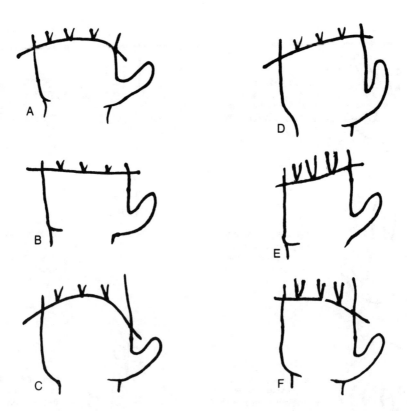

Figure 22. Some variations on finger settings: a) air element formation: b) earth; c) water; d) a variation on the water element formation; e) fire; and f) a variation on the fire formation.

Water element formation: This is an extreme form of the arc setting. Water and air are very low set. This is more common in a water hand. It gives over-activity of feelings and thoughts, thus a neurotic tendency often predominates. Individuals with this formation are often introverted. The palm is narrow and soft in texture.

Water element formation (2): The more low set the fingers are, the more emphasis will there be on the unconscious aspect of mentality. This form is found in water type hands.

Fire element formation: This formation is the opposite of the water formation. Water and earth are high. The emphasis is on preoccupation with the self, conscious projection of ideas and a strong determination and fixity of purpose.

Fire element formation (2): A formation of fire element tending towards extremes. Here the air and fire rise upwards indicating an individual who is deliberate, procrastinating, or who has a rapid response to external stimuli.

The two fingers over the fire area of the palm are of the elements water and earth. The two fingers over the air area of the palm are of the elements air and fire. Considering elemental compatibility gives us an indication of the result of the different settings.

All fingers are distinct from the palm in that they describe non-physical attributes of the human nature. If a digit "sinks" abnormally low, it shows

Table 5. The Various Effects of Sunken Fingers

Sunken Digit Element		Quadrant Element	Resultant Effect
Water	→	Fire	Incompatible. Results in impairment of the development of originality and individuality.
Earth	→	Fire	Incompatible. Results in the adoption of fixed viewpoints and a tendency to extremes of concepts.
Fire	→	Air	Compatible. Although complementary, this results in an excess of energy being generated, and thus the negative traits of Apollo are encouraged.
Air	→	Air	Compatible. As above an excess of energy is created. This formation accentuates the stimulation of ideas and concepts with an often resulting lack of co-ordination between body and mind or emotion and thought.

that the distinction between mental action and physical or material response is weakened. (See Table 5.) Thus we find an impaired quality of judgment in the areas or fields ruled by the sunken fingers. One should note that the settings described in Table 5 do not refer to the length of fingers, which are short by virtue of being low set.

When digits rise away from the palm, mental features are given originality and force of energy. The opposite is the case when they sink. One must take care to recognize when one digit sinks and another rises, as these two features are easily confused. By referring to the "normal" arc continuously, and the relative positions of all the fingers, judgment is fairly simple. Remember that *both* hands must be examined equally to determine the subject's development and growth.

Knots

As we have seen, straightness of fingers or thumb shows that personal energy flows clearly and unimpeded. When fingers curl, hook, or deviate in any other manner from the straight and true, one can see that the energy "bounces," is slowed down, and thus concentrated within specific areas and modes of consciousness. A distinctive attitude or orientation will then arise, either within the subject's consciousness or personal character, related to the area in which the bouncing occurs. It was for this reason that old fashioned palmists ascribed a quality of possessiveness to those whose fingers were curled inwards by habit. When fingers are bent at the mid phalanges, the quality of action and preoccupation with materials and processes would develop pre-eminence. Fingers bent at the top phalanges shows the retention of ideas and veiwpoints.

Joints which are knotty also obey these criteria; knots reveal an innate predisposition towards bouncing. There are three levels of knots. The lowest level is visible on the back of the upper palm. The three levels reveal an arresting of physical energies. The middle joints (on the fingers and visible from the palm) reveal an arrest of actions or expression. The highest joints reveal arrest in the flow of spontaneous mental or philosophical expression.

The quality of the fingers upon which such arrests are found has to be considered carefully. Length and hand element balance show natural orientations. Skin and nail quality show adopted, personally developed, orientations—but we will study these qualities later in this volume.

Flexibility of fingers at the three levels shows the opposite of knots. Rather, flexibility shows the free flowing of naturally directed energies and an acceptance of the world at large. Each level of this can be determined by noting which joint height is involved and testing for flexion at each joint.

THE THUMB

This is a very important digit, for as a whole it shows both the mundane and physical nature and quality of the subject's personal energy. The upper phalange (where the nail is) rules *personal determination*, the lower phalange rules *deductive reasoning* ability. When these qualities are strong, the phalanges governing them will also be long and well formed. One must balance *both* thumbs to ascertain the subject's growth and development in these areas. Ideally they should be equal in size and thus activity. The thumb also indicates, among other things, karmic potential and environmental (geographical and topological) harmony. The thumb is closest to the physical body and was used in ancient times as a symbol of fertility and power. In ancient China the thumb-print often replaced the personal signature upon documents as did teeth-prints—another manifestation of earth element physicality.

The setting of the thumb is also important (see figure 23). Divide the palm horizontally into three equal sections. A thumb coming from the lowest section reveals a practical and dependable expression of mind. If from

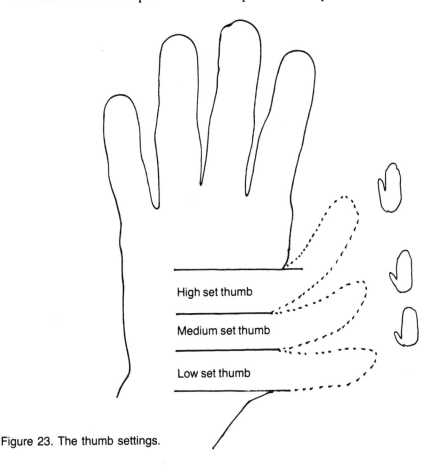

High set thumb

Medium set thumb

Low set thumb

Figure 23. The thumb settings.

the highest it reveals a childish, and often more physically orientated, frame of mind. The central position is the most common and reveals a balance of impression and expression. The angle of the thumb reveals how personal energy is utilized. When the thumb is held close in to the palm, particularly if it is clasped near to the earth or fire mounts, it reveals a surrendering of the power to initiate change in one's life environment—a form of surrendering and opening oneself to determinative and personal karma. It also indicates caution, stress and fear of environment. When the opposite is so, i.e., the thumb stands out, it shows a desire to assert one's mastery over the environmental forces and influences experienced and a tendency towards spontaneous expressions or recklessness. In an earth or fire hand this would be over one's own body, in physical arts or skills, and over other persons: the external, visible world. In a water or air hand the extended thumb shows the desire to master first the internal environment (psychological), the world of aesthetic influence, spirituality, harmony, color and balance. These "worlds" (the inner and outer) are represented by the two hands themselves (passive and active).

THE PHALANGES

The ancient deities were attributed with many functions and responsibilities. As human life became more complex, so likewise did the duties of these deities. In a similar manner the understanding of consciousness itself (which began very simply) gradually developed into a science of intricate ontological significance. Mankind had begun to examine particular manifestations of life and to invest such examinations with spiritual import. Observations in one field were related to other fields of experience, and thus a notion of correspondences developed, which was later to grow into the basis for many religious teachings, of both ortho- and heterodox form.

An early ascription of cheirology was to give a correspondence to each particular phalange of the fingers as had been done to the gods. Each phalange was related to a particular area of activity or endeavor. (See figure 24.) A strong formation of a phalange was taken to indicate that the qualities ascribed to it were predominant in that subject's mind. The level at which these traits and tendencies operated was shown by the overall qualities of the hand itself, its element (energy) levels, etc.

As has been mentioned previously, a predominance of joint knots show an arresting quality of energy and thus an excitation of its action. Smooth joints indicate a quick flow of energy out into the world and thus a more open and accepting attitude towards the world. Joints or phalanges which departed from the natural (straight) finger line were considered to be attracted by the finger they went towards. Thus it could be said that a modification of the inherited energy manifestation and level had taken place.

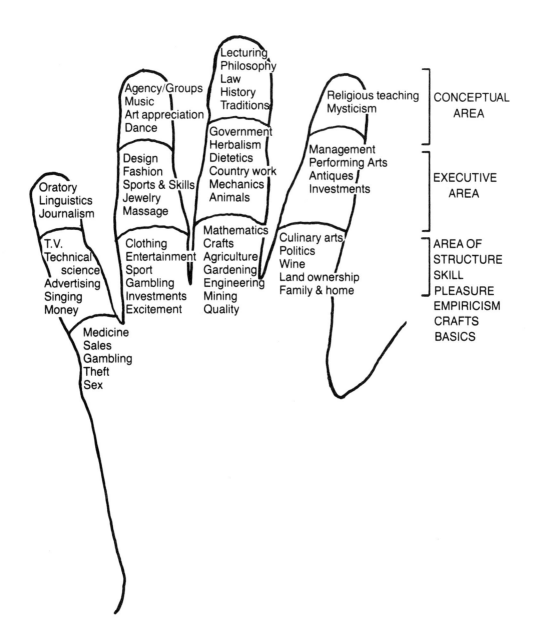

Figure 24. A modern adaptation of an early correspondence chart: interests are reflected in the phalanges. The negative factor of each profession is evidenced when there occurs a degeneration in its relative or digital shape, quality, by lean, or by elemental imbalance when related to the finger, palm line, or ruling element. Achievements in the outer world (the professional world) require good balance of elements, strong thumbs and lines. Achievements in the inner world require especially high quality formation of skin and lines, together with a predominant passive shaping of fingers and palm, along with strong thumbs and lines.

The particular angles, etc., that each finger made in relation to the others could indicate the subtle differences between, say, a religious or devotional philosopher, and a philosopher of medicine; between artists involved in graphics or portraiture, and so on. What prevented Occidental cheirology from developing into a respected form of psychology was that its followers lacked the ability to articulate any systematic philosophy for the art.

When we survey the cheirognomical field, it becomes obvious that there is a limit to the data available for comment—we only have five digits and fifteen phalanges to deal with. However much we research or recodify the potential correlations between digits and fields of consciousness, there lies this numerical limit of inter-relativity. We can see therefore that spiritual philosophies which developed some form of teaching concerning a five or fifteenfold division would render itself amenable to cheirological interpretation. Within India the five became elements or essences (Bhuta); in China the fifteen were used to describe special yogic type ritual exercises (Hsing) and many other things. Different countries used the numerical nomenclature in terms of their own cultural and spiritual environment, retranslating it when and where it proved necessary.

In European cheirology, much influenced by Mithraic Christianity, hands were described as possessing three distinct levels—to parallel the Trinity. In non-Christian countries, different classifications were developed. The system used by our school, being based upon the five elements, interprets the hand in five levels of activity, both physically with regard to its cheirognomy, and cheiromantically with regard to its lineations. Our system has thus more in common with Chaldean theology than with the Egyptian, Greek or Roman theology, for only in Chaldea can we find emphasis placed upon five major planets as symbols of experience and understanding. It is, of course, likely that Chaldea received influence directly from the Orient.

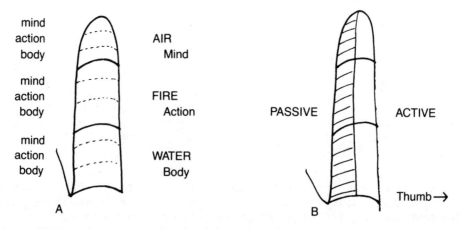

Figure 25. The tripartite division of the phalange is shown in A. When we divide the finger perpendicularly, we delineate the active field from the passive, as shown in B. The active area is always on the thumb side.

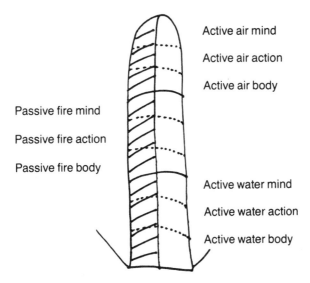

Active air mind

Active air action

Active air body

Passive fire mind

Passive fire action

Passive fire body

Active water mind

Active water action

Active water body

Figure 26. A delineation of specific functions of the phalange is possible when we combine both horizontal and vertical division.

Within our school, the palmar surface is divided into zones and degrees of activity related to the elements. Each finger has three phalanges. The top phalange comes under the rulership of air; the middle phalange is ruled by fire; and the lower phalange is ruled by water. Each phalange, in turn, is naturally divided into three zones as well, by an imaginary tripartite division as shown in figure 25a. So each phalange is also divided into air, fire and water. Each of these elements describes a specific manifestation and act of consciousness concerning mind (air), action (fire) and body (water).

By forming a perpendicular division we delineate the activity field into its active or passive aspects, as shown in figure 25b. The active area is always on the side of the finger facing the thumb. The combination of both horizontal and perpendicular divisions allows us to specifically delineate functions of the respective areas of the phalanges, as shown in figure 26.

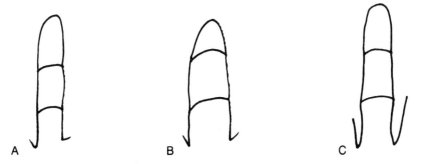

A   B   C

Figure 27. Viewing the phalange longitudinally. Some examples showing a) length, b) width, and c) height.

A phalange or finger can be seen to be orientated toward an element, or away from one by its shape and angle of placement upon the hand itself. Viewed longitudinally as in figure 27 on page 79, phalanges reveal the influence of elements by their length (showing potential) and their width and height (showing actualized energies). Seen endways-on (figure 28), the tendency of a finger quality towards activity or passivity becomes clear. The nail side of a finger rules public life or image; the palmer (volar) side, the inner and private life. Figure 28 compares the end phalange of a famous person with that of a recluse.

The qualities we are dealing with here are deliberately described in energic (i.e., non-specific) forms as the import of these energy forms varies considerably from each country, environment and historical time. What in one place, at one time, means one thing changes completely when placed in another context. The great fault with comtemporary palmistry is that it adheres to this "one manifestation one meaning" tenet. This tenet is invalid to any who appreciate the importance of the principle of energy within cheirological studies. It is enough to understand this principle alone; the individual details must be, and indeed can only be, formulated by the practitioner during practice.

Generalizations have some value, as a teaching aid for instance, but they can never be laws. Due care and attention must be given to the particular environment, time, social and religious ethos one finds oneself in. Granting this care, one can see that in a Western, materially oriented, democratic culture, certain comments and observations can be made about professions and the phalanges related to them. Bearing in mind the profession each energy form creates, one can outline some of the orientations revealed by phalange levels.

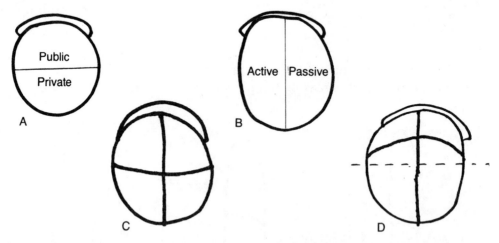

Figure 28. Seen endways-on, the tendency of a finger quality towards activity or passivity becomes clear: a) a horizontal delineation indicates public/private life—the nail side of a finger rules public life or image, and the palmar side rules the private life; b) a vertical delineation indicates the active passive life; c) here we see the fingertip of a famous person, and in d) a recluse.

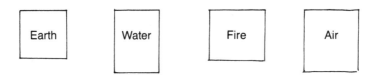

Figure 29. The basic shape of the phalange will give us the first indication of its elemental value.

By relating these professions to the principles discussed here, further directions can be formulated quite accurately. In all cases it is assumed that the hand as a whole shows no degenerate qualities, either in shape, line or balance. These would weaken the qualities potentially available to the subject and make them difficult to develop.

Basic Shape and Elemental Significance

The basic shape of a phalange shown in figure 29 gives us the first indication of its elemental value. Each has a distinctive size and form. Earth is the smallest and square shaped. Water is larger and more oblong (but the same width). Fire is square but covers a larger area. Air is oblong and has the greatest area of all. Earth and water are the same width, fire and air are the same width. Water and air are approximately half as long again as earth and fire.

Flexure

The individual flexibility of each phalangeal joint should be noted. A lack of flexure or flexure restricted in certain directions could indicate an influence exerted by other fingers (or other fields of activity). This would show a blending of two distinct qualities into a third and new type. Theologically speaking, this is equivalent to the degeneration of pristine divinities into composite ones, but with diminished powers. Such was the case with, for instance, the Greek Sun god and even earlier, the Moon goddess.

As long as each finger (and thus its correlate levels of consciousness) functions with individual and autonomous faculties, creative and clear combinations of consciousness can occur. The subject will have clarity of thought and action. When degeneration occurs, this clarity becomes confused and self-understanding becomes difficult. The fingers will reflect this lack of clarity in many ways, often by drawing in towards each other—as if for protection. It is these apprehensive gestures that cheirology notices and explains.

Flexure is a water quality. Stiffness of flexure then reveals an over-development of fire energies and a consequent rigidity of attitude relating

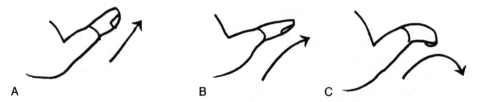

Figure 30. Thumb flexure: a) straight thumb, b) average thumb, c) flexible thumb.

to the area, finger, or joint found stiff. One must compare flexure potential of both hands carefully. If the lower joints are loosest, practical/executive adaptability is indicated. If stiff, the subject will adhere to tradition or tried and tested methods. When the upper joints are flexible, malleability of thought is indicated. Such a feature is common among dancers and actors for it gives the ability to *feel* a role or technique rapidly and to great depth. When the thumb's lower joint is flexible, the subject will have the ability to put thoughts into practice. The upper joint flexive (more common than may be supposed) reveals a possible lack of willpower and an orientation towards impulsive actions. Again it gives great receptivity and is particularly found among those who play musical instruments for it gives this ability to pick up and remember intricate sequences of mind, sound or feeling and to enact them later. (See figure 30.) Such memory does not last. The more fire characteristics present, the more rapidly such sequences are forgotten. Too flexive a thumb shows a lack of resistance, continuity and application of rational endeavors.

Flexure potential of the wrist itself should also be noted, for this gives some indication of general communication between body and mind. An excessively loose wrist reveals a general excess of water element energy; a stiff wrist an excess of fire. (See figure 31.) The joint should be firm but soft, expressive in articulation but not weakly held.

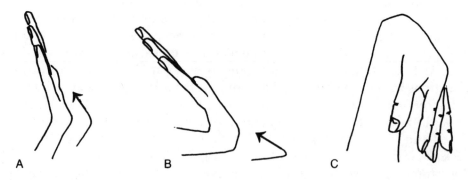

Figure 31. Wrist flexion: a) average wrist flexion; b) extreme flexibility; c) in cases of extreme flexibility, the thumb can touch the arm.

Phalangeal Markings

The presence of lines upon phalanges reveals either discharge or conduction of finger energy. By their presence we can recognize that the phalange is active on a fire or air plane. *Unlined* phalanges show pure, non-structural activity of the nature of earth or water, and indicate a more intuitive function of the form of consciousness governed by the particular phalange.

> *Vertical* lines show increased conductivity and/or hyperactivity of that phalange.

> *Horizontal* lines show frustrations or inhibitions in the area governed.

> *Grills or crosses* upon phalanges reveal simultaneaous activity and inhibition and indicate an unclear or degenerate understanding of that area's function.

Up to three lines, either way, upon a phalange is an average marking. More than this is a regressive sign. Figure 32 shows different levels of phalangeal markings.

Care should be taken in observing the horizontal intermedial lines—i.e., those which occur between phalanges and upon the joints. If these lines are widely set apart (particularly if they occur with knotted joints) they indicate a restriction or holding of the transitive energy flow. This results in prevaricative factors between the phalangeal areas ruled. Depending on air line and thumb development, this indicates a lack of understanding in the relationship between the functions of those areas or the development of excessive caution in activities relating to the translation

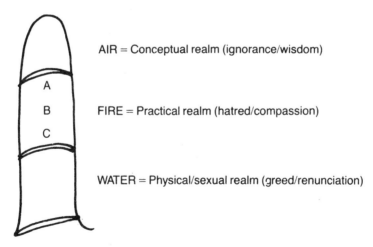

AIR = Conceptual realm (ignorance/wisdom)

FIRE = Practical realm (hatred/compassion)

WATER = Physical/sexual realm (greed/renunciation)

Figure 32. Phalange levels of activity. These are the traditional Chinese values. The air phalange is the conceptual realm, the fire phalange is the practical realm, and the water phalange rules the physical/sexual domain. Note that each phalange also has a tripartite division: of a) air, b) fire, and c) water. The lines between each phalange are called *medial lines*.

of those energies into other areas—for example, the practical/sensual into the ideal, or vice versa. In all cases of restriction within the intermedial area (fire or earth quality), an increased amount of finger tissue will be present. Thus wrinkled joints will be apparent on the back of the hand and/or enlarged joint tissue. The plane or level at which restriction takes place is indicated by the joints which bear this feature, and the section of a particular phalange which shows greatest change in size.

Each phalange can be subdivided into three levels of quality (as is the palm). Horizontal lines indicate by their presence at which level obstruction takes place. If a horizontal line goes across a phalange completely, it isolates interaction between the three areas. What it does this depends upon the line height. Partial lines simply reveal obstruction or hindrances in translating the levels.

Phalangeal Height, Width and Skin

The height of the phalange (away from the bone) is also significant. Generally speaking, a flat phalange has an *earth* function; a slightly raised phalange a *fire* one. A moderately high and firm phalange has an *air* function and a very high full and soft phalange a *water* one. Figure 33 shows the two extremes of earth and water.

Looking at the fingers sideways (see Figure 33) we can also draw a type of imaginary compass which can be of further aid to the analyst in understanding fingers and phalanges. Finger expansion in any of the direc-

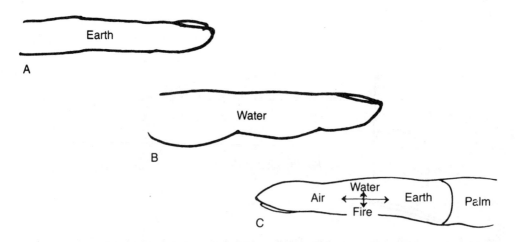

Figure 33. The height of the phalange is measured away from the bone. Here we see the two extremes: a) the flat phalange (earth element); and b) the full phalange (water). Expansion in any of the directions shown (c) increases the qualities of the element indicated.

Table 6. Skin Characteristics

Consideration	Earth	Water	Fire	Air
Texture	Leathery	Very soft	Elastic	Soft but taut
Skin ridges	Visible	Not visible	Visible	Not visible to naked eye
Pores	Medium	Very fine	Largest	Medium sized
Joints	Simple, wrinkled lowest joints	Smooth joints	Wrinkled or knotty midjoints	Slightly wrinkled upper joints
Palmar mounts	Hard, solid mounts	Moist, full mounts	Warm and firm flat mounts	Dry, often cold, high mounts
Skin hue and other features	Deep or dark color, often calloused	White color	Reddish or orange color, deep lines	Fineness, yellowish or pale color

tions shown increases the qualities of the element indicated. For example, a finger which is longer has an increased air element. This gives a greater tendency toward subjective thought or consideration within life. A finger which is fuller towards its palmar end (technically called the proximal end) shows an increased interest in the mundane, practical or physical areas of the earth element. The finger which is full, rising upwards upon its inner (palmar side) surface, shows an increase of water element. This gives a more sensitive and emotional approach to life within the area of activity governed by the finger, and also discrimination in the quality of things.

An increase of tissue, either by fullness or by increased skin folds on the upper and outer (nail) side of the finger, shows high fire element activity. This is often found in the fire shape hand and/or with knotted joints.

Finger phalanges can also be distinguished by their overall width or narrowness. Wider fingers show influence of air or fire elements. These give a larger overall size to the digit and generally show a preoccupation with the qualities associated with that finger. Narrower fingers and phalanges have a water or earth influence. Determining how and which of the two possible elements predominates in the case of wide or narrow depends upon skin quality. Changes in the skin quality in different fingers or phalanges should be noticed, as this can have antagonistic relationships to the ruling element. Both the palmar fascia and the back of the hand should be observed. The former gives information relating to the public face, the latter to the personal image maintained. Compare your findings with those on Table 6. Skin has four characteristic influences:

Fire skin indicates the energies of that phalange are activated and expansive in nature.

Air skin indicates that energy is translated into concepts, not actions, pertaining to the areas governed by that phalange.

Water skin indicates that the area of govenment is internalized and that subjective values predominate in the utilization of that phalangeal activity.

Earth skin indicates that the phalangeal areas of activity will be manifested in their most pracatical and industrious form and an emphasis given to those areas which create solidarity, order and continuity.

One should bear in mind that each elemental skin type experiences the sense of touch differently. The earth skin predominately feels basic shapes and rough textures—its sensation tells it that there *is* an object being touched. Water feels more acutely—its touch tells of its texture and finish. It senses the smoothness and line of an object, and its touch draws the eye to the object for appraisal or dismissal. Fire skin clasps and grasps rather than touches. Its sense is immediate and related to a purpose or motivation. To the fire skin, an object serves a purpose and unless the object "feels" inadequate in some manner it will rarely visually appreciate the object held. Air is the least "touchy" of all skins. It is not in its nature to elicit texture and information by physical sense. Air will more readily observe an object before touching it, and then only hesitantly. Air skin knows that touch results in so much information pouring in that it is better only to look. Touch will confuse its thought actions by a data overload.

One can see, then, that the resultant quality of sensation differs markedly for each skin type, for each utilizes its touch sense in a different manner and for different ends. The mental responses accompanying these different manners also vary and create differing patterns quite unique to each type in accordance with its elemental ruler.

Waisting of the Phalange

Waisting is a regular thinning of the phalange. It can show an inbuilt elemental weakness in certain areas of activity. Waisting takes away tissue from the phalanges and thus reduces the coincidence of that phalange's rulership with the physical plane of experience. By observing carefully where a phalange waists one can determine exactly at which plane this reduction takes place. The opposite of waisting—thick, full finger phalanges—reveals an increased coincidence of that finger's qualities with the subject's consciousness. If the lowest phalanges are largest, the physical coincidence is greatest. The middle phalanges show increased practical activity, the upper mental activity.

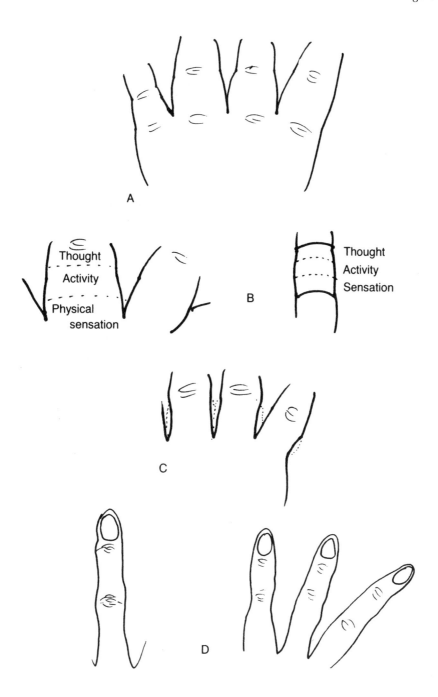

Figure 34. Phalange waisting and thickening: a) lower thick phalanges reveal a general preference for material or physical experiences; b) by determining at which phalange level the thickening occurs, we can see at which level physical experience is preferably generated by the
subject. The waisting of a lower area phalange (c) indicates a reduction of physical desires
and is often found with stronger middle or upper phalanges. Waisting can take place in any
of the phalanges (d) and at all three heights.

Hair

When present upon phalanges, hair indicates an increased activity in that area governed. The nature of that activity is indicated by the hair's color, texture and ruling element. To be in balance, skin and hair should coincide in elemental polarity as follows:

> Fire: Strong, very thick and curly in texture. Black or red/brown hair.
>
> Earth: Strong, straight or wavy. Brown hair.
>
> Air: Soft and sparse. Fair or honey, gray or white hair.
>
> Water: Very sparse, soft and straight. Light brown/fair hair.

NAILS AND FINGERTIPS

Overall, we determine three basic factors of fingertip analysis: 1) Phalange shape, 2) Nail shape, 3) Dermatoglyphic element and general skin quality. These correspond to distinctive functions of consciousness:

- Nail shape relates to awareness of *physical being* and *public image*.
- Phalange tip shape relates to personal awareness of *consciousness*.
- Dermatoglyphic relates to *spiritual/karmic propensity*.

Basic Shapes and Meanings

The top phalanges of the fingers represent that function of consciousness that perceives and deals with non-structural concepts, both consciously and supra-consciously. As each of the fingers themselves correlate with energies symbolized by planets, so the fingertips represent the highest—one could say transcendental—impulses of those planets. These impulses do not belong to the planets; they are merely symbolized by them. In non-Buddhist Chinese cheirology, fingers are related to members of one's family instead of planets, with equal validity and accuracy of interpretation within the Chinese culture.

At this point we must distinguish between the two faces used by the subject. The analysis of volar (palm side) phalanges reveals private, personal understanding and use of energies granted or developed by the subject. The nail side of the phalanges reveals the face shown to the outer world, that is, the professional or social life. These two may not coincide.

Fingertips fall into several types and are primarily characterized by their shape. Each of these shapes indicates the special method of reception

Table 7. Fingertip Shapes

Shape		Element	Quality	Planet
	Rounded tips	Air	Perceptive-ness	Mercury
	Square tips	Earth	Method & order	Saturn
	Spatulate tips	Fire	Activity	Apollo
	Pointed tips	Water	Inspiration	Jupiter

and emission of the various qualities of consciousness available to their owners. (See Table 7.) These qualities are represented and understood by elemental correlation (which can be equally applied to the thumb tips).

The nails on each type of tip also represent elemental energy. The relationship between the nail and the tip of the finger is shown in Table 8. This table shows the "pure" forms; however, there are combinations of the pure types. For example, the spatulate nail has a narrow base (water), and a widening of the fire and air elements at the top (see figure 35 on page 90). Or the base of the spatulate nail may be very narrow (earth-like). The reverse shape—narrow at the top, wide at the base—shows the reverse order of elements and meanings: lack of concept, decrease of activity, increase of preoccupation with material or physical energies.

If the nail is large relative to the fingertip, an excess of air is shown. If small relative to the fingertip, it shows an excess of earth. A circular shape will show restricted energy. An oval shape (wider at the middle) shows an excess of fire and negative energies of air and water.

Nails vary so much in each individual that it is vitally necessary to know how to judge their size and area. In the Chinese system this is achieved by relating nail sizes to other sections of the body. In the European system there is no guide whatsoever. An average nail covers nearly half the area

Table 8. Nail Shapes

Shape		Element	Planet
	Short/wide	Fire	Apollo/Mars
	Long/narrow	Water	Jupiter/Neptune
	Long/wide	Air	Mercury/Uranus
	Short/narrow	Earth	Saturn/Pluto

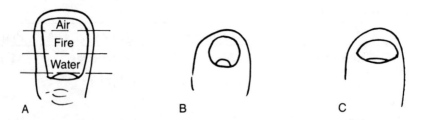

Figure 35. The spatulate nail (a) is a combination of "pure" forms: narrow base is water, and the widening towards the top is a combination of fire and air elements. A circular shaped nail (b) will show restricted energy; while the oval shape (c), wider at the middle, shows an excess of fire and negative energies of air and water.

of the phalange on which it rests. From this key a judgment can be made. A thumbnail should be double the area of the subject's front (large) teeth (see figure 36). This of course is assuming the nail has not been grown long on purpose. The nail on the earth finger is one third larger in surface area than the subject's largest molar. The nail on the air finger should be the size of the incisor teeth. In Chinese analysis, teeth are also interpreted according to elemental qualities—their elemental rulers are indicative of a person's speech. Short (fire) teeth show hasty speech; large (water) teeth show deliberation in speech. Ideally one's teeth and nail shape should correspond in elemental quality.

It is also important to note the *predominant angle of the nail*. Nails curving *upwards*, away from the phalange, show imbalance of earth. Nails curving *downwards*, towards the phalange, show imbalance of air. Nails curving *inwards* (to thumb side of hand) show imbalance of fire. Nails curving *inwards* (to air finger side) show imbalance of water. Observe nail shape from the front and back of the finger so as to distinguish between a nail shape and a tip shape. (Nails are often manicured to an unnatural shape.) Ideally, nail and fingertip shape should correlate with the predominant element of the hand itself.

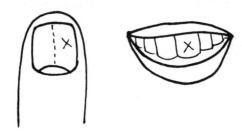

Figure 36. Judging nail size. A thumbnail should be double the area of the subject's front tooth.

Nail Formations and Health

Each part of our body continually grows and develops during our lifetime. Physical, visible growth is the end product of a vast system of inter-connected impulses and actions, each of which is easily disturbed (through illness, etc.). By observing those parts visible—the teeth, hair and nails—we can deduce something about the condition of bodily growth processes themselves. Within our bodies, the hair, teeth and nails can reveal imbalances due to interruptions or imbalances of the growth functions, as well as infections and congenital illnesses.

Ancient palmistry utilized an interpretative key similar in many ways to homeopathy. A certain formation or shape of one part of the hand was always accorded correspondent organic qualities, one favorable, one unfavorable. Of the latter category, three aspects were considered important: emotion, death, and present health condition. These seem to be the main areas of interest to ancient palmists (and to many contemporary ones also!). Health indications were related to specific lineal patterns and palmar shapes. Most of the health indications accorded to the individual finger digits in fact stem from the traits associated with the divinity who was considered to rule that finger. For instance we find Jove, a beneficent and rather indulgent god, correlated with gout and digestive problems! A perceptive observer will easily recognize the illnesses of the remaining digits.

Chinese Wu Hsing cheirognomy developed in a different manner, and of course was Buddhist in religious orientation. We find therefore no equivalent pantheon of divinities being accorded such significant qualities, nor any such interest in theistic correlation providing a valid interpretative or diagnostic technique until very late in the history of Buddhism, with its adoption of spiritual tenets native to the countries within which it developed and extended. Not until the sixth century, with the beginning of systematic Tantric Buddhism, does the inter-relativity of macro and microcosmic patterns become cogent.

Many of the older interpretations of health defects are in fact reliable guides, but lacking a systematic understanding of the workings of the physical body. In China, where the interest was predominantly in the spiritual energy of the body, a satisfactory presentation of formations conducive to health diagnosis was not produced. In the Occident we find fundamental statements made by those considered worthy or authoritative, but no explanation as to how those statements were obtained. Indeed many analysts jealously guarded their secrets, only passing them on orally to their immediate successors.

It may be surprising to some readers that modern Western medicine in fact confirms many of the cheirognomically deduced traditions with respect to health weaknesses. Several of my students who were pre-med students or young doctors have told me of diagnostic techniques that they were taught which were identical to techniques I had shown them several years previously. Occidental medicine occasionally agrees with its Oriental counterpart in its diagnostic interpretations, though usually from a different basis.

Our own method is, of course, based upon the elements and includes holistic principle, rather than specific data, to interpret formations. I shall present some of the traditional interpretations of health indications as shown in nail formations, and reinterpret these according to our Oriental methods. This gives a reader the double advantage of seeing both methods applied simultaneously.

CAUTION: In interpreting nails with regard to health, you should always seek confirming data elsewhere in both hands before stating that such and such a condition is present, if only to avoid frightening a subject! Health analysis is a very sensitive technique, and takes many years of research, study and experience to develop into a practicable art.

Example One

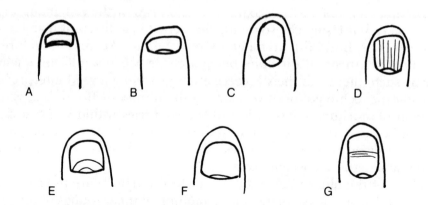

Palmistic explanation: Heart weakness.

Wu Hsing explanation: The palmistic correlation is grossly over-simplified and alarming. Short nails (A and B) reveal a strong fire element which in itself suggests a quickened metabolic rate. Fire, which rules the heart *action*, could suggest tachycardia (heart fluttering), but in many persons this is not abnormal.

In observing nails you must take into account the overall element of the hand itself (this shows congenital health traits), and compare the elements of shape with those suggested in the lineal strengths. A rounded tip (A) shows air element co-joined with a fire shape nail. This suggests a mentally hyper-stimulated heartbeat, not necessarily with a physical cause. With a square tip (B), the fire element is overpowerful and suggests an aggressive mentality and a liking for physical expression. This in turn stimulates the heart rate. Depending on which finger this is found upon, the significance of this formation changes. In C we see a longer and more rounded nail shape (water). Generally this would indicate only a tendency to weakened circulation (*if* found with weak water lines). As water governs the emotions we suspect circulatory troubles, hysteria or menstrual difficulties.

In all cases the quality of the nails must be noted. If they are fluted (lined lengthways) as in D, the water element is over-active; this is especially associated with rheumatism. If they are grooved (lined widthways) as in E, fire element weakness has already been experienced. As it takes not less than six months for a nail to grow, a groove halfway across it reveals some interruption to the growth process around three months previously. All fire element ill-health is characterized by its rapidity, and as nails are upon that part of the finger governing non-structural awareness, one also suspects hyper-active adrenal glands.

If blood pressure is high, the moon at the base of the nail will be larger than average (F). Small or non-existent moons indicate a lowered blood pressure caused usually by lack of exercise. Insufficient or deficient nutritional intake also affects the moons (G). Appropriate advice should be given regarding these to the subject.

Example Two

A

B

Palmistic explanation: Fainting attacks; spinal diseases; poliomyelitis; allergies; neural delicacy.

Wu Hsing explanation: The generalizations here given are alarming! Needless to say they are not reliable. In example A we find a water element nail shape (which is itself associated with hyper-sensitivity) upon an air element tip. Air and water do not mix happily, and there are many adverse effects that result, including sensitivity to criticism, over-reactive attitudes and expressions, self-preoccupation.

Water features, of course, rule circulation of blood and lymph, thus in combination with air (nerves), we could find interrupted flows of both. This could lead to abnormal temperature fluctuations, inability to resist infection, or impaired neural functions (*if* shown in other areas of the hand). All the illnesses shown *could* occur, but it would be foolish to presume their presence solely on this particular formation.

In example B we see a fire element formation again upon an air tip shape. These two are compatible, but in this example the nail covers too much area of the tip. Hyper-activity and stress are indicated. We expect therefore to find this tip much more associated with anxiety, blood infections, and ulcers. If the moon is large, severe internal stress is shown, particularly if this shape predominates in both hands. (This, of course, holds true for all nail shapes described here.)

The one connecting link shown in old palmistry and Oriental techniques is that of shapes revealing the effects of an impaired white blood cell production, or an insufficient lymphatic and liver function. These functions could lead to some of the traditional illnesses indicated. If the nails are sunken deeply into the phalange, air element is weak (neural activation and function), thyroid and thymus imbalances are likely.

Example Three ———————————————————————————

 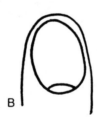 

A   B   C

Palmistic explanation: A) Throat weaknesses; laryngitis; catarrh; sinusitis. B) Chest weakness; pleurisy; bronchitis. C) Lung weakness; small intestine weakness.

Wu Hsing explanation: In our tradition, circular nail formation is related to air element. All air shapes regulate and heighten mental response and sensitivity. Thus worry and stress are likely with this shape, although this will be concealed from the outer world. Thus all respiratory weaknesses are indicated as potential. The larger the moon the shorter the time is taken to fall ill. Air, in this form, is restricted. Thus the European interpretations correspond to the Oriental originals.

The shape in B is also air related. As the nail is larger, congenital respiratory insufficiency should be suspected over infective or virulent disease. This does not mean the bearer is immune to the illnesses stated. The air line should be observed in both hands for confirmation.

The shape in C is again air related, and carries the same meaning as B in example two (see page 93). However we do see a link between intestine and lung blood action. Thyroid, adrenal and pituitary glands are involved here. If through hyperventilation the lung is over-worked, blood pressure is raised. This in turn affects digestive absorption.

Example Four ————————————————————————————

A

B

Palmistic explanation: Lung weakness and infection.

Wu Hsing explanation: This shape (A), known as the "Hippocratic nail," is large in area and height which shows excessive air element. Its association with lung disease, particularly tuberculosis, is long proven. Occasionally it is found as a hereditary factor only. Lung disorders usually involve a swelling of the fingertips. In B we see a distinctive sign of tuberculosis. This nail is also a trait of those prone to muscular dystrophy, particularly if air element features predominate.

● ● ●

In general we must keep the following in mind when dealing with diagnostic techniques: nails are formed of substances, such as keratin, which are directly related to, and regulated by, both the circulatory and endocrine systems. Vibrant health is shown when nails grow swiftly, have full moons and lustre. Generally speaking, length of nail indicates a maturity of the endocrinal balance, while the opposite shows endocrinal insufficiency and occasionally a correlative subnormality. Nail material being ruled by earth element, any insufficiency stresses mineral deficiency or imbalance, as well as all factors connected to or causing this. Color of nails is also significant. After taking into account the season and room temperature, a pale nail indicates lower circulatory power. A vivid red nail shows the opposite. Bluish fingers show pulmonary weakness, while yellow suggests liver or gallbladder insufficiency. If the bluish coloring is found with swollen fingertips, tuberculosis must be suspected. The subject should be advised to consult a doctor.

Modern Discoveries

Research doctors working within the field of endocrinology have conducted much research containing data of cheirological interest. All symptoms of physical disorder reveal themselves in the external body, and glandular malfunctions often show in the condition of hands. Modern work has tended to show that the nail formations illustrated are indicative of glandular condition. Much research is still being conducted in this field.

This formation is rather water-like, except that the nail curves downwards at its tip (air imbalance). The combination has been associated with lung infection, especially when found in a hand type approximating air form.

This type is associated with gonad hypofunction. It has the appearance of fire shape, earth tip, and air ridges.

An unusual type indicating hypo-pituitary action. It has the same basic fire shape nail and earth tip as the one above, but is higher set and of a slightly longer shape.

This shape is indicative of over-active thyroid glands, and is a very common formation. There is no moon evident. This shape has been discussed in the preceding section.

Together with a large body size, this formation is common in hyper-pituitism.

 This is a syphilitic nail formation and shows the presence of infection.

 When this shape is found, and appears soft in texture, it reveals an inherited tendency towards stress and myxoedama (thyroid degeneration).

The nails take between 130 to 180 days to grow fully. In right-handed people, the nails of that hand grow faster. At around thirty years of age, nail growth begins to slow down. The moon of a nail is used as a general guide as to blood pressure or heart action. If full a strong rhythm is suggested, but if small or absent, a deterioration in heart muscle strength and/or blood pressure should be suspected. Examine all fire element manifestations within the palm carefully to check condition of organs and possible causes.

Longitudinal ridges on the nails show a generally sensitive mentality, usually over-active or apprehensive. There is some evidence to link this with a tendency towards colitis or rheumatism, especially if the nail end continually splits. Horizontal ridges indicate periods of interruption in the body's growth cycle, and usually are found to coincide with periods of physical or psychological stress. The timing can be worked out by observing at what height the ridge occurs. Physical injury to the finger can also cause this phenomenon, so inquire from your subject as to whether he or she has ever injured that phalange. White flecks or spots reveal increased and spasmodic air element influence, usually in periods of stress and change or insufficient dietary intake. The timing can be ascertained accurately from the height of the fleck within the nail and the direction of the period from the length. Brittle nails are a symptom of hypothyroid action, especially when found with correspondingly dry hair or alopecia.

Table 9 on pages 98 and 99 is a combined list of endocrinal symptoms as found in the hand and also a chart of elemental shape and size combinations by means of which you can determine the ruling energy of a nail, tooth or face shape, eye, palm, toes or phalanges.

Table 9. Chart of Endocrinal Imbalances as Manifested Within the Hands

Term	Skin	Palm	Digits	Nails	Moons	Flexibility	Thumb	Other Features
Hypothyroid (Cretinous)	Cold, dry, hard	Short	Pudgy, short square tips delicate	Overlong cuticles brittle & dry		Stiff	Broad tip short and badly formed	Few lines hands small and/or deformed
Hypopituitary (Several types)	Lacks hair, delicate	Short	Short, square tips		Full	Hyper	Short	Many fine lines
	Cold-moist	Medium	Long & slender spatulate or square	Small	None	Rigid	–	Few and simple
Eunuchoid	Thin Fat	Elongated	Elongated	Long	Large	Hyper	–	Many lines
Hyperpituitary (Acromegaly)	–	Long	Long & thin (young) Broad (older)	Broad	With & without	Stiff	–	–

Table 9. Chart of Endocrinal Imbalances as Manifested Within the Hands (*continued*)

Term	Skin	Palm	Digits	Nails	Moons	Flexibility	Thumb	Other Features
Adrenal	Moist & cold	Broad & full	Long, square or spatulate tips	Flat, large	Small	Stiff	—	Many deep lines
Hyperthyroid (Several types)	Full & dry and warm	Broad thick	Long, square & spatulate tips	Long curved	Large or opaque		— —	Similar to TB hands
Eunuchism	Thin (female) Fat (male)	Long Long	Long & thin Long & fat	Long Long	Full Full	Fingers only Fingers only	—	Many lines & grilles
Mongoloid	Soft	Large	Short, pudgy pointed tips	Small	Small	Stiff	Short & full	—
Pituitary-Obese	Very soft	Long full mounts	Short, pointed	Small & shiny	Always	Hyper	Hyper-flexive	—

ELEMENTAL PHALANGEAL ANALYSIS

While the primary method of phalange analysis—by area—is quite sufficient for general analysis, a more careful examination of phalangeal quadranture can tell us something more of the subject's particular orientations.
We shall follow the pattern used in the palmar analysis. A line is drawn
from the center of the fingertip on the solar (palmar) surface passing
through the crease at the base of the digit (see figure 37a), that is, where
the finger mount terminates. Irrespective of the angle or tilt of the digit,
the base and top points are *always* used to strike this central, vertical division. Each phalange central line is then bisected by a horizontal line halfway
up. This gives us the four quadrants (shown in figure 37b).

In both hands the fire quadrant is *always* placed on the same side as
the thumb. This means it will be on opposite sides in each hand. We can
thus discern the quadrantal balance of each finger (except the thumb,
which we will deal with later). When we analyze the *top* phalanges in this
manner we can determine particular elemental orientations of the mental
world of the subject (fingerprint element shows the way in which a subject's
best intuition manifests). When we analyze the *middle* phalanges we can
determine a subject's creative or executive orientation. When we analyze
the *lower* phalanges we can determine a subject's physical and sensual
orientations.

The passive hand tells us of the inherited traits in these fields; the
active hand tells us of the created traits or predispositions used most by the
subject in his or her personal, ideal inter-relativity to the world. If you keep
in mind the principle of graduated materiality—that is, energy ascends
from the palm and gradually becomes more refined and ethereal—one can
see that the relative interests related to the phalanges will likewise become

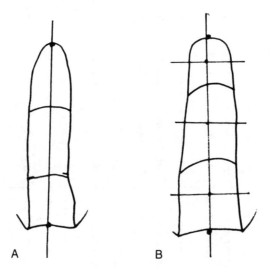

A   B

Figure 37. Quadranture of the phalanges: a) longitudinal division; b) central phalange
divisions.

less and less practical, physical or executive, and transform into more academic or intuitive pursuits and vocations. Analysis of the top phalanges is particularly revealing as it is used to determine the mode of thinking and level of reception in the physiological sphere. In cases of physiological disorder it assumes great diagnostic importance. Other factors are also taken into consideration, and I list some of them here in order to demonstrate the progression of analytical technique to be employed:

Quadrant: Delineate elemental quadrants to determine the quantitative energy possessed by each phalange in both passive and active hands.

Degree of Expression: Note the skin quality of each phalange and note whether it corresponds in element to the phalangeal quadrant, to the elemental height of the phalange, to the element of the digit itself and to the hand shape element. If these elements mainly correspond, the subject utilizes the phalangeal elements creatively and has direct access to their energic correspondents.

Flexure: Determine carefully the phalangeal level of maximum flexure—whether in or outwards. This tells us in which digital element the subject feels most at home. (See figure 38 on page 102.) Test also the rotational flexure of each digit. Determine whether it rotates more easily towards the thumb (which shows a surfeit of outgoing, expressive usage of the energy), or away from the thumb (which indicates an inward, over-personalized usage of the qualities related to the phalange element). Note carefully how far each digit can bend by itself and how far you can bend the digit by exerting pressure. The subject's inhibitory factors are revealed by this test. The greater the difference between the subject's ability to flex and the flexure caused by your direct pressure, so the greater the inhibitory factors in the subject at the time. This is also an indication of a tendency to conceptualize experiences instead of expressing them.

Modifications: Note and balance elemental differences between active and passive hands, seeing such differences as indicators of the personal orientation created by the subject in present times. Balance each phalange with its counterpart. Bear in mind the following:

   • *Nail shape*: In psychological analysis, the nail shape element represents the attitude the subject allows the external world to see.

   • *Fingertip shape*: This indicates the response to intuitive self prompting.

   • *Leaning*: Note if any phalange shows a tendency to lean over towards phalanges of another digit.

   • *Morphic changer*: Knotting of the interphalangeal joints indicates a tendency to restrict inter-communication between the levels indicated by the phalanges themselves. Waisting, in which the phalange decreases in size, indicates an ambivalent attitude towards the material or physical realms connected with the phalange. The subject can take or leave any issue connected or related to the phalange correspondent experience.

The Thumb: This digit is distinguished from the fingers in that it possesses no phalange corresponding to the air element (mounts are earth; lower phalange, water; mid phalanges, fire; upper phalanges, air). We can see that the top phalange of the thumb relates directly not to concepts but to activities and creative influence. Apart from this observation the thumb phalanges are interpreted in a manner identical to the others. Special care should be taken in observing the height upon the palm from which the thumb extrudes and the angle of nail observable from the back of the

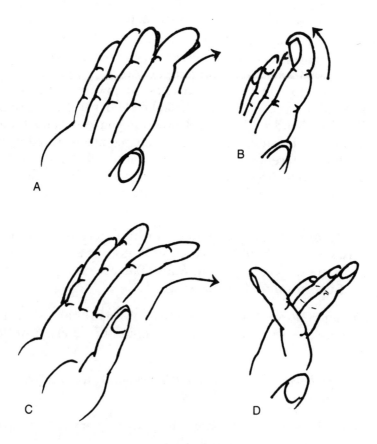

Figure 38. Flexure in the phalanges: (a) and (b) show top phalange flexibility. Mid-joint flexibility is indicated in (c); and (d) shows us lower joint flexibility.

hand. The more nail visible (i.e., the more the thumb is turned 180° from the palm), so the more a subject will externalize his creative energies and seek inspiration in or from other persons and events.

Relationship of Palm and Digit

Each of the digits represents one of four possible areas and modes of consciousness used by a subject. When both the passive and active hands are included, each digit represents the progression or relativity from early formative influences toward present individuality. Each of the four modes (symbolized by these elemental nomenclature) deals with an area or aspect of complete consciousness. By comparing correspondent digits in each hand we can deduce the nature of specific changes away from say, family values, towards that of self motivated goals. We may interpret the correlation between two digits on opposite hands at many levels, drawing from their elemental qualities information concerning all aspects of a subject's being.

When we observe the digit we must decide by the particular shape and one of each phalange to which element they belong to form a tier of three elements. (In practice the fourth mount element is not considered.) This is done with each phalange on each finger of both hands. The elements of corresponding digits are then placed side by side for comparison and evaluation. Before we progress to this evaluation it is well to consider again some of the fundamental values involved in analysis:

1) The palm represents physiological processes and energies.

2) The digits represent psychological processes and energies.

3) When we examine digits exclusively we are examining a reflection of the nature and the quality of the whole usage of consciousness.

4) Each of the digits represents a particular form of energy utilized by consciousness in its understanding of particular goals, aims or ideals.

5) Consciousness is generally considered to be active at the physical, emotional, creative and conceptual levels.

6) When we compare the elemental qualities of each digit we are seeing which of these four levels predominates.

Allied to the above factors we must also bear in mind two other factors that are simultaneously considered in analysis: the overall element of the palm and fingers gives us the manner in which a subject expresses his or her nature; and the overall element of each digit (its ruling element) qualifies the significance of the information we derive from that digit. Thus we can say that comparing overall hand elements tells us of the subject's progres-

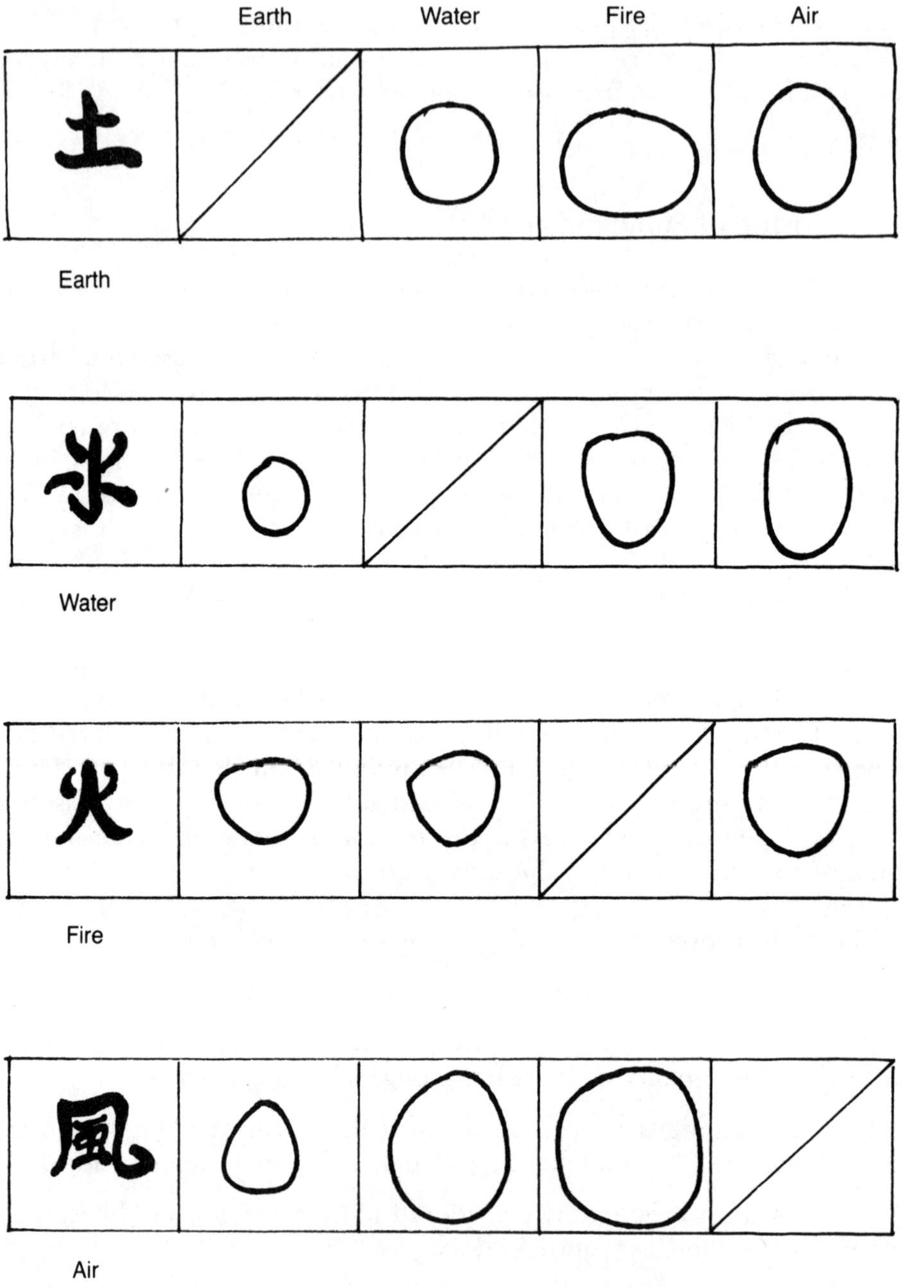

Figure 39. Elemental shapes in combination. When elements combine in the nails, these distinctive shapes emerge. The predominant element is the left hand column, the minor influence is shown across the top. By reading off both columns, the particular elemental shape combinations can be discovered.

sion in individual expression while comparing digital ruling elements tells us about the subject's personal accessibility to and relationships with his or her sources of optimum potentiality.

The palm and digits = one half of a subject's complete consciousness.

The palm = the physical or emotive instinctive energies.

The digits = the subject's usage of psychological or conceptual energies.

Each digit = one fourth of the subject's constitutive conceptual nature.

Each phalange = represents a particular level of expression and impression of the conceptual nature.

Elemental Shapes in Combination

Each element has its own distinctive palmar shape and we can see combinations of the elements by variation or combination of those basic shapes. This is illustrated by figure 39. These shapes prove keys to interpreting palm and finger phalanges. In the holistic tradition of Wu Hsing they are also used to discover the elemental factors of nails, eyes, teeth or head (skull) shapings. If you wish to see the shape of a particular combination, trace the two respective columns vertically and horizontally until they meet. The resulting square bears the shape of that combination.

CHAPTER 9

Dermatoglyphics

Most people nowadays know of the lines in hands, whether they consider them significant or not. Cheirology makes a special study of these lines called "cheirogrammeognomy," which we will make a separate study of in the next section. But in addition to the palmar patterns (called *crease lines* by medical practitioners) there exists another pattern formed by the papillary ridges of the actual skin itself. These ridges are found in distinctive patterns upon the palms and feet—in fact the ridges that give us "fingerprints." The study of these patterns is called *dermatoglyphics*, and in medicine is a relatively new branch of research. Ancient Oriental sources also do not mention it as a special study. The Indian texts by Caraka give details of the effects of various diseases, including incipient leprosy, within the hands, and the Chinese source book of Taoist medicine, the *Nei Ching*, also describes the connections of each finger to the internal organs. But both fail to mention dermatoglyphic patterns specifically. Buddhist texts give specific signs to be found in the hands and feet of a Buddha. These include details of skin color and texture, gesture and shape, and the wheel pattern upon hands and feet. Most now agree that these are dermatoglyphia. This being the case, it is to Buddhist works that we should turn our future research. Other features of Buddhist culture also show an awareness of hands in general. Many paintings originating in western China and Tibet have on their reverse sides the palm prints of the painters or owners. These seem to have been placed there as marks or signs of authenticity, rather as one would afix a personal seal. We can also see this practice in Japan in a scroll written on behalf of Princess Ito during 833 A.D. In this year, she donated estates to Yamashina Temple, and upon the documents concerning this she placed her handprints. These are probably the oldest full handprints in the world.

The police force make probably the most public use of digital dermatoglyphia in the form of fingerprinting. As we have mentioned previously, however, ancient Chinese documents were commonly authenticated by thumb prints, and several examples of these are extant. Both dermatoglyphic pattern and lineal formation begin around the fourth month of pregnancy and all babies are born with fully developed hand-prints. While it is beyond the normal student's ability to make an in-depth study of dermatoglyphic researches, one simple off-shoot of it forms an indispensible aid to analysis, namely the fingerprints.

FINGERPRINTS

There are five main forms of fingerprint pattern. Each relates to the elements and indicates a progression in mind/body communication. There are also several sub-patterns, usually showing negative traits. If we keep in mind the idea of progressing upwards, towards the skies, identification of the major patterns is simple.

The major patterns are the arch, loop and whorl. The whorl pattern predominates among American Indians, Semitic races, Japanese and Eskimos. The pure elemental types are described here. Variant forms of these are described in subsequent sections.

Simple Arch
Earth Element
This is a very simple pattern associated with the fundamental motives of protection, security and inhibition. It gives a sense of rhythm, and often inarticulacy or caution. It is group or tribe orientated.

Loop
Water Element
By far the most common pattern in the Occident, it indicates sensitivity, responsiveness, artistic interests and often lack of concentration. The loop may incline strongly to the right or left of the phalange.

Tented Arch
Fire Element
This is a powerful, hyperactive pattern. It gives deep responsiveness to its possessor, and often over-reaction to stress. Impulsiveness and expression are two of its key traits. It often inclines across the phalange. The basal triadus T distinguishes this pattern from the loop pattern.

Falling Loop
Water and Fire Elements
This confers a dual approach to one's experiences. It gives action and inaction of mind and body, and is thus associated with an erratic nature. Often highly perceptive, its possessors need earth features to stabilize them. It is considered an atavistic sign.

Whorl
Air Element
Chinese tradition calls this "the tree standing in the desert," which gives a clue to its nature. It is independent, freedom loving, original and self motivated—often intense, highly secretive, and emotinally inhibited. It occasionally occurs within the palm, with the same meaning. The whorl pattern is always distinctly separated from other patterns at its base.

Elongated Whorl
Water and Air Elements
This pattern is much the same as the regular whorl except that it gives an emotional overtone to the qualities developed. Original attitudes will be prompted by emotional experiences. The bearer tends to consider others more.

Imploding Whorl
Fire and Air Elements
This is a sign of incomplete energy transformation, and consequently relates primarily to the mundane world as its main point of reference. It indicates materialism, inability to adapt easily, and stubbornness. This pattern is like a whorl or loop folded completely over and pushed together. The pattern always appears as if disintegrating. It—and ones closely resembling it—are also called *composite* patterns.

Triadus
Fire Elements
This is the center of energy within a specific pattern. It occurs upon every digital and palmar mount, marking its effective source.

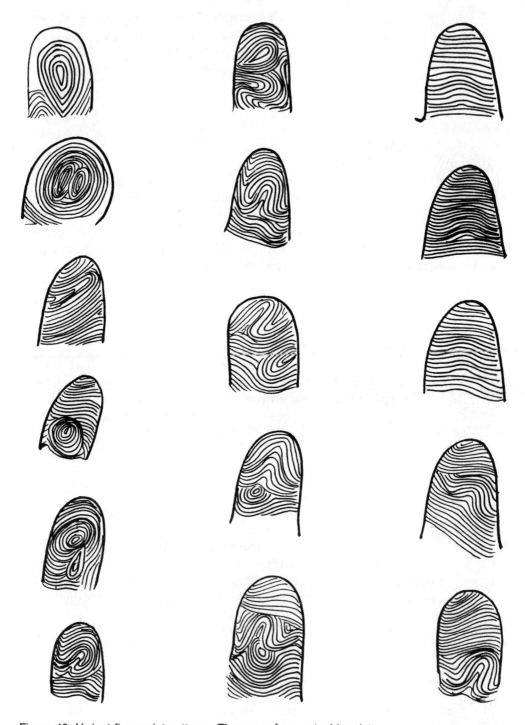

Figure 40. Variant fingerprint patterns. These are from actual imprints.

Flame
Fire and Water Elements
This is a refined combination of the two elements, and shows activity with discrimination in the area it occurs. Note where the tip of the flame points for this is its orientation of resolve. The flame is most commonly found on the palm, but it is sometimes found (in an inverted form) as a fingerprint.

Loop
Water Element
The loop carries the same meanings on the palm as when on the fingertips. Within the palm it often occurs laterally. If the palmar loop points toward the thumb area it indicates a basic need for expression. If towards the hand edge it reveals that the creative urge is internalized, inhibited, or understood only within physical sensations.

• • •

Most of these patterns are readily identifiable on examination of the finger. Figure 40 shows how these patterns can manifest in combination in the actual fingerprint. When patterns incline in any direction, they take on the influence of the element toward which they incline. You would use the same methods of interpretation as you would for a leaning phalange. Inclinations are quite common. Normally, the loop on the air and water fingers should each point inward toward the earth and fire fingers. Other positions—for example, pointing outward—are considered genetic formations. The loop on the water digit pointing toward the thumb is rare—on any other finger it is common.

The spacings between the papillary ridges should be interpreted as with element lines. In the earth formation, the ridges will be large and widely spaced apart. As they ascend the elemental "ladder," they grow closer and finer in texture. One must remember that fingerprints are found on the *mental* phalanges—i.e., the air phalange or tip of finger—and describe particular attitudes held within the fields suggested by the fingers themselves. A simple arch on the fire finger gives a love for simple arts, dance or crafts; a whorl on the earth finger, an original philosophy. A simple arch on the air finger will show speech difficulty. A whorl would be good for a comedian. The patterns of the thumb show how one enacts personal wishes or desires upon the external world.

PATTERNS ON THE PALM AND LOWER FINGERS

The patterns of skin ridges assume definite arrangements within the palmar and digital surfaces. Both the loop and arch patterns were recognized within ancient China. Modern researchers have progressed much further into this area of study, particularly the field of medical (genetic) diagnosis.

There are three main types of dermatoglyphic patterning found within the palm. These will be very unlikely to coexist on one palm. The main types are illustrated in figure 41 and are the loop, the whorl, and the flame. In addition there are also the triadii found in all palms; the center of this pattern forms the center of a mount. Figure 42, taken from a medical chart for purposes of comparison, illustrates common patterns found according to Western medical research. Loops and palmar triadii are common.

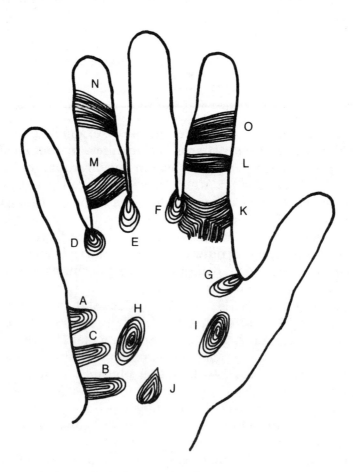

Figure 41. Dermatoglyphic patterns on the palm. the main classifications are: the loop (A-G), the whorl (H-I), the flame (J), and triadii (K). Triadii are found on all palms; their centers form the palmar digit mounts. Digital patterns (L-O) are discussed on page 115.

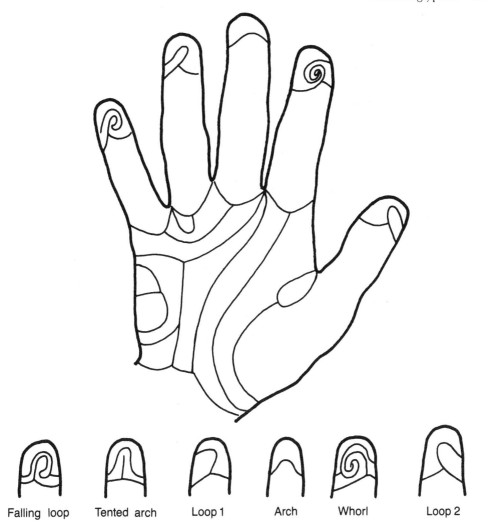

Falling loop   Tented arch   Loop 1   Arch   Whorl   Loop 2

Figure 42. Medical dermatoglyphics—used by dermatologists. Here we can see the same patterns of the loop, whorl and arch. Compare with figure 41.

Palmar Loops

We distinguish three main forms of palmar loops. These are classified according to their elemental quality. Figure 41a shows the earth quality form, which is low in height and widely separated in its ridges. Slightly wider and shorter in length (figure 41c) indicates the fire element. When loops are present in fine and closely packed ridge patterns, as in figure 41b, air element predominates.

Loops can also be found between the digits, as in figure 41d. In general, loops are ruled by water, and impart a quality of sensitivity and originality to the area where they are found. If of the water or air quality and in the lower water quadrant (figure 41b), they indicate interest in esoteric studies, psychic predispositions and a degree of introversion. When the loop is positioned at the height shown in figure 41b, the subject will be inclined toward the arts and the performing arts. It shows a practical expression of the imagination common to designers, architects, actors and surgeons, representatives and public figures of all kinds. A loop positioned as in figure 41a indicates a more material orientation to the imagination, and indicates reasoning and calculative ability—common among salespeople, surveyors, computer and technical science workers. A loop positioned as in figure 41b indicates responsive physical drives, expecially if of the earth or water quality.

In all cases the loop patterning shows that the subject is essentially responsive, working best within fields of activity requiring responses to the public. Wherever it is seen in the palm, this quality will be shaped and modified by the activities signified by that particular area.

Whorls and Flames

When the whorl is seen in the palm as in figure 41i, it indicates that the subject wishes to act as an individual. If found upon the water zone (figure 41h), it suggests originality in that element's activities and, unlike the loop, a penchant to work alone or unsupervised. When seen upon the earth zone, (figure 41i), it indicates pride in the family, racial or cultural background. This marking is often found in those who change cultures (by emigration, marriage, or ideals) or who are highly responsive to patterns of color, sound or smell.

The flame is an energized loop formation which is joined at its top (see figure 41j). Where this top points indicates the resolving area most suitable to the subject's temperamental balance. The flame position is a psychic sign conferring an affinity with non-structural consciousness, inspiration and intuition. Wherever the flame is seen it unifies, activates and orientates the area it grows within.

Flames or loops are found often between the digits. The position in figure 41d signifies a unity of fire and air energies, and this will activate the desire for communication within the levels of body, mind or speech (depending upon the overall quality of the air digit). When the tip of the flame points toward the air digit, the realm of ideas is stressed. If pointing toward the fire digit, the realm of action is valued. Figure 41e shows a unity of fire and earth elements. These are not compatible and incline towards "scorched earth" attitudes. They indicate fixed viewpoints, mental stasis, and intensity or seriousness of thought. When flame tip points toward the earth digit, it indicates that the subject has an excessively sober and often solitary nature. This is a good marking for academics, religious leaders or financiers. When inclining towards fire, more constructive attitudes are suggested. Figure 41f shows a unity of water and earth quality, indicating strong idealism, independence and leadership, if found with good thumb formations. If not, it confers physicality, a liking for self-indulgence and pleasures. The subject will tend to dislike personal restraint.

Digital Patterns

The digital phalanges themselves indicate particular traits and qualities of consciousness, irrespective of dermatoglyphic patterns. However in Wu Hsing form, elemental formations are identified and serve to indicate an underlying karmic propensity towards their particular elemental experiences. The angle of the dermatoglyph provides the identifying trait. Let's look at some examples found in figure 41. The pattern in figure 41l is of earth element and indicates an underlying tendency to maintain and remember experiences. The pattern in 41m is of the water element and gives sympathetic and emotional receptivity to the phalange correlate. The peak of this loop type points to either external or internal actions of consciousness. The pattern in 41n is of the air element and indicates that an active and thoughtful attitude is maintained or appreciated within the field of phalange rulership. Pattern 41o is the fire type, which energizes and activates the phalange correlation into conscious awareness. Each of these elemental patterns usually bears an air or water quality of line. Since they are digital formations, they relate to patterns of consciousness above all else. However, one should look for variations in these two elements. Although it is rare to find an earth or fire dermatoglyphic quality on the digits, such a trait, when found, tends to decrease the intellectual capacity of the subject, making him or her more materialistic in outlook.

FINGERPRINT EPICENTERS

Chinese metaphysical teachings say that each fingertip phalange is a sensor for natural energy, and that the tips are receptive to both earthly light and inner light. This energy is called *Chi* and manifests in many forms—and one of these forms is the fingerprint. If we take as an example the whorl patterns, its center point—from which the actual dermatoglyphic pattern emerges—is said to be the source print between physiological and natural energy. In Chinese medicine this point is associated with the eyesight (sight itself being a feature of light sensitivity). The actual placement of this center tells us something about the subject's fundamental reception to all forms of energy, within the limits of the ruling features and objects of that digital phalange. Thus the earth tip, wherever its center, is concerned with matter, order, principle, etc.

The commencement or energetic point (the *epicenter*) tells us much about the subject's predispositions. When the epicenter occurs nearer the thumb side of a phalange, the qualities of that finger, on the mental level, seek external expression. The reverse is true when the epicenter occurs on the air digit side of the phalange. The higher an epicenter the more idealistic, conceptual or spiritual the reception of Chi becomes. The lower the epicenter appears, the greater the desire for physical or material expression. Figure 43 shows a simple chart of the epicenter positions and also the secondary points. The secondary points will give us combined meanings.

The epicenter should always be regarded as the commencement of a finger dermatoglyphic. The triadus represents its predisposition in non-energetic terms—such as environment of birth, family or inherited traits. We expect therefore to find a stronger formative environment in cases where the triadus is strongly and clearly marked. When the triadus is not visible—for example, when it occurs on the edge of the phalange—the formative impulse is directed predominately by the subject and will be either expressive or inhibitive, depending on which side of the phalange it rests.

It will help your interpretation if you visualize the epicenter as if it were pushed away (or around) the "waves" of the dermatoglyphic. Thus in a loop formation the waves are pushed upwards from the bottom of the phalange. (We know this because in the loop formation the base dermatoglyphic lines are unclosed.) There is here a direct entry from the lower section of the phalange, and thus a greater receptivity to the earth/water aspects of that phalange's qualities. In the case of a pure whorl, this base is completely closed up and the epicenter acts in its own right according to the height at which it rests. There is thus more significance in its position

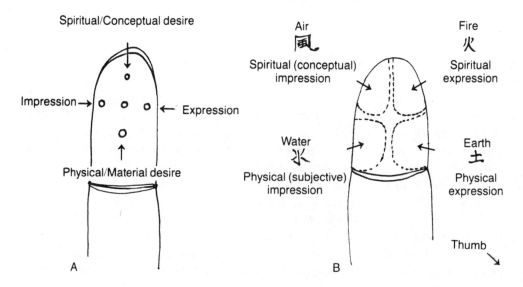

Figure 43. Epicenters. Primary points are shown in A, and secondary points are shown in B.

and less significance in its contact with the lower elements of that phalange. Seen another way, the whorl effectively bars influences from the medial phalange by emanating the dermatoglyph pattern, rather like the concentric circles formed from a pebble dropped in a pool.

In the simple arch pattern, the epicenter is only just being formed within the evolutionary process of the subject. In the tented arch, the epicenter has accelerated up high and its triadus serves to stabilize its energies—as if to remind the epicenter of where it came from. The falling loop shows the epicenter has over-reached itself; the composite, that it is dividing, disintegrating, and transmutating.

By combining the epicenter placement, level and direction together with the triadus position, and considering the field of activity ruled by the phalange itself, a very accurate plan of the subject's interests and influences can be understood.

EPICENTER INTERPRETATION AND ANALYSIS

Because fingerprints never alter, the Chinese system associates them with one's personal karma, that is, events or attitudes that one has created in previous existences. This has little relevance for most cheirologists, but it is worth considering. Every other feature of the external body changes or develops except this primary pattern, and it is very interesting to see the link being made between fingerprints and genetic disease by medical researchers, as inherited illness is a form of karma itself. Indeed one could view the RNA or DNA code as the "fingerprint" of our genes.

In Wu Hsing analysis, two points within the fingerprint are used as references: the high point and the low point. The highest part of the inner patterning is the "eye" of the whorl, or the point on top of an inner loop (or tented arch) formation. This will be the epicenter, and examples of different variations are shown in figure 44. This point indicates the highest

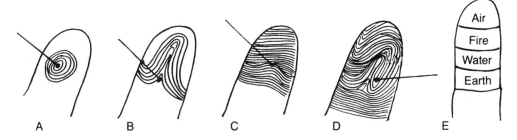

Figure 44. Various placements of epicenters: a) the epicenter of a whorl pattern; b) of a tented arch; c) of a simple arch; and d) the epicenter of a falling loop. The epicenter may lie at one of the four heights, shown in (e). These heights refer to levels of expression utilized by the subject within the areas governed by the overall element ruling the phalange (finger).

elemental *level* available to the subject in question. This element is judged by the height upon the fingertip at which this center point is found. Most central points will be found to lie within the fire zone. A tendency towards a higher position is said to be a sign of spiritual potential. A lower placement gives a more material or physical orientation to the subject.

The lowest point used is the *triadus* of the dermatoglyphic. This is the triangular point found towards the edge of a fingerprint pattern. The illustration of medical dermatoglyphics shows where these commonly occur. (See figure 42 on page 113.) Certain patterns, such as the simple arch and some forms of the loop or tented arch, often have no discernible triadus, for they may lie far to the side of the phalange. Such a formation indicates a direct flow of energies up into the central point and an excess of body stimuli to its bearer. Such an individual may be hyper-active or responsive to external environments (or persons), and not easily able to separate feelings from thoughts. When this offset triadus lies toward the thumb side of the finger, it shows such responses to be active. If found on the auricular (air) finger side, responses are passive. If both are clearly visible, the subject possesses an ability to synthesize thought and feeling in a creative manner. Such marking is often found on the hands of designers, musicians and artists of all types.

In Master Print One we can observe the different epicenter heights in the fire and earth digits. The fire digit is higher and the left hand triadus is clearly visible. Observe also Master Print Two. The right-hand fire and water digits have no discernible triadus. The earth is clearly visible. On the left hand, triadii are not visible either. In this print all the central points are lower than usual, lying in the earth or water levels. This gives the subject strong instincts. On the right palm, the loop dermatoglyphic is clearly visible in the water quadrant. Such loops show great physical sensitivity and take two distinctive forms: those that point towards the thumb side of the hand and those that point away from it. If the loop points towards the thumb side, it indicates an outwardly directed desire for comfort, pleasure and artistic or cultural satisfaction. When the loop is pointing inward, it usually heightens the subject's physical responses.

PART THREE

Shou Hsien

Study of the Lines

CHAPTER 10

An Introduction to Cheirogrammeognomy

The concept that hands and their lines respond to an inner energy flow was particularly popularized in 1900 by William Benham within his work *Scientific Hand Reading* (NY: Putnams), but it was not originated by him. Chinese medicine had already clearly stated such principles around 2000 B.C. Benham presumably lacked any understanding of this earlier teaching, but did remarkably well in his presentation and development of it. Other hand analysts, lacking his perception, failed to appreciate the significance of energy flow. Some of Benham's more renowned contemporaries were completely ignorant of it even though certain of them claimed to have access to esoteric or pristine traditions. This is probably why Benham called his work scientific, in order to distinguish himself from those who made unsupportable claims to authenticity. Later researchers also ignored Benham's teaching regarding flow. One psychologist, C. Wolfe, authored several perceptive works upon cheirological diagnosis that pay great attention to both cheiromorphognomical and lineal balance; however she by-passes their metaphysical significance and completely avoids discussion of their paradigmatic implications. When we come to appreciate the subtlety and metaphysical implication inherent in lineal formation we can experience and express their meanings in terms of a subject's personal life, but we are still not brought any closer to our question of why they are there. Chinese tradition considers such a question as invalid, saying that "first causes" are ineffable and not worthy of persistent enquiry.

When we try to discover the etiology of what the Greeks termed *Mantika* (prophecy) as a practice or ethic, we are faced with great problems. There are many questions about other subjects that cannot yet be answered—ones about history and agriculture, architecture and science, and so on, of the countries within which we can find Mantika. To know its source we would really have to understand the purpose or initiating cause of life itself. We can, however, work with what we actually observe, and, by noting recurring lineation patterns, draw tentative conclusions as to their origins. This principle is not new; it has originated many sciences and philosophies. Hand analysts claim that conclusions can be drawn from such observations and that the principles governing what is observed can be deduced via common and specific hand line patterns. The Occidental students of Wu Hsing cheirology call these patterns *paradigms*. They are viewed as keys to energic manifestation at many levels of existence.

HEALING AND ENERGY

There are many teachings that connect specific lineal formations with certain physical organic processes, but these at their best are only diagnostic techniques and not therapeutic. Only from personal experience can we know that the Oriental methods of natural healing and diagnosis actually work, for they are based upon holistic teachings inaccessible to specialist and modern European medical tradition. We may perhaps see or suspect that it is this specialist manner or criterion of observation and examination that pervents us from understanding the significance and import of lineal formations, and hence a fully preventative form of healing. Happily there have been many dissenters from over-rigid forms of diagnosis within Europe and these may have paved the way towards an acceptance of Oriental techniques, philosophy and practice.

In Oriental tradition the energies contained within the physical body are not expected to be visible to the naked eye; they can only be sensed by someone of a particular attitude and ability. This sensitivity takes a long time to develop and refine; thus not all persons can be either cheirologists or doctors of Oriental traditional systems. We may perhaps then wonder how we can assess the energy if we cannot see it? This is a reasonable question; Chinese naturopathic doctors have, however, developed special forms of pulse diagnosis which are related not only to the heart or blood circulation but also to the energy circulation of the physical organs. We see that in this Chinese tradition a physical process is allied to a metaphysical one. A similar process occurs in the medical interpretation of palmar lineation. Lineation patterns are regarded as a "thermometer" of the quality of life itself—not just organic life but also spiritual life—in that they are understood as describing metaphysical forces innate but active in nature.

In cheirology there exists both an energic pulse and natural beat for each function of the human being—spiritual, mental, emotional and physical energy manifestation, which is determined by examination and comparison of both hands. It is not possible to prove the existence of this energy, though we can subsequently validate its prognostic interpretation. That we cannot prove this principle is not strange; in our daily life we use, measure, and receive benefits from another mysterious and as yet unseen force, namely, electricity. A connection between the energy form we call electricity and the metaphysical energy present within the body was suspected almost as soon as electricity was discovered. Ancient Chinese manuscripts describe the currents and tides of metaphysical energy in a manner similar to the ways we describe electricity nowadays (in certain cases I would suggest they do it better). That this energy flow is active within the body is best discovered by direct personal experience, either through traditional Oriental medicine, Chinese massage, martial arts or cheirology itself. Each of these opens a specific form of access to it. The principle implicit to cheirology is that such energy is capable of influencing the structure of physical and paradigmatic patterns, and can then be subject to codification or analysis. Greek philosophers such as Democritus and Pythagoras held this latter view and sought to describe its manifestations via the physical symbols in nature (i.e., the elements). The Chinese never considered justifying its presence philosophically; it had already been used for over 2000 years as a living experience.

When we analyze lines, it becomes apparent that we can do so at several levels. In the old, popular viewpoint of palmistry, the manifestations observed are given significance in direct relation to human emotions, events and personality patterns. Palmar markings are equated with a system of simple correspondence; if you have marking "A" then meaning "B" must apply, and so on. All European hand analysis grew up with this format. Such correspondences cannot be denied—but they are not so simple.

In the old system, when we came across a marking or lineation which was found inaccurate, nothing could be said or done about it. It was wrong and that was that. If there was any blame, it fell squarely on the shoulders of the analyst (called then a palmist). It never occurred to those ancient or not so ancient palmists that their fundamental criteria may have been misunderstood or even misinterpreted. No one could correct them—for they lacked knowledge of cheirology's metaphysical principle. Consequently all analyses were kept safely within the bounds of character interpretation and prediction of the future. The implications of the latter principle were never pondered very deeply. It was assumed that everyone had a fate which was, in the main, unchangeable. The palmists' task was to prognosticate concerning it. Not until the 1800's did anyone in Europe care to seriously relate health to the hand or attempt to correlate the two descriptively. A few early attempts were made by medical doctors, but it wasn't until recent times that others seriously sought to improve upon those early pioneers. With the advent of more recent discoveries concerning the bio-physical electrofield, Kirlian photography, the refinement of dermatoglyphics and the research of the Cheirological Society, discoveries have been made that appear to confirm that the correlation is possible. To make it applicable to the average individual, only a suitable descriptive nomenclature is required.

In our tradition, the nomenclature used takes the form of elements and, like the early Greeks, Chinese Buddhist sages explained elemental powers in manners both direct and inferred. The elements are eminently suitable for this task in that they can be either physical, amorphic, or metaphysical in nature. By utilizing them as symbolic representations it became possible to place equal emphasis on both their symbolic and physical values. Dual and tripartite levels of understanding thus became accessible. If—as in the Chinese system—organs of the body were held to be under the rulership of specific elements, then their related lines would also describe those same organs. Based on this, the art of physical diagnosis, *Chen Tuan*, was born and with it the possibility of prognosis.

For the early cheirologists, working within a Buddhist philosophical framework was a great advantage. There was no concept of an omnipotent deity, no fate as such and a strong emphasis on self help and self understanding. It was only within such a framework as Buddhism that cheirology could have made progress and attained such clarity. Early Indian Buddhism was formal, but with the spread of monk missionaries into China the sect know later as Tai-Cheng (Greater Vehicle) developed. This was more liberal and integrative in its outlook. From around 200 A.D. on, China had hosted Buddhist monk doctors. In the late 4th and on through the 5–6th centuries A.D., the esoteric Buddhist teachings emerged. These were of a school which, though stemming from Indian Buddhist traditions, had developed its esoteric and integrative aspects further, eventually becoming an important, separately developing form of Chinese traditional belief. It was within the esoteric schools of Buddhism that cheirology developed, for a central tenet of Tantra was that enlightenment could be won through the human body. Thus we find Tantric teachers embracing physical training methods such as martial arts, medicine, mudra, physiognomy and yoga along with meditation. It was from within the Buddhist esoteric physiognomy that the division of the hand into elements began. All subsequent cheirology is dependent upon this beginning. Indian Hindu cheirology as an organized study was not known until long after this, though Hindus quickly adopted Buddhistic improvements in other studies and arts.

HANDS OF BUDDHAS AND DEITIES

The earliest lines we find to have been recorded within both statuary and iconography are those popularly called the *head* and *heart* (upper and lower transverse). These are much in evidence in statues of the Buddha made within 300 years of his death (see figure 45). Prior to that time there exist sets of palmar lines found upon statues and icons of the Hindu deities, particularly Shiva. This Shivaite palmar format appears to have been adopted by the Buddhists around and after 200 A.D. The main Shivaite

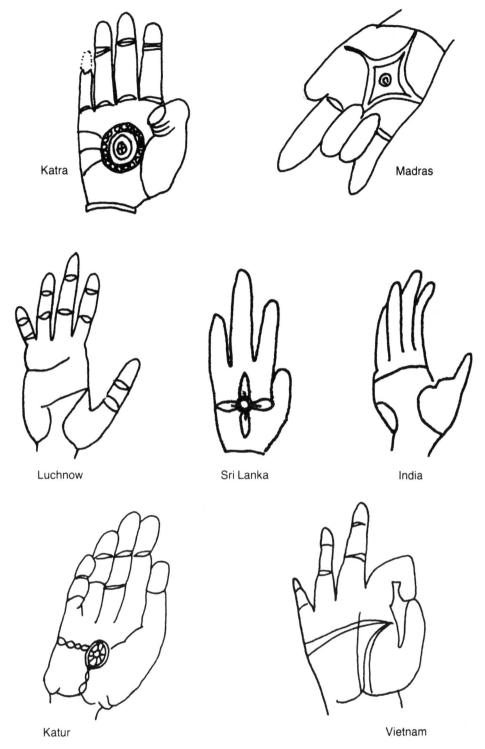

Figure 45. The hands of Buddhas and deities. These are copied directly from actual statues of the Buddha Shakyamuni and are faithful reproductions of both cheirognomical and cheiromantical appearance.

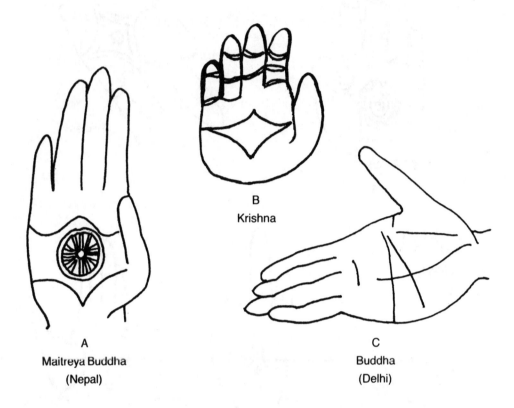

Figure 46. Special markings of the future Buddha Maitreya are shown in A and C. The hand of Krishna is shown in B, dating to 1600 A.D.

pattern is diamond shaped and occurs without further markings, isolating all peripheral corners of the palm. In its Buddhist form, we find a sign added to its center—usually an eight–spoked wheel or a swastika. What is especially distinctive of the Buddhist statues is that in quite a number of cases they bear fingerprints and often both loop and whorl patterns are shown. It was perhaps from these Indian statues that the Chinese devised their own system of fingerprint classification. In fact, the Chinese used fingerprints to replace signatures on documents. Within the statues of the period 300 A.D. to 750 A.D. we find evidence of the head, heart, vitality and a Moon line appearing. It is significant that only a very small amount of Apollo or Saturn lines are found. Absence of Saturn is explainable doctrinally in that a Buddha has risen above all fate.[1] Absence of Apollo is not. One of the many honorific titles of the Buddha in India was *Surya*—the Sun. This is a notable iconographic and cheirological omission. The diamond shape referred to earlier is symbolic of mastery over the four elements (a basic teaching theme of Buddhist meditation). The fact that head, heart and vitality lines are reproduced (and within a reasonable period of living memory) shows that the Buddha indeed had lines upon his hand and that such lines were considered significant. In those early times every mark upon a Buddha's body had extreme significance; they had been foretold prior to his birth and the Buddha himself also described markings the future Buddha Maitreya will possess (see figure 46).

Apart from such supernormal interpretations of the palmar features, another level—and one which has not escaped the gaze of modern Western doctors—is that of psychology. The earliest detailed and systematic descriptions of psychology and epistemology are found in India. Hindu scriptures concerning meditation give refined and detailed accounts of the various mental processes. Buddhist meditation masters developed these findings even further; they postulated access into the transcendental state of meta-consciousness—a state never previously taught within India. Our modern art of psychology (from the Greek *psyche*, the spirit) is not really sufficient in its linguistic scope to describe the nature of Oriental transcendentalism. This transcendentalism extends far beyond the realms of the ordinary mental concepts. We have yet to catch up linguistically with these ancient systems.

Not content with mere earthly psychology, Buddhist Tantrists also described the mental states of deities, demons and ghosts. I am purposely laboring this point to show that the potential range of information regarding the workings and patterns of the mind available to Oriental students and teachers was (and is) vast. It is not trapped within the rigid framework of either European or Middle Eastern religious or psychological dogma—it exceeded them long ago. Consequently when we begin to wonder at what point Oriental cheirology stops, the answer is: it doesn't! Its principles are said to continue after death in an unceasing scope and cycle.

The individual has to be considered from the various levels of mind, spirit and body. To do otherwise would lead to a divorce from the significance and implications of our study itself. At each of these three significant levels we must examine fully their holistic and constituent formations. From such formations hand analysis as an art of macro/microscopic discovery developed.

At this very point we may ask the question: What is the purpose of lines? A valid reply would or could only be at the level of answer you require. From the spiritual view of theistic teaching we could answer: To demonstrate the unity of God and mankind by revealing their nature. From the non-theistic view of Buddhism we could answer: To remind us that life and evolution are complex; not until we fully know that which creates this complexity can we touch the wisdom of enlightenment or understand its basis. From the animistic viewpoint we could answer: To appreciate the glory of nature itself and to evidence its domain. From the medical doctor's viewpoint we could answer: To describe the interconnection and development of the genetic and endocrinal system within the physical being.

Which answer is it to be? Any or all of them can be your choice, for they all have validity. What we can say is that the hand is the most natural, perfect, faithful and true reflection of the individual and the cosmos we have ever known, and even if one planned for a thousand years with sophisticated computers we could never produce an artificial replica so simple in structure yet so profound in meaning.

LINE FORMATION AND GENERAL HEALTH IMPLICATIONS

Everything in nature has a flow, an unceasing quality of change that responds to the environment. The most obvious natural changes are the seasons. In addition to such obvious flows, there are further, not so obvious ones also taking place. For example, light changes occurring within the seasons bring responses in plant growth, human fertility and overall health balance. The physical body manifests these changes, and renews and develops itself according to patterns that can be detected if one knows how and where to look. Chinese medicine tells us of a 24 hour cycle that our organic energy undergoes each day. Cheirology also knows of such cycles, and they are revealed not daily but annually for a period in length varying from seventy to ninety years.

Each line of the hand represents a specific form of energy—that is, one governing a special purpose. From a qualitative analysis of lineal presence one can come to recognize the "thermometer" of potential existing within the subject. This quality is articulated in terms of the four elements. Each line relates to an element, and therefore an organ or function ruled by that element. The earth line, for example, describes bones, minerals, etc. The water line describes the circulatory system within the blood, lymph and joints. Air describes respiratory functions, neural efficiency and mode of consciousness. Fire describes digestion, movement, physical power and metabolic rate. To assess a subject's particular form of energy balance— whether organic or psychological—one has to be aware of which potentials are available to the subject.

Theoretically, each lineal formation can be fully present on a palm. This is called "100% presence." Lines which *must* be present are those we term *major*. These are concerned with basic functions of the life itself. We cannot have weather without, for example, wind and rainfall; in the same way, thought, vitality, emotions and activity (each corresponding to an element) are all essential to the balanced human being. If we observe only 50% of each of those lines present—that is, if they are all present but in only half their natural length, or half are present in full length—we know that a cycle of degeneration is present, an imbalance which will evenutally terminate the structure as it now is. Sometimes this coincides with death, and sometimes with a complete change of life style, attitude, or organic function. The lines that deal with organic processes and are activated by the unconscious or parasympathetic nervous system are termed the minor lines. When minor lines are very pronounced, we know that an organic function has been made conscious; it or its paradigm has been brought to the surface for some reason. This is not natural; it is like snow in July. We find that most minor lines appear only when major lines are functioning at less than optimum energy. By noting the percentage of appearance and the element ruling the apparent lines we can begin to assess the area and nature of imbalance present and arrive at some form of preliminary diagnosis. Imbalance is revealed not only by length, but also by elemental quality. We expect a line ruled by an element to show that element's characteristics—for example, a fire line should in principle exhibit a fire form. If it evidences another we know that something has affected it. A fire line that has an air form has been dispersed and has weakened in its function. A water line showing a fire form has become intensified and overloaded to a dangerous degree. Each line, by length and elemental quality, should be assessed in this manner (see Table 10). No one line formation within the hand expresses completely a single element. To a degree each is composed of the others. Certain lines are connected in action or effect on certain physiological functions to a greater degree than others—we therefore consider such to be of this predominant elemental energy ruled by that function.

Table 10. General Qualities of the Elemental Forces

Air Energy	That which communicates, balances or understands experiences derived from external conceptual sources.
Water Energy	That which identifies, personalizes or relates internal experiences into emotive patterns.
Fire Energy	That which challenges, leads, or directs experiences into recognizable boundaries of expression.
Earth Energy	That which relates to, contains, or preserves experiences of one's own or other's being and continuity.

Table 11. Comparative Names of Lines

Line	European	Roman	Medical
Earth:			
major	Life line	Vitalis	Thenar crease
minor	Fate	Fortuna	Radial longitudinal
subsidiary	Influence	Amicus	Medial longitudinal
Water:			
major	Heart line	Via Cor	Distal crease
minor	Via Lasciva	Via Lasciva	—
upper	Girdle of Venus	Cinculum Veneris	—
lower	Ring of Moon	Cinculum Lunaris	—
subsidiary	Travel lines	—	—
	Affection lines	—	—
Fire:			
major	Mars line	Soror Vitalis	Inner thenar crease
minor	Success line	Solaris	Ulnar longitudinal
subsidiary	Ambition line	—	—
	Ring of Apollo	—	—
Air:			
major	Head line	Cerebal/Mensal	Proximal crease
minor	Health line	Via hepatica/via lactia	Hypothenar longitudinal
subsidiary	Worry lines	—	—
	Ring of Mercury	—	—
	Hyperactivity lines	—	Striations
	Obstruction lines	—	Transverse striations

The basic elements control, direct and are expressed through their four major lineal formations. For the student's reference, these are shown in Table 11 under their old names, elemental rulerships and more modern forms of description. Figure 47 shows the major lines and figure 48 shows the minor lines. Minor lines are termed *reflections* of the majors as they tend to show their subtle activities. They are not therefore present in every hand. If we view the hands with a specific orientation in mind—for example, to discern ill health—certain minor lines are very important and assume a significance almost as great as a major. Major lines show the causes of imbalances; minors show the symptoms of imbalance. One should not, therefore, be led into thinking of major and minor as being terms describing their overall importance upon the hand; this classification is purely practical in nature.

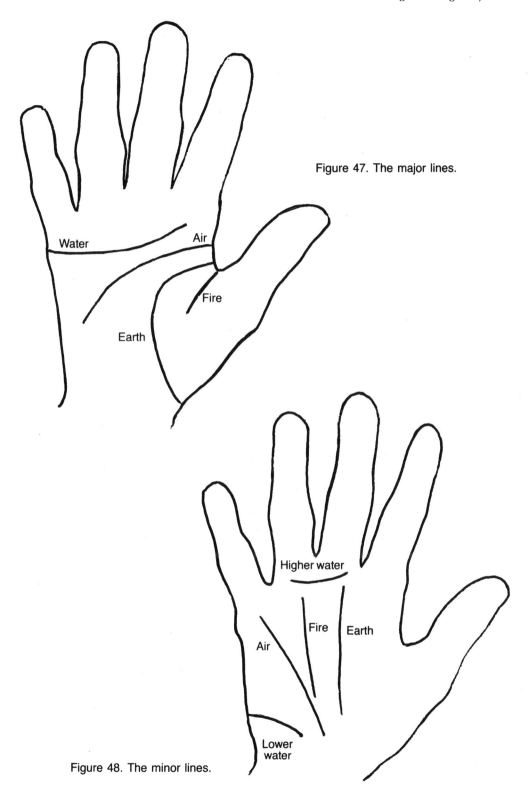

Figure 47. The major lines.

Figure 48. The minor lines.

LINE FORMATION AND PSYCHOLOGY

Psychologically speaking, major lines deal with primary mental directions, minor lines with unconscious orientations. There is thus a direct connection made in Wu Hsing method between fundamental organic energy, or action, and psychological orientation. This complex interaction is what all lines manifest. A comparable interaction is found within Occidental medicine in the action and effects of the endocrinal system. An imbalance in these often manifests drastic temperamental changes. Such changes are either congenital or can be caused by insufficient dietary balance. *Fire* lines are related to energy, enthusiasm, bravery and physical power. *Water* lines are related to emotional sensitivity, imagination and introversion. *Air* lines are related to intellectuality, truth seeking and communication. *Earth* lines are related to group activities, simplicity in outlook and constancy. In very general terms, we can say that predominant elemental lines indicate that the individual feels most at ease within those thought processes or orientations natural to that element; thus fire dominance shows an active type, water, a feeling type, air, a thinking type and earth, a physical type. Each of these types perceives things more rapidly within the orientations of their elements. Each feels most uneasy when confronted with or placed within their opposite polarities.

Most of us possess two palms and two sets of digits. These portray basic family or ethnic feelings, thoughts, activities and bodily orientation. They also show how the subject has modified, denied or extended these realms at the present time. A clear psychological development can thus be traced by observing line elements within both hands. Fears and phobias can often be recognized by accurate evaluation of elemental presence. The various fundamental ones common to the types form reverse crystallizations of the governing elements:

Fire fears water, restriction, envelopment in all senses.

Earth fears heights, public exposure and lack of identification.

Air fears caves, rigid enclosures of thought and emotionalism.

Water fears fire, rebuttal, insensitivity and lack of expression.

In evaluation, the manner in which elemental predominance manifests within personality is dependent on many things. Religious, educational and social levels modify how we respond to and receive elemental energies, so it is necessary to make some allowance for this.

One of the early modifications devised in Oriental countries was that of the tripartite quality. In different cultures this took various forms. For example, the Buddhists viewed life experience as being the prime source of spiritual evolution. This experience was developed in mind, speech and body. The Shamans and Taoist followers viewed all life as falling under the domain of heaven, earth and mankind. The French cheirologist Desbarolles innovated a similar idea in his classification of the hand surface into the zones ruling mind, materiality and physicality. Later commentators ascribe his classification to the Semitic Kabbala but the Kabbala does not have such a classification at all. It is instead more likely that Desbarolles drew his inspiration from Far Eastern, rather than Middle Eastern, sources. The three systems here outlined can be interconnected:

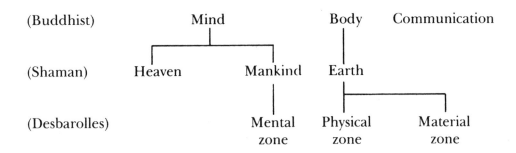

Despite their apparent differences any system founded on tripartite qualities tends to resemble others with a similar basis. Practically speaking, it is more the cultural environment that decides how we articulate the tripartite pattern.

What emerges from such patterns is the awareness that each and every factor present with the palm can be understood at different levels, whether they be the three mentioned above or other similar ones. In analyzing lines we can see that there emerges a tripartite manner of understanding their import. This can be termed the lineal high, medial and low function (see Table 12). The high function relates to spiritual, non-structured understanding. The medial function relates to practice or executive experiences. The low function relates to physical and mundane experiences. The high and medial levels usually describe the internal nature and basic orientation of a subject's psychology. The lower level describes the external and consciously exhibited factors of a line's rulership. If we consider the four major element lines of the palm, we can see the value of their significance alters considerably according to the level at which we analyze them. As we begin to combine different factors seen in the hands, the resultant combinations

Table 12. The Four Major Elemental Lines
and Their Three Levels of Significance

Air	High	To indicate the chronological sense and macrocosmic aspirations of the owner and to show how he or she perceives them.
	Medial	To describe the quantity, quality and orientation of mundane consciousness and its effects upon the temperament.
	Low	To indicate the result or effect of physical desires/impulses within the psycho/neural activities of the subject.
Water	High	To indicate the degree of intuitional or devotional sensitivity attained by the subject.
	Medial	To describe the quality of emotional energy, its control, usage and orientation.
	Low	To describe instinctive, physically based wishes for intercommunication. To indicate the functioning of the circulatory system.
Fire	High	To describe the amount of source energy used in maintaining the harmonious interaction of mind and body.
	Medial	To indicate the power of present and inherited forces governing physical power, endurance and fertility.
	Low	Absence of this line indicates low function. This implies a lack of drive, family influence and exocentric individuality.
Earth	High	To describe the amount of metaphysical regenerative energy possessed by the subject within his or her physical body.
	Medial	To describe the harmonious functioning of the whole body and its constituent organs. The ability to resist infection or inflammatory illness.
	Low	The amount of physical power utilized by the subject within his or her normal life pattern.

of line meanings, their elemental level, and quality we can see that cheirognomy enables a high precision and accuracy.

SOURCE COMPATIBILITY: LINES AND QUADRANTS

Each of the lines we observe on the palm indicates a certain activity that has been initiated by either body or mind. The beginnings of such lines can tell us something of their nature and action when considered in elemental terms.

The major *water line* begins in the air quadrant and is therefore fundamentally antagonistic to this quadrant's energy action. Air describes, in particular, those methods of communication based upon knowledge (structured systems of understanding). Water departing from this quadrant tells us that the function of water is the opposite to it—non-structured, or emotional, intuitive, understanding. The course of the water line describes the success or failure of the subject's attempts to realize this intuitive consciousness.

The *major earth line* generally starts just within the fire quadrant and, again, these two represent opposite polarities. Earth is static and solid. Fire is active and non-material. Earth departing from fire shows us that earth's function is to stabilize the hyperactivity symbolized by fire and to channel its energies onto rhythmic, repeatable forms. Both the water and earth lines describe the attempts made by human consciousness to attain an ordered energy pattern within life experience, particularly by transcending forces serving to inhibit the primary function or orientation.

The *major fire and air lines* both commence close to each other, within the fire quadrant, which is compatible with them both. This gives them a natural hyperactivity that is channeled, via the physical senses, into either mental concepts or physical responses. While the eventual termination of the air line is highly variable, both usually end within quadrants of opposite and antagonistic elements. Fire goes towards earth, air goes towards water. In energic terms this is necessary so that if each over–develops (and grows longer) their eventual end is within an energy form that will sedate rather than activate. Earth sustains but exhausts and modifies fire; water diffuses air.

Many of the so-called chance lines reveal the passage of energies to and from the various quadrants. It is by observing these passages that we can determine the personal balance (or lack of it) within the individual, for they form a record of all the stabilizing actions taken within the mind/body organism during one's lifetime.

DETERMINING SKIN AND LINE QUALITY

There are four major types of skin described in Wu Hsing hand analysis, one for each element. These may be found not only as a general type for a whole hand, but also in particular areas—a hand may possess two or even three different types of elemental skin, particularly on the finger phalanges as opposed to the palm. You will be able to identify elemental quality by sight and touch. In general, fire and water skin tend to be warmer, earth and air, cooler. By touching each phalange, differences in temperature may be noted. Water skin is soft and warm; fire is hot and has a feeling of strength; earth is hard in texture and leathery; and air is fine and taut. The warmer a digit, the more active and responsive it will be. The mounts in the palmar surfaces should also be felt. It is usually fairly easy to feel zonal excess (warmth) in the beginning; as one gains experience subtle temperature differences can be noted quite accurately.

One can determine a hand's ruling skin element in several manners and most cheirologists will use several. After you have learned to identify the appearance of the basic types, one of the most accurate ways of determining rulership is by skin pore and dermatoglyphic texture. Fire skin has large, clearly visible pores. Water has fine, almost invisible pores. Air pores can be seen after careful examination. Earth pores are slightly smaller than fire but much less clear due to skin thickness. If one could illustrate them within a certain area, we would have patterns as shown in figure 49. The pores form skin ridge lines across the hands, and one should observe both the palm surface and skin upon the back of the hand to determine ruling elements.

As with skin quality, there are also four elemental types of lines. The elemental nature is revealed by the form of a line, and within a short period of careful observation all the main types can be readily identified:

Earth: These lines are broad, wide, and roughly formed, often short in length.

Water: These are fine lines, often wavy and pale.

Fire: These are deep, intense in color, and straight.

Air: These are deeper than water, pale in color and curved or straight.

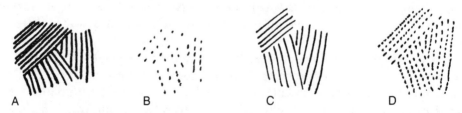

Figure 49. Judging skin pores to determine elemental rulership. Here we see a) earth pores, b) water pores, c) fire pores, and d) air pores.

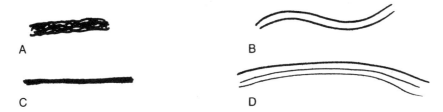

Figure 50. The quality—thickness, depth, etc.—of the lines will also help determine elemental rulership. Here we see a) earth quality, b) water quality, c) fire quality, and d) air quality.

Comparatively they assume forms as shown in figure 50. Using the following determinators, correct elemental classification can be readily made of the line and skin formations:

1. Pore and dermatoglyphic features of the skin.

2. Temperature differences in the various areas of the palm and digits.

3. Color of hands.

4. Length and width of palm and digits.

5. Direction or curve of lineal formations.

LINES OF ELEMENTAL REFLECTION

The principle of reflection is explicitly stated in many Hindu and Buddhist scriptures and was incorporated in various forms into the Wu Hsing method of China. This adoption was probably to affirm that the Taoist accredited energic polarities of yin and yang—unknown as a practical evaluation prior to Chang Chung Ching (circa 160 A.D.)—postdated other, non–Taoist systems. Native Chinese lay great importance on antiquity. To show that a teaching was old was, for them, to demonstrate its truth. The principle of reflection states that each major function of the body and mind has a correspondent lineal formation. One is usually active and obvious, the other passive and hidden. If some obstruction or breakdown occurs in one, the complement takes over its function. This function is predominantly energic rather than physical, although similar processes do occur in the human body. It is through these physical correlates that we can reveal the energic sources.

For practical purposes we will concern ourselves with the main functioning activities rather than the infrastructures. Each major line has its

Figure 51. Foot lines (cartopody)
from an ancient Chinese text.

reflection, termed a minor line. Thus the major air line represents consciousness and structural concepts. Its reflection (the minor air line) relates to metabolism, governed by the structure and action of the endocrinal glands. Consciousness produces thoughts; metabolism attunes the bodily action to those thoughts; and vice versa. Consciousness is produced or directed by sympathetic nervous action, metabolism by parasympathetic action. As a general rule, reflections are not a good sign, for they usually reveal a condition of past and present imbalance. It is therefore better for the hand to be free from their presence—however, most people have reflective lines. The nature and formation of each reflection reveals information concerning the imbalance present, and it is from this nature that ill health can be diagnosed.

Within the hands there are many balances and inter-reflections evidenced. The basic pairs relate to fundamental activities of body and mind (see Table 13). However, there are other pairings of major and minor reflections used to determine specific physical or psychological conditions. Let's consider some of these combinations.

Table 13. Fundamental Reflected Lines

Elemental Name	Functions
Major Air	Consciousness balancing
Minor Air	Metabolic balancing
Major Water	Emotional balancing
Minor Water	Intuitive balancing
Major Fire	Physical energy balancing
Minor Fire	Social balancing
Major Earth	Physical body maintenance and balancing
Minor Earth	Inner, environmental balancing

Minor air and major earth: These form a "thermometer" of the nervous system. Major earth shows the total amount of energy available at that time and determines the quality of the sympathetic nerves. Minor air reveals the quality of the parasympathetic nerves. Often minor air is not visible, as the parasympathetic nervous system acting autonomously needs no prompting. In cases of imbalance, however, it appears clearly. It is also related to the spinal cord. If it appears simply and clearly (without defect, doubling or break), it shows a general hypersensitivity of the parasympathetic nervous system itself—which is often due to continued stress situations or nutritional deficiency. As the function of minor air is to communicate, the line is straight and direct, having a fire/air quality. The major earth line should curve, and have the earth/water function to aid harmonization of energy. Most often it has fire or air quality (i.e., in color and depth) in Occidental hands, and water or earth quality in Orientals.

Major air and major water: These describe the inter-balance between structural consciousness and non-structural consciousness if present within the hand in a naturally curved formation. The major air line "filters" physical energies into recognizable and orientational forms or aspects, then recirculates them back into the water quadrant. Major air is, of course, air-like in action. The major water line acts as a second and more refined filter, preparing the energies radiated from the major air for passing into the digits, and thus is definitively conceptualized and directed. It works at the physical and mental levels simultaneously and has a water-like action carrying the air quadrant into fire. Acting together they transmutate feeling or physical stimuli into general concepts and then identify and redirect those stimuli into specific fields of action/impulse. They should ideally be of equal power and quantity. A straight major air line has a more prominent fire orientation, as does a straight major water line. When intermingled or connected in some manner they "shortcircuit" the interpretive function of structural and non-structural awareness, and cause extreme polarizations to manifest. In relational terms, this is emotional trauma and mental unease.

Minor fire and minor earth: These two describe the balance between internal (self) and external (other) relationships. Since they are communicative, they are naturally direct and straight in their finest formation. Minor earth describes the crossover from unconscious to conscious. Although it is more on the conscious side of the palm, it in fact reveals the unconscious or uncommunicated inner mental balance maintained towards others. Minor fire shows the conscious wish for approbation and respect. It occurs on the unconscious side of the palm. These two are best thought of as the edges of a central energy channel running upwards to a point between the earth and fire digits. When present and of good quality they show that harmonious balance (internal or external) is present, in an active form, within the subject.

Subsidiary reflected lines (higher and lower minor water; water quadrant hyperactivity lines, earth quadrant stress lines): These are minor water element reflections telling us something of the physical and mental interaction of the individual. The higher and lower minor water lines each describe the presence of an ultra high sensitivity—the lower within the physical body, and the higher within neural response. Heightened sensitivity means the subject reacts quickly and metabolically to stimuli on either body or mind. Lower water indicates the need for care with alcohol and foodstuffs, physical and sexual activities. Higher water indicates the need for mental calm and a peaceful environment to dwell within. Higher water type people are more prone to nervous ailments and psychosomatic illness. Lower water types are prone to infections and fever. Ideally neither should be present in a palm. It is better to have one, than both, present. Both high and low minor water show the same effect at different levels. Lower water has a fire action upon water, higher water has an air action upon earth. Both lines reveal the same effects of stress inducement upon the unconscious, image producing mental plane.

• • •

When you examine a hand and do not find any lines of reflection, ask your subject if he or she has experienced any of the above temperamental changes associated with the reflected lines. If there are no reflected lines, then a condition is either just about to develop or has just cleared up. You will only be able to ascertain this by questioning your client. When a line or element action breaks down, a short period elapses before the reflected line appears—if the condition cannot be dealt with by the normal processes of the body. When you notice the absence of a reflected line, you know the subject is either in this mid-way stage, or the illness or condition has just recently been overcome. When the condition passes, the lines fade away. So don't jump to conclusions in your diagnosis—ask your subject.

You must keep in mind that we are discussing here reflected lines which appear *when there is a defect in the major line or lines*. If there is no defect in the major lines, then lines of reflection—the minor and subsidiary lines—have a predominantly psychological significance rather than a physiological one. This is an important point: you cannot consider the minor and subsidiary lines alone. In cases of psychological disorders, this distinction is crucial to bear in mind.

When observing the progress of illness, you should also pay great attention to the condition of the lines after the period of illness has passed. This will let you see if the illness has, in fact, been overcome. The cessation of symptoms is not necessarily the cessation of illness. If the lines look healthy at this time, be confident that the illness will not return. In the Oriental tradition, a regular inspection of the hands is considered essential. This usually takes place yearly, but in cases of suspected illness will occur more frequently.

CHAPTER 11

Studies in the Elemental Lines

The following sections explain the major, minor and subsidiary lines individually, elucidating their psychological, health and spiritual relationships. Each line is explained in a general introduction, then details of specific features are given.

THE MAJOR EARTH LINE

In ancient times, the earth line, under its traditional name of life line, was considered one of the most important in the hand. As its old name suggests, a correlation was drawn between it and the life span of the individual. In some cases this correlation appeared to be accurate but in others woefully wrong. As any patient observer of lines will tell, the line's termination, when interpreted chronologically, can occasionally coincide with the time of earthly death. We can see therefore that there is some link—even if of a tenuous nature—between this line and the subject's life expectancy. The real meaning of the earth line, however, is understood by exploring the underlying significance of this link. There are several things to consider before we can approach an understanding of this line's significance. We have to ask ourselves, how do we define life itself? When we talk of "life" or "life span," do we mean conscious life or physical life? (These can exist independently.) Or could we mean another kind of life altogether?

In the Wu Hsing teaching, however, the problem is gotten rid of by reassessment of the line's significance. We call it the earth or vitality line, which indicates that we see it not as a measure of one's lifetime but instead as a measure of vital force or energy within the body. This is a physical concept; our interpretation relates to the function of the human body. It is also a spiritual one, as the vital energy is not *only* earthly in nature. It is but another manifestation of that energy considered and used in Chinese traditional medicine—*Chi*. Each of us has a certain amount of Chi when born, and as we go through life we supplement, circulate and renew it from various natural sources, such as food, sunlight, air, etc. We also receive Chi

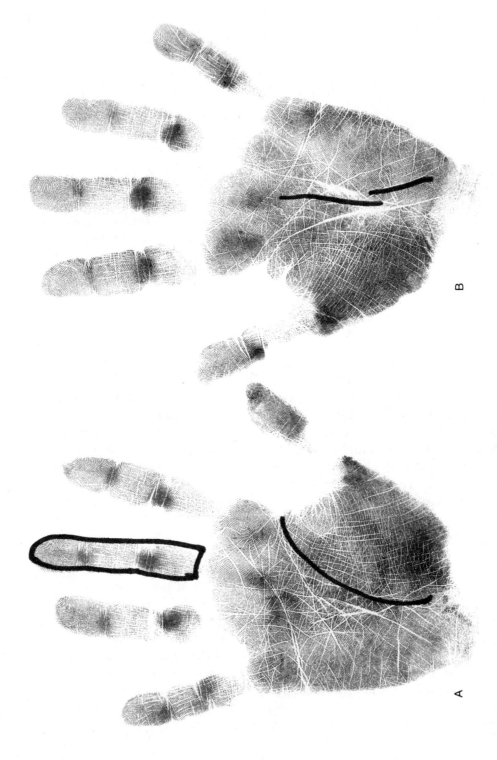

Figure 52. The major (a) and minor (b) earth lines. The earth digit is shown.

through our various external organs and circulate it through our internal organs.

There are certain areas more receptive to Chi than others. Some of these are in the hands. According to tradition, we receive Chi from the earth through our feet; we receive Chi from the air through our mouths; Chi from fire (the Sun) we receive through our skin or eyes; and Chi from water when we wash, drink or bathe in the sea, lake or stream. The Chi of earth also circulates within our fingers. At birth its main inflow is said to enter via the tip of the forefinger. One result of this inflow is that the creative energy flows down through the hand at precisely the point our vitality line commences. This is one reason why the line can be understood as a "thermometer" of vitality. Certainly the longer it is (assuming a good formation of the line), then the more energy has been attracted into our bodies. Remember, however, that possession of a long line may not mean fine health! The organs and other physical attributes may not be in accord with this energy—they may burn up a good flow continually. A very ill person may need a great amount of energy to sustain life and yet still possess a fine and strong vitality source.

If one's energy circulation stops or is seriously interfered with, rapid physical deterioration and even death will ensue. If the line shows such impairment we have to think in terms of source energy only. Where, why or how the deterioration will happen has to be seen in other parts of the hand. The vitality line encircles the major part of the quadrant related to the earth element, thus primarily relating it to physical being and foundation. If the foundations of a house sink, and or the roots of a great tree rot, sooner or later they will topple. Before this occurs the house walls will crack or the tree's leaves will begin to fade. The signs of the hand show this metaphorical equivalent by evidencing lineal degeneration. It is this degeneration that reveals the nature of the source energy stoppage or blockage. It is to the lineal patterns in both hands that we must look for signs of deterioration or death and not to the thermometer of vitality.

Location and Description

The major earth line encircles the mount at the base of the thumb (called the *Tubercula* in ancient Rome). It commences below the base of the water finger and travels downwards arching outwards into the palm. It terminates by turning inwards towards the base of the wrist bones (see figure 52).

As it is a fundamental line it always commences in the same general area of the hand (see figure 53a on page 144). Figure 53b shows a slight variation of this, for in this formation the beginning is high on the water mount, but the terminus generally encloses or roots the earth line to its correct place. If you bear in mind that this line commences close to the meeting point of the active and passive regions of the palm, you can see

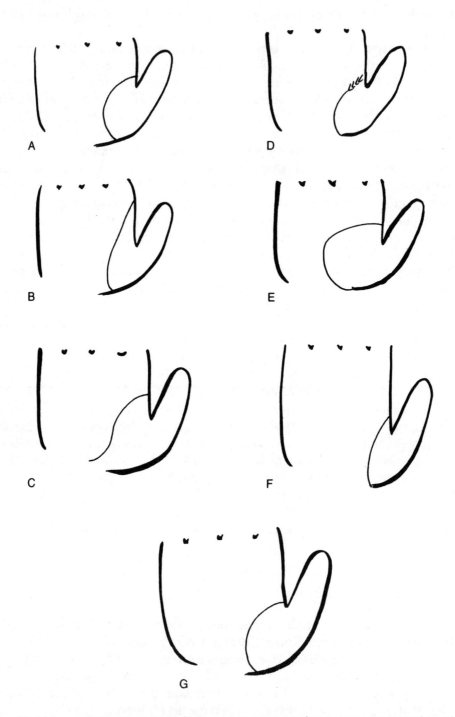

Figure 53. Major earth line formations. Here we see a range of commencements and terminations: a) this is the usual commencement and termination; b) a high commencement; c) a
wandering earth line; d) an interrupted earth line; e) wide formation; f) narrow formation; and
g) a low commencement.

that its essential function is to unify and provide a base for these two aspects of mind and body.

The quality of the line at its commencement indicates something of the environmental influences inherited from birth. The formation in figure 53a shows a strong and normal early life. The formation in figure 53d, bearing a furring quality, suggests physical or nutritional deficiencies present in either mother or child. As the earth line describes energy, any impairment of it indicates difficulties of some form or another in the early years. Temperamentally it reveals a lack of foundation, difficulty in originating or organizing the basic requirement of life. Depending on the elemental balance of the hands themselves, this may show anything from an inability to cook or lack of dress sense to lack of confidence or poor health habits.

The line in figure 53b shows an inborn desire for balance, the fact that the subject experiences some sense of imbalance in the fundamentals of life. It is often found in self-made individuals, religious leaders and all who by nature strive for improvement in mind, body or speech. On this formation, the line usually moves closer to the thumbs, making the area it encircles smaller. Since this area is related to family, security and harmony, it shows that the subject will tend to relinquish these in order to improve. If the rooting terminus mentioned above is absent, this tendency is heightened, although the minor air line will usually compensate for its absence. The rooted or enclosed line shows a sense of duty and responsibility, particularly to one's ethnic group, country and family. Nationalists or sectarians always have this clearly defined ending. It is as if their conceptual understanding of their base is complete, enclosed and fixed.

The overall significance of the high set commencement (figure 53b) is a vital energy that responds forcefully to the external, social, environment. The placement is often seen in those to whom tradition or status quo is important. Physically it indicates a highly sensitive, liquid balance in the body. Such a commencement invariably shows a wish to exceed personal limitations. Conversely, a low commencement (shown in figure 53g) reveals the influence of low quality fire. This gives a powerful impulse to the temperament, and a tendency to aggressive use of the body. Sportsmen, violent criminals and surgeons often have this commencement. There is usually a raised earth quadrant with this commencement, and the level within which the subject dwells (shown by hand shape and so on) indicates the subject's utilization of this increased power.

The usual starting point of the earth is about halfway between the base of the forefinger and the thumb. This position gives plenty of scope for development of the fire lines and quadrant. Theoretically, the earth line can terminate in several areas, but practically speaking, we find only two important terminations. The first in the usual one described above and shown in figure 53a. The other is called a "wandering end" and is shown in figure 53c. It shows a desire to change and move one's source energy and possible bravery in doing so. One often finds this marking in the hands of world travelers. The wandering feature imbues the line with a water element quality and its presence indicates an urge to seek out emotional or mystical balance. With a strong thumb, it can give ability and interest to the mind of its owner. With a weak thumb it gives unreliability and dislike of self-responsibility. It is common among itinerants.

Curvature

The curvature of the earth line should not go on beyond a vertical line drawn down from the earth finger. If it does (as shown in figure 53e), it reveals too powerful a water energy within the earth element. This confuses it and makes it mud-like. In terms of temperament, such a wide sweep gives a highly responsive physicality. The subject will be strongly motivated towards things or persons of the nature of water. This usually brings a hyper-emotionality of outlook, a strong and sensual intercommunication with others. At a high level it can give good judgment of objects (antiques, furnishings, etc.), but at a low level and with weak thumbs it gives an over-sexual approach to life.

A lack of curvature (see figure 53f) reduces the earth influence and channels the responses exclusively into conceptual areas. There is often sensitivity but almost always a very strained, apprehensive or rigid code of personal ethics. From the ordinary viewpoint, such a narrow curvature may manifest as a reserved or even cold nature, but in reality it shows an orientation away from physical things, a desire to evade or avoid those situations or circumstances that could activate the subject's hypersensitive emotions. This is not a contradictory statement. Such lack of curve is found upon those who possess a high physical responsivenes but not the attitude to accept such responses, hence the adoption of strict standards. These individuals need to take great care to cultivate meaningful, emotional rapport with others, for lack of curve predisposes them to sexual fantasy instead of feeling. As a health indication, this lack of curvature shows an air orientation of earth energies, which particularly relates to neural illness, fatigue and lack of appetite.

Quality

Ideally the earth line should possess a firm, strong appearance showing that its vitality is vibrant and that resistance to infections are high. It's interesting to note that nowadays this is seldom seen, and the line is more likely to exhibit weakness than strength. If the earth line exhibits an earth quality, it reveals a basic lack of vibrancy, and insufficient energy being circulated.

Temperamentally, this predisposes the subject towards lassitude and a lethargic outlook. In health, it indicates weak bone marrow and body posture. Care should be taken to eat lots of vegetables and take regular exercise. Earth quality is uncommon and is usually only found in the hands of those who have been ill for a long time already, for example, invalids or those suffering from congenital diseases. The earth line is also connected with the wish to live—at least on the cellular level. A weakening of the line suggests the giving up of this will.

Water qualities in the earth line show hyper-responsiveness in matters of health and environment. Hypochondriacs or busy bodies (those who fall ill due to worrying about their neighbors) are the first types to spring to mind. Water usually blends well with earth, but it is not favored for the earth line aspect. The threadlike appearance of this element predisposes one towards digestive and urinary infections as well as making one apprehensive in temperament. Water features are found in the earth lines of those who suffer from psychosomatic illness (skin rashes, asthma, etc.). You must always bear in mind the hypersensitivity of the individual in such a case, and advise restraint in foodstuffs, alcohol and temperature extremes. You will often find this feature present in those who take frequent baths.

A fire quality earth line is healthy, except when occurring with fire markings. Fire indicates good reserves of energy. If deeply colored, the individual may be predisposed to infections or feverish complaints in general, but these are generally ably coped with and recovery is rapid. Temperamentally, the fire quality confers enthusiasm and good appetite. In illness the fire type wishes to recover quickly and usually does.

Air features in an earth line are not often observed. This element brings an inherent weakness to the physio-psychological unity and is most common in those suffering from mental illnesses of one type or another. It rarifies and degrounds the physical body, making it prone to too rapid changes in metabolism and therefore temperament. The air features are similar in some respects to those of water, except that with water illness is often absent, whereas with air it is over-present but sublimated. The individual with air quality in the earth line suffers from being externally orientated and thus ignoring the natural balances of health. Rest and play, food and drink, pleasure and pain are often exaggerated or juxtaposed, and form negative environments for harmonious health development. Due to the exocentric attitudes of air and earth lines, we often find illnesses of the nervous system (neurosis, paralysis) occurring suddenly. The air quality is well able to prognose these, but because of the manner in which they orientate themselves within life, the person doesn't have the time to notice symptoms. Nervous exhaustion is common to this formation, as is cancer. Wu Hsing relates air to metabolism, which itself regulates cell growth. Cancerous conditions occur when this growth rate falters and hyperactivates. If the fundamental vitality area (earth) has air features, a predisposition towards abnormal cell growth is shown.

Length

As has been remarked previously there is little connection between length of the earth line and length of life. Length does, however, show total quantity of energy available. If we see a shortened line, we know that resistance and healing ability does not have deep resources to draw from (though this must be modified when the line has fire quality). In the case of a short line, illnesses that are of short duration will not have much effect on the subject. In the case of long term or congenital illness some caution is needed. As earth shows internal balancing ability—the will to live and amount of source vitality—the shortened formation reveals a significant insufficiency. The cause of this must be ascertained elsewhere in the hands. A shortened line is uncommon and particular illnesses usually manifest in malformations of the line rather than absence. Mineral imbalance can cause the line to disappear or fade, and elementally speaking this is what we would expect. As earth (minerals) decreases, air (faded lines) increases. Obviously there is a limit to the amount this can occur within the body and by the time one has reached a point where lines have begun to disappear, something is already obviously wrong. Examination of the air lines is of great importance here for they will also imbalance or develop more fire like intensity when the earth lines are weakening.

Health

The central function of the earth element is to preserve and balance the body's energies, to protect it from infection and to rebuild it in cases of injury. When the line is degenerate, all these functions are impaired. The greater the presence of degenerative features the more vulnerable the subject. Earth is intimately related to water, and in the body these two govern the growth of skeletons and bone marrow. Deficiency in either of these always causes organic and circulatory imbalance elsewhere. Physiognomically considered, the first third of the line rules the neck and head bones, the second third the chest, arms and spine, the lower third the hips and legs. Deficiencies thus can reveal skeletal weakness or bad posture and movement in these areas of the body. The wide curvature of the line is usually found on those with a full body shape (see figure 52e); the narrow curve (figure 53f) more often on tall, thin frames.

Distinctive Markings

Each line may also have distinctive markings as shown in figure 54. The significance of these markings is as follows:

Bar: The bar signifies an energy interruption and thus a condition of vulnerability to sudden changes such as are found in accident, shock, critical infections or skeletal breakage (see figure 54a). Being of a fire nature, a "scorched earth" condition is shown within bodily energy. The condition of the line following the bar must be examined carefully to determine its effect. If no bar appears on correspondent lines, suspect that accident or infection is indicated.

Dots: Shown in figure 54b, this occurs when fire energy implodes within the organic processes of the body. They tend to show a predisposition to excesses of conduct—i.e., over-eating or drinking—and are temporary. Observe water lines since, in some casees of an extreme nature, thrombosis may be indicated.

Cross: An enforced sudden change from outside of the body. One must observe where the cross comes from so as to determine something of its elemental meaning.

Rising branches: Branches that leave the earth line and extend outwards beyond it are caused by an infusion of fire energy into the main line (see figure 54d). This itself can be the result of increased demands on the self made by the subject (or by others). The direction of these rising lines gives us some idea as to the nature of this demand, for they tend to orientate toward that elemental source that will stabilize them. These lines are also health indications—if they occur after or during a period of weakness within the major earth line, they show an attempt to overcome this weakness by "casting off" the excess energy within the line. A proper rising line leaves the major line rather than runs into it. We can distinguish between these two by observing the thickness of the rising line. A line that leaves a major line is thicker at the major line end. A line that runs into a major line is thickest at the point furthest from the major line. Such a line is not a rising line at all. Rising lines do not reach the mounts toward which they orientate—they fall short of them. If they do actually go into the mount area they become indicators of a specific form of weakness or illness and are not thus classified as rising lines. Rising lines are usually of a fire nature. All branches show a wish for change—either on the part of the body or of the consciousness.

Internal branches: Often termed "stress lines" these lines do not extend beyond the perimeter formed by the major earth line (see figure 53d). Their presence again indicates a build up of fire energy within the organism but, as they do not extend out beyond the major line, indicate that the mind/body interaction is capable of containing their causative forces. In many cases this will indeed manifest as stress, be it physical or mental. The important thing to note with these lines is the internalizing disposition the subject assumes towards imbalance. A few lines only are of little import but many, particularly when of air and water quality, show that stress is never

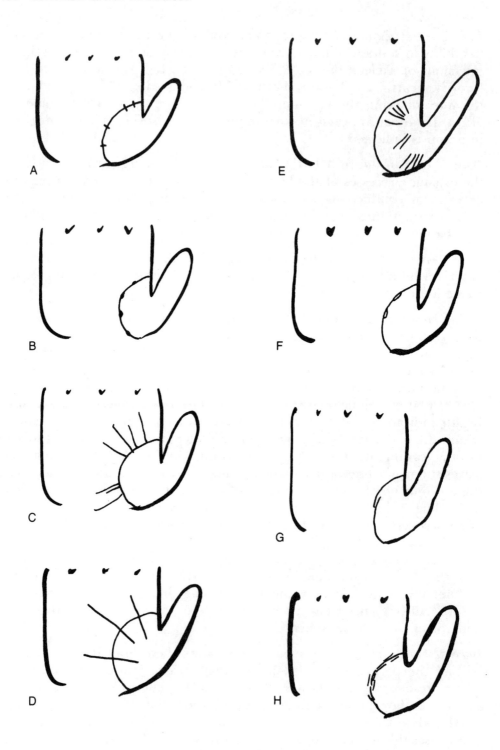

Figure 54. Markings on the earth line: a) bars, b) dots, c) rising branches, d) internal branches, e) cross lines, f) islands, g) overlaps, and h) striations.

far from the conscious mind. If these lines touch the major earth they can be interpreted chronologically and cross–related to the other element lines elsewhere in the hands. Disorders or unforeseen changes within the subject's family will often produce these internal branchings.

Cross lines: In most cases imbalances in body/mind energies are aided by sending a branch to earth. It is therefore common to see lines coming into or going across the earth line from various areas of the hand (see figure 53e). By tracing their beginning one can diagnose their effects, particularly in the organs related to each element, finger or mount. This effect is shown by the condition of the line after crossing has taken place. Lines that come from the *inside* of the earth line show attempts by earth to balance itself. The direction of cross lines indicates the nature of the balance—if they go towards an air mount or digit there is an excess of air (stress, mental disturbances, neural or response upsets, etc.) affecting earth ruled actions and organs. Be sure to distinguish clearly the origin of a line so as to recognize whether it comes from or goes to the earth line. The thickest or deepest is the commencement point.

Doubling: This is more common a feature than might be supposed. The inner line is generally the major fire line and a useful, invigorating sign. It shows a greater depth of energy and an abundance of spirit and zest. If a degeneration of the earth line occurs, the inner fire line compensates automatically giving reinforcement and power. It is thus a good sign. In the presence of a weakened earth line however, it shows the change in the earth element activity. Since 1960 the incidence of fire line has (in Europe) increased dramatically and, if present trends continue, it will become a common sign in hands. On a fire or earth hand it indicates a tendency to physical excess.

Absence: Very rare indeed but if seen is always coincident with an over-development of air and fire elements. It occurs temporarily in conditions of psychological disorder, neurasthenia or extreme emotional stress causing introvertion or catatonia. The absence of markings, partial or whole, shows that only the barest minimum resources of physical life are acting. It, of course, gives great vulnerability to infection. Absence shows that nearly all physical energy is under control of the parasympathetic nerves. Air lines should be carefully examined.

Islands: All islands reveal a division in fundamental energies and a weakening of the subject's mental/physical readjustment to change of all types. Physically viewed, they suggest a weakening of the body's ability to digest or metabolize foodstuffs (this failure could be caused by attitudes as much as direct physical illness). The whole length of the line should be divided into three equal areas and each area related to the body. The top third relates to head, neck and chest, the middle third to chest, lungs and other thoracic organs, the lower third to intestines and reproductive organs.

Islands at these heights suggest some weakness of the organs related. Figure 54f shows some examples of islands.

Psychologically, islands always indicate periods of duality, be it indecisiveness or multiple external pressures. This is felt for as long as the island exists. Chronological assessment should be made and the period related to other lines. The condition of the line prior and subsequent to the island should be noted.

Overlaps: These occur when the subject has consciously reorientated his or her attitudes towards fundamental issues. Overlaps, shown in figure 54g, indicate a new start in life and are thus a creative sign for they indicate the ability and vitality to grow from old to new circumstances.

Striations: Striations, an air effect, occur when the source energy is failing to distribute itself correctly. They are a sign of organic or metabolic dissynchronicity. Overall they produce physical or psychological spasmodicity. This often results in poor resistance and recovery to illness of all forms. Striation is most common upon water and air hand shapes. It is important to trace the reason for striation—a careful overall assessment of the hands is required. Psychologically, it can create difficulties in communication and a jerky spasmodic manner of talking, writing or moving. Striation can occur simply by the earth line exhibiting regular changes in its depth or color. The line does not necessarily fade away altogether. (See figure 54h.)

THE MAJOR WATER LINE

Water is, of course, essential to life and its correlate in human life—emotion or (more accurately) non-structural consciousness—forms the basis for the majority of spiritual teachings. Understanding of emotional experiences is the base from which our conception of both spiritual and mundane life springs. The import of emotional or conceptually non-structural experience is vast, as it underlies the development of our everyday methods of communication at many levels. It forms a substratum to every thought we formulate.

To fully understand its significance we must arrive at some familiarity with the principle of non-structural understanding itself. The theme requires considerable thought; you aspiring analysts should practice this heuristically as a preparatory study, for it will enable you to appreciate correctly any statement or judgment concerning consciousness. In the Chinese Wu Hsing method this is particularly important. One has to prepare the materials properly before commencing any "building" work.

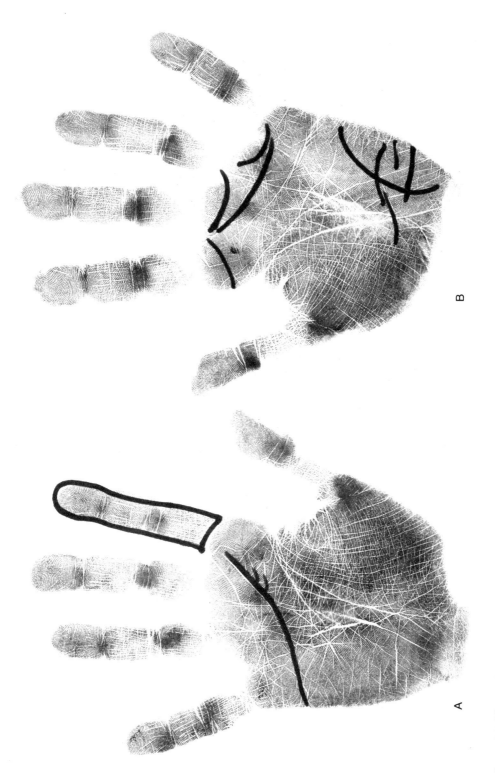

Figure 55. The major (a) and minor (b) water lines. The water digit is shown.

In terms of personality the major water line usually relates to our emotions; for this reason the water line was termed the *heart* or *love* line. However, as mentioned before, non-structural consciousness also covers the realm of intuition and spiritual wisdom. These relate to love, but are not restricted to the usual understanding of the word. In combination with other elements the water line can reveal conditions and states of consciousness normally inaccessible.

Location

The major water line begins in the area below the air finger and proceeds below the finger mounts towards the opposite edge of the hand, crossing both the air and fire quadrants equally. The water line always begins in the same general area. This itself is a remarkable feature for it shows that certain forms of experience are always governed or set according to inviolate principles. Since water relates to emotional experiences, it reveals a pattern to which all humankind is subject. Oriental schools relate this line to our ability to formulate experience itself, to remember, relate and regenerate non-structural consciousness.

The termination of the water line is much more variable, revealing the individual orientation of the subject. It describes the optimum non-structural consciousness available at that time. Terminations can readily change direction, quality and element according to the degree of self

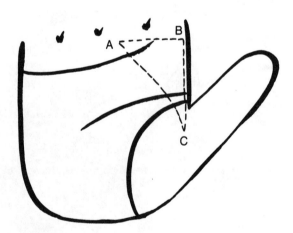

Figure 56. Major water line terminations. All terminations near the center of this triangle indicate gregarious, balanced and harmonious developments of the non-structural consciousness. Terminations in the lower sector (a) indicate inhibited sensual/personal objectives; b) terminations near the water finger indicate idealized and group shared objectives; and c) terminations near the thumb indicate personal and self-orientated objectives.

understanding attained by the subject in the water ruled realms. There are three basic orientations, as shown in figure 56. The most common formations are shown in figure 57 on page 156.

The water line can terminate on any of the areas below the finger digits, though the majority find their home in the area between the earth and water digit mounts. Taking the water finger as an apex, we can form a triangular area within which exist a number of significant terminal points. All terminations occur in the fire quadrant. This signifies accessibility to consciousness, and motivating energy. In addition, each has an individual significance.

When the water line ends under the earth mount as shown in figure 57a, this indicates a fire-like, physically expressive kind of self-understanding. However, since this makes the line short, it limits the range of the higher intuitive emotions and emphasizes the inward, personalized nature of experience and goals. Often associated with emotional caution, inhibition or over-sensuality, it brings a keen sense of the lack of intuitive or emotional fulfillment.

Figure 57b shows a healthy ending, which aids optimism, practicality, kindness and sensitivity. This ending unites the energies of water and earth, and develops a blend of idealistic romantic and practical emotional and intuitive development.

The water line high on the water mount indicates a high level development of non-structural emotions, and is associated with mystical or spiritual friendships, devotion to persons, causes or places (see figure 57c). It may also make the individual susceptible to emotional disappointment owing to the over-optimistic attitudes it creates. This placement is common to those in the healing professions and devoted religious followers as well as faithful spouses.

The termination shown in figure 57d indicates a balance between physical objectives, idealistic wishes, and sexuality. This ending makes the water line very long—overlong in fact—and thus it increases the range of emotions available to the subject who can often exhibit sudden changes from love to hate and vice versa. If the whole line is curved, it adds sensitivity to others. If straight, fire-like—it gives power to the emotional drives. It is present on strongly motivated individuals.

When the water line is curving down over the air line, a need for manifesting physical drives and contacts is emphasized. We find this ending on subjects who like to touch and have more physical contact with others (see figure 57e). On a fire or air hand it controls the verbal expression of emotion, but increases the physical needs. On the water and earth hands it tends to increase sexual inhibitions. It may create a great potential for jealousy on a low level hand; on a high level hand, an intense wish for emotional and mental identity with oneself and others.

The termination shown in figure 57f brings receptivity to external stimuli and needs a good air line to balance it and give strength. It shows

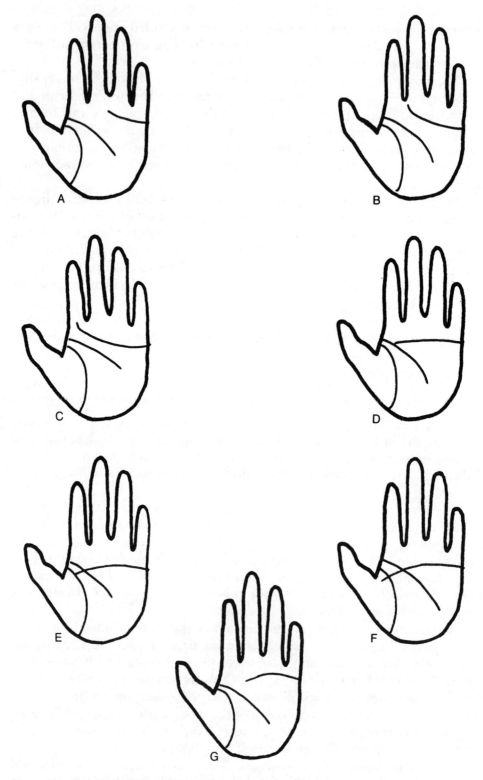

Figure 57. Some common water line formations are shown in illustrations A-G. These are discussed in length in the text on pages 155-157.

great idealism concerning physical/sexual compatibility and a need to be completely fulfilled in one's expectations. In female hands it gives a masculine, dominant touch; in male hands, a feminine sensitivity to the emotions. It is often a sign of hypersexuality or sexual deviancy—in all cases strong drives are present. The level of the subject is important in deciding how he or she uses this energy. This is a more extreme form of figure 57e.

When the water line terminates in, or strongly towards, the air line it shows the dominance of conceptual processes over the intuitive, and thus a nullification of the emotional energies (see figure 57g). This is not usually a beneficial sign, for it predisposes the subject to think rather than to feel. In daily life, it proves useful; in emotional life, inhibitive. Observe whether there are compensatory or reflected lineal markings to offset the inhibitive trends.

Curvature

The perfect water line curves similarly to a crescent moon. This degree of curvature indicates a delicate blend of affection, sensitivity, sexual drive and emotional grace. When the line lacks curvature (and thus becomes more fire element ruled), the emphasis is placed on the object of consciousness rather than the means of attainment. A completely straight water line shows a direct flow of wish and desired end. Owners of such lines are direct and open, plain speaking and energetic in their means of obtaining fulfillment, be it metaphysical or sexual. The quality of emotional style is indicated particularly by the curvature. Analysts should always distinguish between the orientation geared to specific aims (straight) to general means (curved).

Quality

The water line is subject to the four elemental qualities as are all other lines; but in this case its significance has to be interpreted in terms of non-structural awareness and its normally inevitable concomitant manifestation of emotion. A brief outline of the elemental qualities follows. However, real understanding of water lines can only be gained via development of water consciousness itself.

The water line having an *earth* quality shows a development of instinctive responses. It is non-verbal and predominantly physical in response to external stimuli. It is simple and dislikes embellishment of any nature. Fertility and stamina in generation are shown by such a line.

Water quality makes the line very feminine, but also fickle in its orientation. It suggests a very high level of intuitive response to subliminal or unrecognized situations or environments. Commonly found on religious devotees, mystics, actresses and artists, it indicates a great sense of color and design. Its chief detriment is lack of reliability, its greatest asset the ability to be highly receptive and malleable to changing environments.

A water line having *fire* qualities indicates energy and intuitive physical responses, and a desire to express experiences physically. It can be found on doctors, soldiers, prostitutes and violent criminals—all, in fact, who need to sublimate pure receptivity of emotion for professional reasons and who physically enact their non-structural awareness. It has a great potential for both good and bad. Special attention needs to be paid to the structures revealing willpower, logic, intelligence and spirituality with this formation.

The quality of *air* shows intellectualization of the line's actions, and indicates that responses are subject to external direction. It is easily misdirected, submerged or dissipated. Though air in length gives a wide range of accessible responses, they are usually too much for the conscious mind to relate to efficiently. We then find the subject victim to numerous emotional attachments basically caused from emotional projection onto others. As emotional projection is a clearly structured mental format, it is alien to this line's action and will always be insufficiently experienced. The air quality also indicates emotional fear or hesitancy—almost as if emotion is a source of worry to the subject.

Length

Deciding dominant element by the length of the water line is simple: one observes under which finger the line terminates:

> Under the air finger: gives earth rulership
>
> Under the fire finger: gives water rulership
>
> Under the earth finger: gives fire rulership
>
> Under the water finger: gives air rulership

Each element of the line relates to its opposite element finger. The active male elements of the line are under the passive (feminine) fingers, and vice versa.

It is very important to decide the level at which individual operates, his or her intelligence, and willpower—for these can alter the manner in which the subject expresses the non-structural awareness. The ability for swift, decisive action indicated by a fire quality water line could, in the uneducated, be the mark of a thief or robber. In an educated individual, it may be the mark of a surgeon, chemist or political leader. It is essential to decide at which overall level the subject uses talents found and at which educational plateau he or she resides.

Health

The major water line indicates the quality of fluids within the body. Lymph, synovial fluid, stomach enzymes and blood are of an active (fire) nature. Perspiration, intestinal juices and bile are of a passive (earth) nature. Urine and saliva are of a passive (water) nature. Spinal fluid and pleural liquid are of an active (air) nature. The water line also indicates the supportive, parasympathetic actions of the physical organs and nervous system.

Any distinctive elemental quality of the water line in itself suggests delicacy in one of these areas, whether created by the subject or genetically inherited. Examine closely the quality of the lines to determine which predominates. By length or quality, the water line can reveal hidden weakness. If distinctive formations are found in the first half of the line, suspect inherited weakness. If in the latter half, suspect created weakness. This principle holds true for all lineal formations.

Distinctive Markings

All markings on the water line reflect interruptions to its natural flow. These interruptions have a greater significance than in other lines, for the water line is the most sensitive one in the palm. Therefore you should give special attention to observing all related lines when reaching judgments concerning markings.

Dots and bars: Being of a fire nature, these show sudden shocks to the circulatory production and flow. They indicate accidents involving loss of blood or synovial fluids, and gastric infections or poisonings. Psychologically, they suggest emotional shocks or periods of severe and unexpected stress. Dots are intense forms of bars.

Islands: A water malfunction; these reveal congenital weaknesses or malfunctions of either a persistent or valvular nature. These tend to weaken the system as a whole, producing compensatory illness or desires for food (earth) or warmth (fire). The period of weakness lasts as long as the island lasts.

Overlaps: These show periods during which the body's metabolism is adjusting to a new rate of activity. In itself, the overlap is suggestive of a complete change of internal and/or external environment and should be verified in other lines.

Branches: Branches from the water line reveal insufficiencies in its action, and the branches themselves reveal a seeking out of extra energy. Where a branch goes to usually reveals the element required. In this sense, they can be considered as roots seeking nourishment. The cause of a branch coming into existence must be searched for, as occasionally deficiencies in the air line will attract a water branch. It would thus not be indicative of a water element weakness, but rather the opposite. (This occurs in many other lineal formations.)

Furring: This occurs in cases of sclerosis and incipient thrombosis—a sign of earth element.

Cross: A true cross on the water line is extremely rare. It has the same significance as a dot except that it suggests external causes.

Striations: Striations reveal multi-level presence of catharsis and, occasionally, wasteful dispersion of emotion.

Dots, bars and crosses all indicate acute illness. Branches, islands and overlaps all suggest more debilitatory illness. As terminal marks, they have similar interpretations. If you bear in mind the elements of the digits under which the water line passes, the specific markings of the line beneath these digits will give you information as to the nature of congenital illness. One classic example of popular palmistry states that islands in the water line under the fire finger indicate eye illness or blindness. In my own researches I had never found this to be accurate. Experience has shown conclusively that islands in the air line (which logically connects with sight) do show such weakness. The difference in interpretation is really one of causation (for which palmists have no philosophy). Islands in the water line under the fire digit refer to conditions in the eyes in which movement (water) of the eye muscles (fire) are impaired through atrophy or misuse (fire). Islands in the air line under the fire digit refer to eye weakness which is neural (air) in source or caused by optic nerve injury (fire). Many such examples can be reasoned out by the aware analyst in the course of study and research.

Doubled lines: These are more common than is generally supposed, particularly on the fire element hand shape. Doubled lines have to be examined closely in order to determine which of the two lines present is dominant. We can determine which is the predominant line by observing which is the stronger—i.e., which has the most fire characteristics. This will make the stronger line more intense or deeply colored. If the upper distal formation predominates, it indicates a hyper-sensitive parasympathetic response. This is common in subjects with high blood pressure, tachycardia, body temperature regulation insufficiency, heart weakness and emotional neurosis. If the lower line predominates, it indicates that the subject's emotional drives are very intense in nature. Negative markings on either line thus indicate either emotional or physically induced imbalance.

Considered at the level of temperament, the doubled line shows an ability to perceive non-structural intuitions and impulses. If the upper line predominates, it indicates a receptivity to idealistic goals and pursuits. The subject will have an interest in charities, social and medical professions and a sacrificial nature is shown. The length of the doubled line reveals in which field this idealistic conception will be expressed. If the lower line predominates, a more mundane and emotional outlet will be sought by the subject. Compassion, sympathy and a wish to do something to help others are indicated. It is also a marking of those with a very sensitive physical response, and is sometimes a marking revealing sensuality and a love of bodily sensations. A love of food, clothing, sex, and massage all come within this category. Observe the strength of will and intelligence of the individual and you will will be able to determine how subject uses the increased energy. Again, the length of the water line will show you to which area the subject will gravitate in order to express this energy.

Absence of line: The water line is never totally absent except in the case of the simian formation (in which it is obscured). The function of water is fundamental to life itself. Nor has it ever been seen to fade in illness or death, though its coloring may alter. When extremely short it may not appear to be present, but closer examination will always reveal it, perhaps masquerading as another line in the same palmar area.

●   ●   ●

If we take the ideal water line—fully curved, free from imperfections and terminating on mid water mount—we can see an archetypal emotionality from the point of view of European fashion. The subject is loyal, optimistic, earnest, graceful, coy, feminine (or masculine) and fully fascinating. When the line is shortened or badly formed it takes away these high level qualities and replaces them with coldness, self-preoccupation, avarice and crudeness. If it is very long it increases physical expression, impulsiveness and a lack of grace. Somewhere between all these meanings probably lies the subject whose hands you will analyze.

The water line also symbolizes the ability to communicate, not only spoken words but also in body language, energic attraction, and subliminal suggestion. When the water element is strongly present, it tends to give the individual an aura of mystery. On an earth ruled hand, it indicates fertility and intuition, on water, a psychic ability, on fire, physical energy, style and dash, and on air, a refined and moderate expression of affections. When hand shape element and water line element agree, the resulting non-structural awareness will permeate the whole subject. It is almost a Karmic trend.

When you are assessing the meanings of the major water line, you should always consider it in relation to other factors of the hand. The function of the water line is so fundamental to the human being that any special quality it demonstrates will manifest throughout the other features. Some of the features you should consider prior to finalizing your assessment are:

The thumb. The thumb indicates the degree of the individual's self-reliance, consistency and determination. Each of these is important in expressing the quality of the water line. A weak thumb will always impair a high quality line (and this is true for the other lines also).

The fingertips. By determining the predominant elemental shape of the fingertips, you can see how the subject perceives and expresses the water impulse within.

The hand element. This tells you the overall expressive capabilities of the subject—how they will enact the water impluses within the daily life.

The major air line. This will indicate the nature, manner and orientation of the subject's mental capacities.

The water finger. This will give you some idea of the individual's capacity to express the water element in general and, by observing which phalange is largest, in which area this capacity is most likely to be used.

The air finger. This digit describes a wide area of human activities, one of which is sexuality. Sexuality itself is expressed by the air digit's lowest phalange (the water level phalange). If this phalange is large in terms of its area, the subject's sensitivity to stimulation is high. When it is small the subject responds more readily to direct physical approaches rather than to hints or suggestions.

You should also consider the waviness (itself a water trait) of the water line, for this indicates changeability of affections and a rather unreliable emotional balance. It also, of course, shows metabolic discontinuity, which increases the likelihood of moodiness in a person. Striations and bar lines on digital phalanges often reveal much about the emotional difficulty a subject will experience. The height of the mounts also reveals the degree of sensitivity possessed by a subject and the level at which they are capable of making useful experiential judgments.

Although some writers, both ancient and modern, have invested the water line with predominantly sexual significance, many other factors are shown by it. Some of these, particularly the health interpretation, override sexuality modes. Glib definitions of sexual types are misleading and unwise to assume without deep consideration of all other facets of the subject's life and patterns reflected in each hand.

The circulatory condition should always be considered in conjunction with hand and nail color; the condition of synovial fluid by the subject's flexual ability. Other circulatory systems have to be considered in relation to past illnesses until a firm understanding of the subject's water element manifestation is reached. Only with this attunement can accurate diagnosis of health and emotions begin. The finely tuned metabolism and depth of emotions go hand in hand—actually like a glove and hand. Each complements the other and imbalance in one produces a like condition in the other. The simple palmar patterns of ancient Occidental races have now been increasingly replaced by striated and stressful lineations, and the water line reveals this response to modern living and eating. Deterioration of awareness, intuition, dedication, trust, loyalty, health and emotional identity results. Lines that run alongside or join into the main water line were interpreted in olden times as affections or marriage signs. If these states caused the subject to adopt a complementary emotional or intuitive awareness or even caused indirectly a change in metabolism (such as adopting a different diet), then the "love" meaning can be accurate. However, it is more often a health indication than an emotional one. Modern day hands are commonly striated, clearly revealing contemporary values concerning marriage and emotional communication. Ancient prints are much clearer but largely irrelevant to us now. This is one reason why we cannot use many of the traditional interpretations. We have different understanding of time, value, society and ethics.

THE MAJOR FIRE LINE

The Western mind is predominantly of a fire and air nature, and these two hand shapes are commonly found in the West. In Eastern countries by contrast, water and earth are much more evident. The growing dominance of fire has caused the development of fire lines to undergo a remarkable process of change over the ages. For although fire is a major foundation of our environment, its continued development within the so-called civilized nations has led to its gradual recession grammeognomically. On the modern hand, fire lines in general occupy a much lesser value than before. It is as if the "flame" has to burn now much more brightly to be noticed, as everywhere else is brightly blazing! The major fire line is shown in figure 58 on page 164.

In Wu Hsing, the major fire line's function is supportive of the earth line, acting as its energizer. It is most commonly found running at an obtuse angle to the major earth line; sometimes it appears parallel to it, other times not. It is always deep and strongly colored. In old palmistry, its nearest equivalent was referred to as the *Mars* line, but this is really a different line altogether. The Mars line was considered to be a rare and auspicious sign. Ancient palmistry often confused the fire line with the influence lines, which run parallel to the major earth line, for these lines sometimes resemble the fire line. However, if you remember that the major fire line always possesses a fire depth and color you will not confuse it with other lines. The fire line is not a fact rare at all. It describes the amount of active energy within all fire organizers of the body (heat, blood, muscles, etc.), and is thus vital to a fully balanced physical organism possessing plentiful energy supplies. Modern lifestyles—with their unhealthy foodstuffs, lack of exercise and fresh air—have no doubt contributed to the decline of the

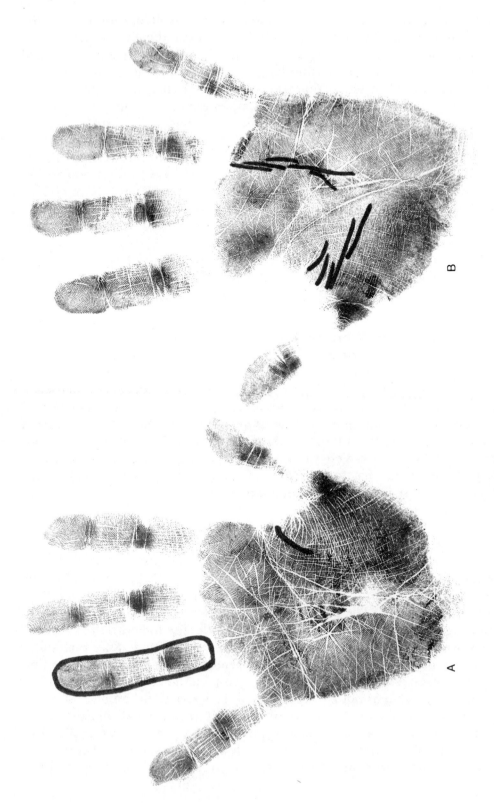

Figure 58. The major (a) and minor (b) fire lines. The fire digit is shown.

major fire line, and have caused its minor deflection (the minor fire line) to assume a more prominent function within everyday life. One result of this has been the development of the cult of "personality," the "public" image, along with its supportive media cohorts. In Eastern countries, personality projection occurs only within areas dominated by Western cultural interest. Such lands are also far more spiritually aware and often more health conscious in daily life.

As the earth line reveals the total energy production of the whole physical organism, so the major fire line demonstrates energy in motion, renewing and repairing damage. While it is present, the body is capable of utilizing that percentage of its energy relative to the earth line. For example, if the fire line is 50% present relative to the earth line (50% the length of the earth line) then renewal is 50% effective parasympathetically. In other words, one is "half ill" before the imbalance is noted.

Considered predominantly as a health gauge, the fire line is a valuable aid. It is most effective when found following the path of a major earth line. It becomes less revealing when it is partially present or distant from this earth line. It has no special psychological indication save determination and capability to overcome health imbalance in the manner mentioned. It does suggest a certain intensity of spirit but this feature will be recognized in other lines more readily. The major fire line has only minimal meanings in interpretation, and there is only so much one can say about it. The reader will notice that the space devoted here to the fire line is relatively shorter than the descriptions of the other major lines.

Quality

The fire line is predominantly of fire color and depth. If found pale but deep, it indicates a tendency to nervous upsets or psychosomatically induced imbalance. If it is pale or weak looking and continuous with the earth line, it suggests a tendency to infections and muscular (rheumatic) diseases. One should check a suspect major fire line with its reflection (minor fire line) and the strength of the fire finger in general. If these are strong but the major line appears weak, the line is more likely to be a subsidiary earth, rather than fire, formation.

Length

Modern research into Wu Hsing methods now leads me to believe that within contemporary Occidental civilizations, the fire line has reached a norm of one third the earth line. This should be considered an average length. As the major fire line relates directly to sexual virility, it should occur parallel to the commencement of the major earth line, thus corresponding to the period of early childhood and puberty. It will often be found fading when an influence line takes over (suggesting marriage and another source of sexuality apart from the subject's own body). It will often appear in a fragmented form much later at a time coincident (in women) with menopause. Total absence of this line therefore suggests a congenital lack of potency in conception, or other difficulties associated with child bearing.

If the fire line develops later, it indicates a period of physical or mental activity within the subject. It may be professional advancement, a new environment or illness. Each of these requires the extra vitality provided by the fire line. When the fire line exceeds the one third length given above, it brings with it a more physical outlook on life. The subject tends to interpret experience through physical activities or stimuli.

THE MAJOR AIR LINE

The major air line acts as a significator of the extent, quality and orientation of consciousness. Figure 59 shows the location of the air line. The Romans knew this line as the *mensal* or table line, by which they meant something level, stable and supportive. Consciousness, as we now understand it, is often far from stable, for modern day life demands we understand ourselves more fully. It is useful to think of the air line as a T.V. aerial, picking up signals and helping to conduct them to the screen of our minds. Here they are turned into knowable pictures and concepts which the mind then acts or reacts towards. The longer the line the more signals are picked up, and the slower their significance is realized. If the line is short, only a few signals are received and the resultant image is quickly formulated. With long lines there is danger of mental dispersion or indecision, and short lines tend towards superficiality. The longer line requires more coordinative discipline. If this is achieved the resultant information is more detailed and thus fully accurate. The danger inherent in long lines is to become mentally distracted by all the information received. The shorter line requires mental patience and thoroughness, to offset the innate hastiness of its decisions.

The air line always begins below the mount of the water finger, above the earth quadrant. Its termination may be any other position on the opposite side of the hand or palm. The termination of the line indicates the orientation the mind most naturally works towards. Whereas termination varies widely according to the individual temperament, commencement has only four important placings as shown in figure 60 on page 168, all within an area spanning about three-quarters of an inch. They are: (1) the mount

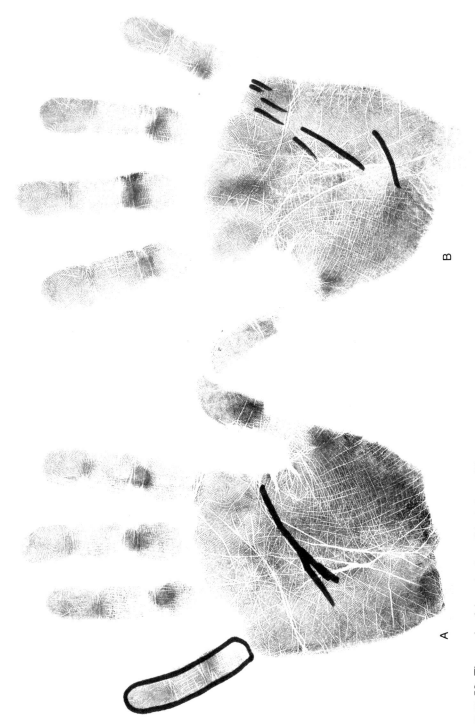

A

B

Figure 59. The major (a) and minor (b) air lines. The air digit is shown.

below the water finger; (2) just below this mount, above the major earth line; (3) attached to the major earth line; and (4) just below the major earth line.

When commencing just below the water finger, the influence of the water element is strong. This gives the consciousness an independent and idealistic tone. Such a temperament seeks to ground experiences in a higher form. An air line commencing just below this mount, above the major earth line, indicates a lessened idealism and more individualism is shown in the development of personal attitudes towards the self and others. This is the position of an independent mind that separated itself from family influences early in life.

A commencement attached to the major earth line is a common position, being a blend of individualism and caution. It show the influence of the early environment. When present on both hands, an apprehensive temperament is shown. When the air line begins just below the major earth line, a strong earth element attraction is indicated and a wish for stability and self-protection. It is often seen in those who feel they lack these qualities. The closer the air line comes to the earth line, the more earth qualities

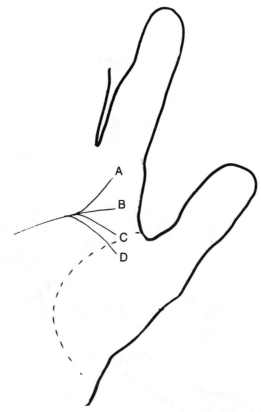

Figure 60. The major air line has four important commencements: a) the mount below the water finger; b) just below this mount, above the major earth line; c) attached to the earth line; and d) just below the earth line.

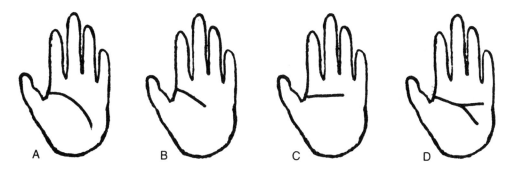

Figure 61. The various terminations of the major air line: a) ending on the water quadrant; b) ending on the fire quadrant; c) deep, straight form; and d) a divided ending.

are needed by the subject. Domestic national, political, racial issues are felt to be significant. The further from the earth line the air line commences, the more the wish for independence from the home, country, family, culture, etc.

The longer the air line is tied to the earth line the greater the part played by early environment in the development of attitudes and evaluation of experience. Terminations vary a great deal, but figure 61 shows us the most common. The air line ending on the water quadrant (figure 61a) imparts sensitivity and imagination. Ending on the fire quadrant, (figure 61b) the air line indicates construction and aggression. Curvature is a water quality; straightness is a fire quality. The deep, straight line ending under the fire finger (figure 61c) is very masculine and practical. The long, deeply curving line going deep into the water quadrant is feminine and emotional in nature.

Strongly divided lines (shown in figure 61d) show unifications of both feminine and masculine, structural and imaginative faculties. By noting which branch of a division bears the most masculine or fire quality, you will see which is predominant and which acts as a supporting function. Divisions are always marks of versatility.

The air line rising upwards or sending a branch towards any of the digits indicates an orientation in attitude towards the activity described by that digit, particularly in purely conceptual, non-physical areas of interest. The effect of this is an intensification of the elemental energy ruling the line, which produces almost a mania of interest in the field shown. It is as if a magnetism were being manifested between similarly polarized elements. When an opposite polarity branches off—i.e., a water quality branch to a fire ruled mount—a health imbalance is shown (see figure 62a on page 170). This is intensified if the length of the line itself is of an opposite polarity to that which it rises towards—for example, a water length branch up towards the air finger, as shown in figure 62b. Generally speaking, such manifestations primarily relate to metabolic imbalance. Rising lines or ris-

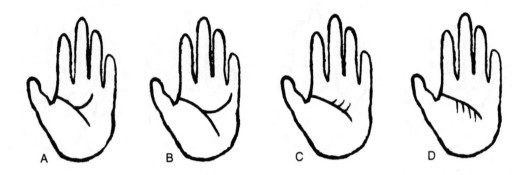

Figure 62. Various features of the major air line: a) water branch to fire mount; b) water branch to air digit; c) rising lines; and d) falling lines.

ing branches of lines (see figure 62c) show an attraction towards non-material and non-physical manifestations of consciousness (unless they reveal opposite polarities as stated). Descending lines (figure 62d) show attraction towards emotional, imaginative or physical realms of consciousness.

Occasionally you may find a major air line which possesses several distinct beginnings, as shown in figure 63. In such cases, you should first ascertain whether this actually is a beginning. Note if the thicker end of the line is found towards the major earth line itself. It's common mistake to miscredit this line as a beginning when in fact it is a branch line. If it is a proper multiple beginning, then it shows the influence of different factors in the development of consciousness. In figure 63, we can see a unification of the water influence (shown by the line rising high into the water digit mount) and the usual fire/air influences of the quadrants in which it always begins. Often such a doubled beginning occurs where a child has parents of widely differing temperaments. At any rate, this position shows you that the domestic pull of earth and the idealism of water are united in the life views of the individual.

Figure 63. The major air line with a double source.

Quality

The quality of the line indicates in what manner the mind translates its signals. *Earth* quality shows slow and pedantic attention. *Water* quality shows sensitive and humanitarian concerns are strong. *Fire* quality shows decisiveness and intensity of thought. *Air* quality shows conceptual and intellectual awareness. The less interrupted the major air line, the more clearly source information is received and comprehended. A fuzzy line results in a fuzzy picture and, therefore, mental confusion.

Length

By considering the air line's length, quality and termination, you can get an accurate understanding of a subject's store, articulation, habit and orientation of consciousness. The first is easily perceived if we relate length directly to element. Earth is shortest and extends to the middle of the earth finger. Water is a little longer and extends beyond the earth digit. Fire extends to the fire finger and air to under the air digit. (See figure 64.) Remember this is a classification only for length and not quality.

Earth length is under-developed and reveals a primitive mode of perception and mental awareness. The senses, rather than the intellect, are used to gain information concerning the environment and little original thought is evidenced. Water length is a little more active but still is the consciousness of the servant or follower, and suggests a lack of organizational ability and a preoccupation with material objects, senses and pleasures. In fire length we find the average of humanity. Fire is active and structural, and registers, regulates and orders mental phenomena into workable foundations for thought. Air is rather overlong for ordinary lifestyles and when, as is usual, it descends into the water quadrant, more suited to the artistic professions. Being long it reveals a wide panorama of

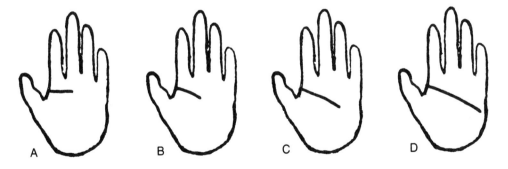

Figure 64. Length of line is related to elemental quality. Here we see an air line with a) earth length; b) water length; c) fire length; and d) air length air line.

influence to which the individual is subject. We can often find air length in those who see both sides of a situation equally and who find it difficult to make decisions. It is also inspirational for it receives stimuli of a perceptual and super-conscious nature equally. It gives hunches and guesses, and (when descending) confers the ability to remember emotional (or non-factual) events more easily. This is not good for the mechanic, scientist or mathematician, but ideal for dance, art, mime poetry—all the arts.

Relation of Major Air and Water Lines

In human beings the balance of emotions and intellect is of prime importance in establishing personality patterns. The air line reveals its distinctive traits and affinities in this balancing action by its height on the palm. If the line is set high up and close to the major water line as in figure 65a, it reveals a strong emotional bias in thought. Judgments are made as a result of feelings, rather than fact. If set low, forming a wide space between the water and air lines (see figure 65b), consciousness is independent of emotions and more inclined to make judgments solely on the factors involved.

The amount of space between the air and water lines varies considerably. Even on one hand, we may find them close at one part and wide apart later on (figure 65e). These divergences show how the attitude develops according to experience. Generally, the air line curves downwards towards its end, revealing the maturity of old age and the accumulation of many years of interpersonal experience. A narrow space between air and water must be assessed in elemental terms. Is it because water has dropped or because air has risen? When this area is narrow it reveals an insufficiency in both water and air attitudes, so much so that they draw together to reinforce each other. As these elements are antagonistic, such an occurrence cannot take place without mental and emotional stress. Rationality is interfered with by emotion, and emotion is repressed by rationality. Neither works properly or towards inner balance and the development of intense feelings and attitudes is likely. As a health sign it reveals that respiration (air) or circulation (water) are not harmoniously connected and it is a common sign found in asthmatics. Psychologically, it reveals a tendency towards fanaticism or narrow-mindedness and over-subjective evaluations.

Sometimes the air and water lines fuse into one line across the palm as shown in figure 65f-h. This is called a simian formation (so-called because it is often found on the palms of apes). Much misunderstanding of this feature exists and many palmists give it too much credit. In many cases palmists credit lines with simian characteristics incorrectly. True simian formation occurs when there is only one line present and there are no traces of any other major water or air lines. When major air and water lines fuse, we can easily see that emotional response and intellectual action

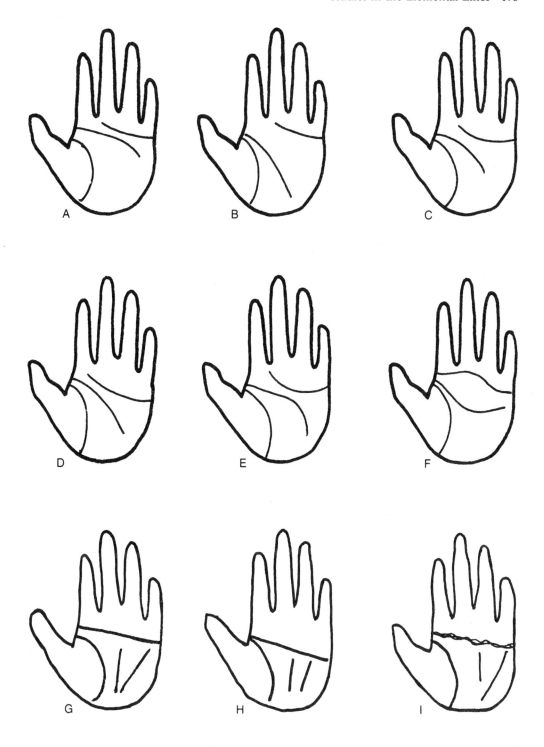

Figure 65. Relating the major air line to the major water: a) air line is high; b) air low; c) average relationship; d) a low water line; e-f) here the gap varies as the lines curve; g-i) various simian line forms—the air and water lines fuse into one.

become inseparable and intertwined. Individuals with such lines do not know if they think or feel their experiences, and thus find it difficult to attain self-understanding and detachment. Simian formation always brings intensity and tenacity of purpose—the subject pours his or her heart and mind into whatever is of current interest. The formation is often inherited and serves to show family attitudes or ethics which have been implanted from birth. Simians find it difficult to separate themselves from their family standards, and many would never think of doing so. In these cases, the simian always occurs in the passive hand.

You should attempt to judge whether air or water energy is predominate in the simian formation and this is usually evident from its height. If the simian is high water as in figure 65g, then emotion is the basis of their intensity. They will feel emotions deeply. If the simian is low set (figure 65h) air element predominates and a detached, intellectual basis of great intensity is present. The water element simian is good for social and charity work, supporting the underprivileged, etc; the air simian for scientific, mathematical work and research, philosophy, electronics and the armed forces. In fact one can interpret the true simian as an absence of the subordinate element line.

In most cases the simian line bears fire element characteristics: straight, deep and red. Often it actually looks like two lines intertwining around each other (see figure 65i). Only when these factors are present should you judge the line as simian. Many formations may approach the simian but none has the depth of feeling and thinking that the real simian possesses. Channeled into the correct environment, simian bearers can make great progress. Many famous research scientists and doctors bear this mark. It is also found in those guilty of brutal crimes of passion.

Healthwise, the simian reveals a direct and close link between psychological health and emotional balance—which is why it is so powerful in effect. Each needs to be developed equally. Organically considered, respiration and circulatory functions are sensitivized. Heartbeat fluctuations and bronchial weakness are common in simians. Due to the interconnectedness of bodily organs, the heart and sympathetic nervous system are also very sensitive to stimulatory responses. Simians should not live in an atmosphere of uncertainty, change or deprivation. This is especially so if the simian marking is present in both hands (although it is more common in a single hand). One should also interpret the marking in conjunction with the fingerprints. With whorls predominating an intense love of freedom is indicated. Such subjects function best alone in self-motivated professions. The fire and water fingerprints reinforce (or balance) the simian, depending upon its height. Earth fingerprints physicalize the drive and tend to restrict its expression. Often this is found with a rich inner life but an inability to communicate with others. The individual with a simian marking tends to like secrecy or has an innate ability to ferret out others' secrets as well. Intelligence work, forensic science, police work, insurance and all forms of investigative work (including industrial espionage) are easily mastered by the simian bearers.

Distinctive Markings

Ideally, the air line should be clearly formed, free of obstruction and gradual in its angularity. This demonstrates both physical and mental balance with one's internal and external environmental demands. When debilitating signs appear they reveal a weakening of this clear balance. The weakening signs can be classified elementally:

Earth: brings a total absence or widening of the line, giving it a brutal scar–like appearance. In consciousness it vulgarizes perception. In health it dissipates fine neural responses.

Water: brings wave-like meanderings of a line, islands and a delicate quality. In consciousness it brings poor concentration, emotionally based perception, and a subjective response. In health it indicates hypersensitivity and lack of rhythmic energy and application.

Fire: distinguished by its deepness. Fire traits are bar lines, multiple lines (striations) and sudden terminal markings such as the cross formations. In consciousness it brings shock, intensity of purpose and speed of response. Healthwise it shows a sudden draining or stoppage of the energy flow.

Air: gives a delicate and pale appearance to a line. It produces many small lines seemingly placed randomly over all parts of the palm. Air also produces a fine fluffing, in which small protuberances drift from the line, too small for bars or cross lines, yet not detached enough to reveal clear influences. Fluffing reveals unclear patterns of thought, mistaken judgments, and lethargic attitudes. Healthwise it reveals a lack of inner adjustment to the outer world, mental stress and apprehension. It can also indicate neural inflammations when present with other signs.

Each of these debilitative markings relates to all other lines, but in the case of the air line their support is reflected in structural consciousness and neural action.

Not all markings on the major air line are debilitating however. Consider, for example, breaks. Occasionally we find the air line breaking off and recommencing elsewhere. This coincides, psychologically speaking, with a fresh start in life: a new direction unrelated to previous environments or persons. It is usually beneficial for it takes both courage and opportunity to change, and the break shows both exist. Breaks may be either overlapping or direct, as shown in figure 66 on page 176. When breaks overlap, some influence from previous conditions is shown, since for

Figure 66. Breaks in the major air line may either be overlapping (a) or direct (b).

a period there are two lines in action. It is often found when beginning a new business, home or similar endeavor. Breaks should occur clearly, that is, the first ending should be simple and not occasioned by a bar, cross line or anything else. If these negative markings are present, the formation is more likely to relate to health and reveal an accident to the head or some form of shock to the nervous system. Check reflected lines carefully in this case. Let's consider some of these lines in detail.

Islands: These are rejoined divisions within the line and reveal a change from the intended function of air element. Division occurs because of interruption in flow (in this case the flow of perception and cognition) strong enough to cause a "billowing out" of attitude, which then returns back to its original flow. The commencement of an island is thus an incipient forking of the air line. This feature could have been fortuitous, leading as it does to a more open and aware perception of personal experience. However, in this case the forking has halted and returned, showing an intrinsic inability in the usual function to meet demands made on it. Because air relates to attitude and outlook, we know that it is this which has proven faulty and therefore that external, environmental factors have been the cause.

Experience shows that islanding occurs in times of personal stress when decisions assume a significant value to a subject. The internal consciousness is not in harmony with external requirements and a breakdown has occurred. All situations in which a radical reassessment of attitudes is called for produce the island formation, even if the cause is emotional. Change in religion, domestic or marital crises, or business worries all produce islands. We most often find this sign when the air line is not balanced in itself—such as when it terminates in an opposite polarity (that is, the water or earth quadrant), or when the elemental balance of the hand shape itself is not harmonious.

Considered from the health viewpoint, islands show a temporary obstruction in neural function somewhere within the body. They divide and thus weaken the energy current. Before we diagnose the island formation, it is essential to inspect it in both hands and to examine the reflected air line running down from the air finger. An inspection also of the earth line should be made as this reveals fundamental constitution and resistance in general to ill health. If the island formation is evident in both hands, and the reflected lines (minor air) and the earth line also shows weakness, then you can consider that a condition of ill health is present or at least incipient. Experience and tradition show that a clear island on the air line under the water digit reveals spleen malfunction and thus lymphatic disorder and anaemia; under the earth finger, liver or digestive malfunctions; under the fire digit, vision problems, tachycardia, valvular malfunction or kidney insufficiency; and under the air finger, neurasthenia, epilepsy and catatonia, respiratory weaknesses, phobic states and mental imbalance of many kinds. In all cases of diagnostic procedure, analysis of elemental balances on both hands must be made.

Many conditions shown in the hands are inherited from the parents or are of a temporary nature. An effort should therefore be made to discover the family health history, particularly grandparents, as their health conditions seem to be exhibited much more frequently than those of parents.

If the island is formed of lines of a fire quality, suspect inflammatory illness. If it is on water quality lines, suspect circulatory problems or exposure to infection. An island formed of earth quality lines (very rare) indicates a direct organic malfunction, often inherited. An island on air quality lines shows a respiratory or neural cause or effect.

One other indication of the cause or effect of illness can be seen by observing the type of island present. There are three types as shown in figure 67. These are:

1. Island caused by root line dividing and rejoining itself—suspect infection or direct accidental cause.

2. Island caused by an ascending (weaker) line rejoining—the cause is often psychosomatic in nature or at least non-organic. This is also common in specifically air diseases such as neural infections.

Figure 67. Islands on the major air line can be caused by: a) a root line dividing; b) an ascending line adjoining; or c) a descending line adjoining.

3. Island caused by a descending (weaker) line rejoining—look for organic (perhaps inherited) illness. This is a mark of physical importance.

Consider the overall elemental predominances and then associated illnesses. Familiarity with physiology is, of course, important and any analyst venturing into the field of cheirological health diagnosis—even if only exploratorily—should ground him or herself in basic anatomy and endocrinology so as to be fully cognizant of all major bodily actions.

Dots: These are sudden and small indentations within a line's structure and are evidence of sudden and often inflammatory attack. Dots are of the fire element, so the predispose the subject to organic shock or failure. Dots are seldom present on the hands for long. If also present on the major fire and water lines, they should be considered possible indications of thrombosis, epilepsy or nephritis. Thrombotic condition of cranial blood vessels would tend to produce sets of dots in a confined area of the air line. One should inspect the water and earth lines carefully. In most cases a mild nephritis is indicated. Accidents in which the neck or skull is fractured also produce dots. Irregular dots occasionally occur in cases of venereal disease, malaria and jaundice. They are always sudden in their health effects and can often be recognized by their deep coloring, which makes them distinct from the usual line shade. Pale dots are rare but are evidence of insufficient blood supply to the brain. Epilepsy is a common symptom of this, as is the tendency towards holding the neck and shoulder areas too rigidly. Observe the subject's posture. Headaches and migraine caused by bad posture are also shown by pale dots. If there are many dots, fainting attacks can occur. Remedial posture training is the only cure. The deeper a dot is, the more sudden (or debilitating) its effects. Coloring is always the guideline in this case.

As a temperamental factor, dots indicate periods of great intensity (if deep red) or of stress (if pale). They reveal a situation in which currently held attitudes are discovered to have drastic shortcomings; they indicate a response to the immediate environment, usually in the form of shock. They can also be evidence of an accident, so great care must be taken to inspect other lines. If the dot is found with no complementary signs in other lines, mental shock is indicated. This is usually caused by loss (especially of a loved one) or failure of some form.

Bars and cross lines: Bars are short, unconnected markings that are not part of major or minor lines and that cut across the paths of these lines. On the air line they reveal influences and attitudes that run contrary to the basic mental pattern of the subject. The effect of these can be seen by observing the nature of the air line after the line has been crossed. Longer lines, whether of a major, minor or seemingly unclassifiable nature, which cut across the air line (or any other) are termed cross lines (see figure 68a-c).

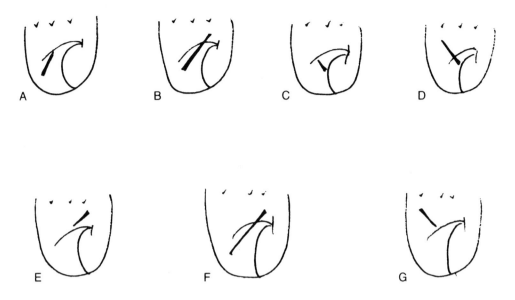

Figure 68. Chance lines (cross lines): a) from water to fire quadrants; b) again from water to fire quadrants, but a longer form; c) from earth to air quadrant; d) a longer version going from earth to air; e) fire to water quadrants; f) a longer form going from fire to water; g) air quadrant to earth quadrant.

In matters of health, bars have similar significance to dots, except that in most cases a bar indicates an external rather than internal cause for illness. Cross lines, on the other hand, show a channeling of energies across the air function, which can either aid or hinder its action (depending on the state of the line after it has been crossed). All cross lines which carry energies across elementally antagonistic quadrants are health indications (water to fire or air to earth). The point at which they cross the air line reveals how they manifest within consciousness, either by causing direct symptoms or by altering metabolic rate.

Generally we assess the direction of a line by regarding the thickest part as the source. Thus a chance cross line from water quadrant towards the fire quadrant (shown in figure 68a) shows an overload of energy concerned with liquid circulation in the body—this will cause or is causing, distress. If the line continues into fire quadrant as shown in figure 68b, it reveals a need for heat and is correlated with an anemic condition (lack of red [fire] blood cells) or with circulatory (water) stagnation, as is found in low blood pressure. If a line crosses from earth quadrant towards the air quadrant and stops at the air line (see figure 68c), it suggests respiratory malfunction, infection, or simply insufficiencies caused by bad breathing habits. Extreme slouching or kyphosis can be suspected with this latter trait.

An analyst can usually determine them by simple observation of the subject's outward posture or respiratory volume. Respiratory rate can also be directly correlated with emotional condition—water lines will confirm this. If the cross line carries on over into the air quadrant (see figure 68d), suspect a more entrenched condition. Again, one must enquire into family history to see if relatives are prone to respiratory ailments. I have seen many cases of these indicated strongly, in one hand only, in subjects whose grandparents died of TB, bronchitis or pleurisy.

Any changes in the elemental quality of a line after it has been crossed should be noted. The dispersion or intensification of the air element affects the subject considerably and in a subtle and slow manner, so he or she is often unaware of an impending tendency towards stress or neurosis.

Cross lines that descend usually reveal that internal organs are acting to offset overloads upon them. In the case of a line approaching the major air line from the fire quadrant towards water (as in figure 68e), the fire energy is over–intense and seeks to "blow" away. This is seen in cases of alcoholism or extreme fanaticism, depression (which is caused by other things of course), and lack of confidence (which can cause an unreal persona to be maintained). Hypersexuality also produces this. If these conditions are severe, the line will cross the air line and proceed onwards towards water (see figure 68f) in an attempt to extinguish itself.

In the case of a line commencing in the air quadrant and approaching (or crossing) the air line towards earth quadrant (figure 68g), we see an attempt to ground a neurasthenic condition. This can assume many forms; respiratory hyperventilation is one, neurosis is another. In China this is often considered a sign of psychic imbalance. Deficiency in those minerals which conduct electricity is also suggested. This line is known as the minor air line. We will discuss minor lines further in this volume.

As the major air line reveals consciousness, much of what occurs in ill health is directly related to temperament. The air line delineates the quality and breadth of outlook, so all markings that interrupt this line disturb and set out of balance the internal balance of thought and perception. This can result in the development of psychological illness, phobias and apprehensive states (given that the form and quality of the line demonstrate an initial stability). When analyzing the air line, a clear understanding of its basic nature is necessary prior to interpreting any of its modifications. In this manner the significance of change can be understood in the terms of the subject analyzed.

Cross lines are more commonly found than bars, and often—if a print is regularly taken—you can see that bars are often created by a cross line fading away and leaving only the cogent part remaining. Conversely, it can occasionally be observed that bars grow into cross lines; but this is more common when the air line changes direction or quality after the bar has cut it. If this is the case, it reveals a change of attitude (or method of self-communication) on the part of the subject. As this new attitude develops, so the bar grows and describes this change, eventually forming into a definite auxiliary line.

A bar that is changing into a cross line can be identified by its depth— it will be deeper at its crossing point. A cross line which is changing into a bar will be deeper further from the air line. Careful observation of the hand will identify the source of bars or cross lines clearly.

MINOR AND SUBSIDIARY EARTH LINES

This formation, known in popular palmistry as the *Fate* line, occupies a central and longitudinal position in the palm. (See figure 69 on page 182.) Commencing from the lower part of the palm, it runs up towards the middle finger. The line as a whole has to be considered in conjunction with the minor fire element line (see page 196) for together they form a thermometer of the objective and subjective. It is this action of internal stabilization that gives the minor earth line its distinctive qualities. In China it is equated with the Buddha of Equality and non-discriminatory wisdom, the Buddha who has realized an all embracing compassionate attitude. This line manifests the ability to harmonize inner mental conflicts or questions with the outside world of change, and by doing this, achieve balanced resolution between actions, thoughts and feelings. When the line is present, the degree of inner harmonization is greatly enhanced, depending, of course, on the actual quality of the line itself. If absent it reveals a restriction of stability, meaningful working relationships, and a tendency to allow oneself to be dictated to by external circumstances. Underlying this absence is a deficit of those attitudes which serve to cohere experiences, persons and thoughts into a relational pattern. Cohesion itself is not appreciated as a valid quality necessary to personal development. We find absence of this line common among those whose lifestyle requires little social responsibility or command.

The position of the minor earth line falls between the conscious and unconscious zones of the palm; indeed it usually divides those zones. We can see simply from this fact that it acts as a form of osmotic barrier between structural and non-structural thoughts and feelings. Absence of the line, either partially or completely, shows an uncontrolled intermingling of imaginative, relational urges together with consciously oriented motivations and aims. This only leads to confusion and diffusion of personal energy. The minor earth line fulfills essential tasks within the palm, and because it is connected to so many vital aspects of human development, it will be dealt with here in greater detail than the other minor lines.

The things of the earth are very important, be they foodstuffs or bodily minerals—we cannot live without them! The lines associated with the

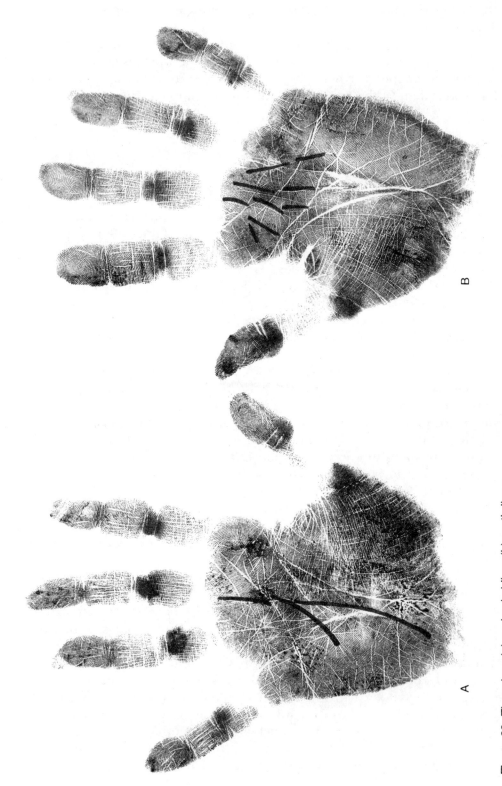

Figure 69. The minor (a) and subsidiary (b) earth lines.

earth elements in our hands are likewise concerned with fundamental activities. Whereas the major earth represents our ground within the body, the minor earth represents the *social face* of the ground, our balance within the world at large. The total absence of the minor earth thus immediately tells us that something is lacking in the subject, that his or her sense of balance and inner communication has atrophied for some reason. When absent, the subject sees life as a great struggle or battle; there is an inability to develop adaptable relationships to circumstances or persons. Many finer efforts are wasted because the subject is unable to fully discriminate between useful and useless endeavors. Great amounts of energy are expended to no avail. Goal orientation and creative friendships should be much encouraged in these subjects.

Although it is termed a minor line, the function of this line is as great as the major line. As long as it is present, our relationships with the outside world and our own inner natures remain balanced and inter-communicative. In fact, the minor earth line reveals our sense of mental adaptability and our ability to attain creative experiences. When fully present such qualities are strong in our temperament and confer a serious and firm sense of justice, ethical regard and respect for traditional values or institutions. In a negative form (having a fire or air quality) the line can make the individual rigid, strict, and a stern disciplinarian—but absolutely reliable: one who would rather die than lose honor.

Commencement

The line rises from four common positions: the water quadrant; the earth quadrant; the middle of the wrist; some way up the palm, in the middle. (These are shown in figure 70.) When it rises from the water quadrant, it indicates a degree of sensitivity in the line, a feeling for external balance from friends, family or supporters. Such a commencement is elementally compatible and is often found in those who can adapt to others' personalities skillfully and adroitly. When it rises from the earth quadrant, it indicates that the centering function is very strong, and responses to fundamental harmony and well being are paramount in mind. This is often a characteristic found in those closely influenced by their families (the fundamental unit), or by music (the fundamental vibration). Musicality is also often manifested by a minor earth line that is tied to the major earth line. If this attraction to the earth source is shown clearly, there will always be a great liking for all types of pleasures. With a long (high) minor earth line or stiff earth finger, these pleasures will be strictly traditional. If found with a short minor earth line or very flexible earth finger, they will be of a more indulgent and sensual type.

A commencement rising from the middle of the wrist is a blend of both indications above. This commencement reveals a complementary development of imaginative responses and ideals conjoined with dedication

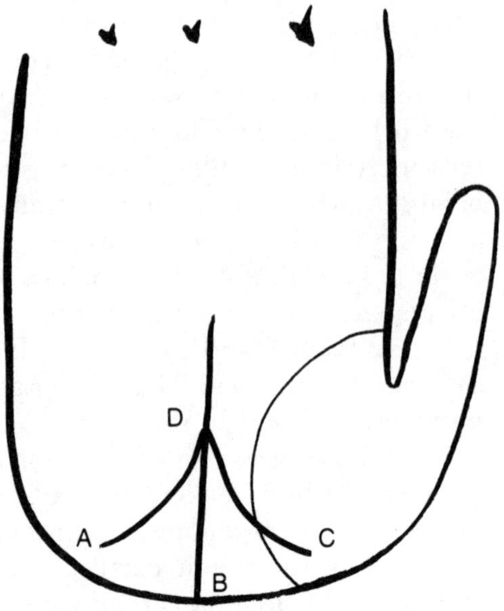

Figure 70. Minor earth line commencement positions, beginning from: a) the water quadrant; b) the earth quadrant; c) the middle of the wrist; and d) in the middle of the palm.

and responsibility. If the line starts late (up the palm, in the middle), it reveals that the subject's internal balance did not develop in childhood. Such a marking is suggestive of family disturbance or deprivation. Everyone should have inner balance and security when young and wherever the line absence is observed, so also is shown a period of some form of deprivation or loss of well being.

Special Commencements

The secondary earth line can occasionally begin from unusual areas of the palm, particularly from the mounts. If this is the case, a specific and special motivation in internal communication is indicated, making the subject less free in his or her choice of relational attitudes and more "fadic" or fixed in nature. This loosely corresponds to what psychologists call neurosis, and can take many forms. The positioning indicates that internal harmony can only be attained by or through particular orientations, and that the development of variants will in fact hinder fulfillment. As these commencements are not usual, it suggests a separation from the usual attitudes of the general society or environment. This may be very helpful in the case of persons with special vocations or callings, for it gives power to the consciousness, but much depends on the element quality and nature of the hand itself.

The more common of these special commencements stem from the areas of the major fire line, the base of the air quadrant, the earth quadrant and the top of the water quadrant. We can see that each of these positions causes the line to run roughly at right angles to its usual position and acts as a direct conductor, rather than a mediator between the various forms of consciousness. It must be remembered that special commencements can only be present when the ordinary line is absent. If you remember this, no confusion will occur between the secondary earth line and other chance lines. If we find several sources to the minor earth line, we can see that multiple influences prevail in the subject's fundamental psyche and means of attaining internal balance and relationships.

Figure 71 on page 186 illustrates several examples of special commencements. Figure 71a shows that emotional and traditional sources are sought to establish relationships. This may sound normal, but in fact is often accompanied by emotional alienation. It gives warmth and impressionability. In old palmistry, these joining lines were interpreted as marriage lines, despite the obvious fact that many join at a point in the line which, if viewed chronologically, covered the ages one through eleven! However, the fact that the individual would find balance in another person is a possibility, but only at a higher point of the line. Figure 71b shows a diverse source balance, utilizing family and extra-family values and standards, or alternatively earth and water energy forms. This could indicate parents of widely differing temperaments who have been taken as sources of stability.

Figure 71d shows classic marking of the "son and heir." It is found in those strongly energized by the earth quality. On a refined hand it gives stability and a sense of harmonious unity. On a weak hand it shows apprehension or indulgence with material assets. An islanded commencement, as shown in figure 71e, reveals a fundamental imbalance or deprivation from birth. Old palmists called this the "illegitimate" birth mark. If viewed as indicating an absence of balancing points (i.e., parental influence and guidance), this interpretation could contain some truth. It is more significant healthwise, as it indicates that secondary earth (growth processes) are hindered. If the island extends into the Neptune area, karmic retribution is suggested. A hindrance of bone formation or growth is indicated by this island, as is mineral utilization, especially if an island occurs in a branch joining from the water quadrant.

The minor earth line always ends on, or is orientated towards the earth mount—and it is named because of this feature. A line ending anywhere else—for example, twisting at the top towards the water mount (see figure 71h), is *not* an earth line and should be considered as a separate and distinct line formation of its own. If, however, a line takes over the minor earth line (figure 71i), then that portion of the line orientated towards earth finger alone should be considered as the earth line.

The nature of the terminal section reveals factors relating to the balance ideas in the subject. However, in most palms the line does not occur fully present; indeed this is quite normal, for few of us have a full view of life so early within it! More commonly the line appears fully formed in our later years as we grow mature and experienced, and have come to know our own capabilities and modes of experience more fully. If fully formed, the following special markings are of interest.

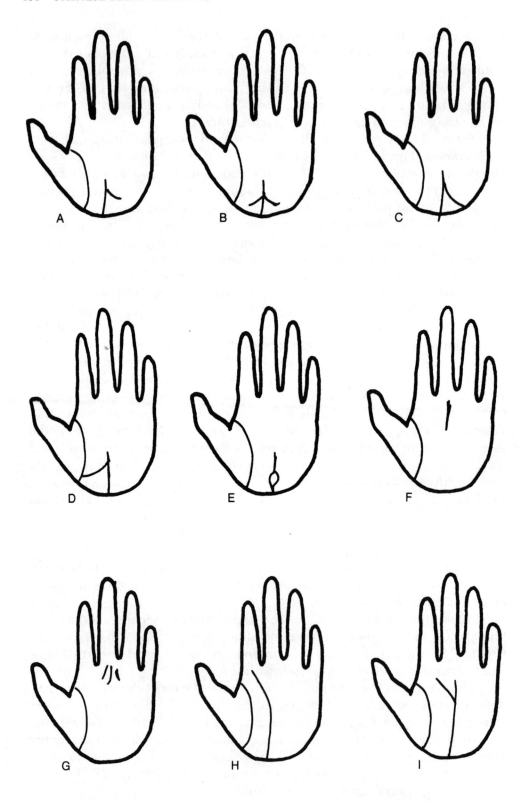

Figure 71. Multiple and special minor earth line commencements and terminations.

Striation: The presence of five (or more) parallel lines upon the earth mount reveals an excessive fire action. This shows an excitable and often over-optimistic attitude to business or professional contacts. The development of objectivity is needed when this termination is found.

Star or cross: This marking was often given ominous meanings in old palmistry; in fact it indicates an inner conflict between the public image desired by the subject and that which he or she is capable of maintaining. It thus carries with it the overtone that the individual is vulnerable to being discovered in nefarious or unethical deeds. Elementally it is an overload of fire on earth, revealing a tendency towards obsession, fanaticism or self-destruction. Subjects with this marking clearly present need to be careful in their motives and try to insure that their capabilities match their desires.

Bars: Several horizontal bars crossing the line at mount level reveal frustration in endeavors through lack of sufficient foresight. It is not a good sign for financial matters. Air qualities (i.e., understanding) need to be developed further.

Curvature

The minor earth is predominantly straight in appearance. Any curve in it indicates influences of environments, persons or states of consciousness affecting personal balance. The nature of earth is simple and direct and curvature is seldom found. When it is, think in terms of balance lost and try to determine which aspect of consciousness is being over- or under-developed.

Quality

The minor earth line reveals the nature of a subject's balance by its elemental form and length. If the line is of a *fire* quality it shows subjects that take stabilizing power seriously, forming definite relationships along fixed and active lines. Individuals with this quality tend to keep themselves and others firmly in their place, respecting protocol, decorum and status. Straightness and directness are the fire characteristics. If the line is of *earth* nature, internal communication is inhibited and we find a rather solitary nature and outlook, tending to concern itself primarily with internal considerations and natural or physical processes. A *water* quality weakens the stable qualities of the line, making it tend towards vacillation or imitation. Such lines are usually found on those in the performing arts, for these individuals show great dependency on the environment or public. The balance is obtained primarily through external responses rather than internal understanding. These lines are usually wavy in formation. *Air* quality lines indicate a concern with the theoretical or non-physical aspects of the chosen profession, as well as a pronounced awareness of the subject's own thought processes. This line is thus suited for consultants or advisers in the professional field. Angular or striated in appearance, air quality shows a hypersensitive outlook and a tendency to be sensitive to criticism. Air quality is best in the design or advertising professions. It also indicates a great affinity for science and research.

Length

The usual line is around seventy percent present. If longer than this, a specialization in earth-ruled consciousness should be suspected. When long, the line is usually found very straight and fire-like in presence. Such a marking is usually associated with the so-called "establishment." It indicates a strong respect for traditional values and methods and—although creating an imminently respected mental skill—often indicates pedantry, lack of tolerance and narrow mindedness. It is often found in the law profession, religion, medicine and academia, and implies acceptance of society's demands. A wish for external, easily recognizable standards is strong. The stern school teacher and drill sargent are found with such long lineal formations. The longer and more strongly formed, the greater the ability to dedicate oneself to some cause or study. If found with a strong thumb, achievement is almost certain. With a weak thumb it is merely respect for, or fear of, superiors.

Health

The minor earth line relates to fundamental functions of the body, particularly the skeletal system and nutritional balance. When the line commences from the water or earth quadrants, unnatural curvature of the spine is suggested. If you relate the lower palmer area to the sexual organs and the highest part of the line to the neck, the respective organs upwards along it will relate to the organs found in the body itself. The minor earth line itself relates directly to the spinal column—we relate the lower section of the line to the lumbar vertebrae, the mid-section to the thoracic, and the higher part to the cervical vertebrae. A sudden turn in the line reveals a misalignment of vertebrae in the respective areas named. Because the spinal nerves connect to internal organs, these will also be affected according to where the line travels, breaks or fades. The line also is correlated with the earth finger itself in its flexion. If the top joint is flexible, it reveals a looseness of the cervical vertebrae (this often shows an unnatural backward curvature of the spine). The lower two joints of this finger also show flexive ability, or lack of it, correspondingly.

Distinctive Markings

Striation: Striation always indicates a dispersal of energies. When striation occurs on the minor earth line, it indicates that the subject's inner balance is disturbed, probably because the individual is over-concerned with trifles. It can also indicate that the subject takes things and people so seriously that the creative self becomes restricted. Striations can also symbolize wasted time, when the individual should be doing something else. It can also indicate an over-apprehensive outlook towards things.

Dots or bars: Since bars are of a fire nature, they show sudden setbacks to personal psychological balance. These are usually from external causes. Regular bars indicate the persistent adherence to out-moded methods of self-communication. Healthwise, bars indicate back injuries and spinal troubles.

Overlapping: This feature reveals that the subject is, or has, adapted his or her attitudes to a new level and towards a field different from that implanted by family tradition. It therefore suggests independent development and activity within the subject. Often branch lines will reveal the elemental source or nature of the new balance.

Islands: Islands indicate that the subject has a divided attitude. Islands are often of a temporary nature and may be formed by striations or overlappings joining together during periods of stress. They always indicate the presence of stress in relationships and, being of a water quality by nature, show excessive consideration of environmental pressures or other people's viewpoints. As a health sign, islands usually reveal weakness in the organs served by the spinal nerves in the correspondent position. If an island occurs in the middle of the line, it indicates a weakness in the spine. If it occurs at the top of the line, it will reflect neck weakness. Islands often occur as a result of unsuccessful psychological development; the marking can be an attempted overlap.

The old palmistic correlation of this marking with both prostitution or financial deprivation should be understood in terms of the elemental indications. Any period of indecision or instability always affects healthy creative relationships, and makes the subject more likely to be unemployed (or unemployable) with subsequent financial distress.

Branches: All branches show adaptions towards or from specific causes in the subject's consciousness. Branches joining from the earth or water quadrants reveal the nature of the influence. Those from water usually relate to attitudes developed from other persons and are often indications of business or romantic attachments that give rise to changes in the manner or method of achieving internal stability. Branches joining from earth relate to changes concerned with family, professional or domestic stability. The individual will invest time and effort into producing this stability.

The condition and quality of lines after a branch has joined should be noted carefully, for this reveals the effect of new influences or attitudes. Branches that rise from the line indicate activities initiated by the subject and their direction reveals the nature of this activity. Periodic observation of this feature is useful because branches often develop into new and separate lines completely. When this happens, it reveals that the object or nature of the new balance has been attained and adopted as the basis for future consciousness and inter-relationships. Health factors are only indicated by branches if they leave the line. You will be able to recognize a "departed branch" because the thickest part of the branch will be closest to the main line. The direction of such lines always goes towards an elemental area ruling the illness itself. In most cases these are found in falling rather than rising lines. Direct health indications by branch lines are quite rare, for these lines are primarily concerned with attitudes rather than organs—although attitudes can, in themselves, interfere with the balance of health!

Doubled lines: The nature of earth in general is to solidify and join; therefore doubled lines would normally indicate that optimum quality is absent. However, as earth tends also to dullness, doubled lines can show an active, fire-like use of its qualities. The doubled line shows that a two level balance has been created. This may take the form of satisfaction gained in different areas of life—probably in a part-time hobby or profession. Generally, the doubled line can be interpreted as a minor fire line, for these functions are very similar, dealing as they do with public and private image.

Fadings: When the line appears to fade away it indicates a period during which the subject was externally orientated to achieve inward balance. Fadings must be interpreted chronologically. Such a sign is not particularly fortunate, for it implies that previously such balancing was achieved independently within the subject's consciousness. The lack of this ability automatically suggests a failing of consciousness in some manner. There are always reasons for such signs and they must be determined by examination of the other lines in both hands.

Foreshortenings: Sometimes the minor earth line appears to be prematurely halted. This indicates that it has failed to reach its full potential. This halting usually occurs at two distinct points: at the point where the minor earth touches the major air line (as shown in figure 72a); and where it touches the major water line (shown in figure 72b). The first placement indicates that the mental energies represented by the air line disperse the cohesive abilities of the earth line. In personal terms, this often indicates that the subject's attitude or mental abilities are not sufficient to meet the demands that are placed on him or her. The second placement indicates that the subject's emotional attitudes or experiences somehow interfere with integrity. This marking is not uncommon to find in the hand of someone who has just gone through a divorce or an unhappy love affair. In the case of

 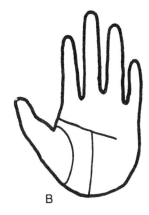

Figure 72. Foreshortenings of the minor earth line at a) the major water line; and b) the major air line.

both types of foreshortened lines there is hope. The line can regrow itself, and regular inspection of the hands for this feature will determine whether or not the individual is overcoming the difficulties or inabilities.

MINOR AND SUBSIDIARY WATER LINES

When early mankind graduated from nature and earth presiding deities, the next deity worshipped took the form of the goddess. The religions devoted to the female deities were very similar to one another and all gave importance to the prophetic and divinatory arts. The old earth gods had presided over the autumn and winter periods (harvest and the end of December being important); the goddess ruled spring and summer, fertility and growth. She had as her special attribute intuitive, mystical, non-structural understanding. It took no form, shape or name, but developed from close contact with the growing things of nature. In today's world such forms of knowledge are devalued and consequently the line describing feminine, passive, and natural understanding is frequently absent.

Unlike other minor lines, minor water takes two forms on the palm. Each form is concerned with a different aspect of the water consciousness and serves a different orientation—although the manner in which they do this is the same. The two forms are known as the *higher* and *lower* lines, referring to where they are found on the palm. (See figure 73 on page 192.)

The *higher minor water* lies above the major water line and below the digital mounts. It is usually seen as a straight line or series of straight lines, commencing in the air quadrant and coming across into the fire quadrant. Occasionally it may be slightly curved (but nevertheless quite distinct from

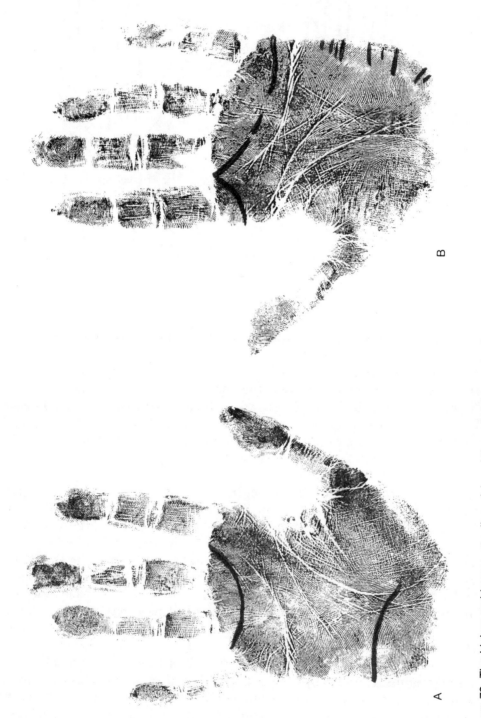

Figure 73. The higher and lower water lines (a) and the subsidiary water lines.

the circular or crescent ring pattern that can occasionally be found below the digits). The higher water line show the higher, mental function of the major water line and indicates and increase capacity for mental, platonic emotion. It is usually found when the major water line is overcharged (or hyperactive), and it serves as a stabilizing influence to it. If the major line isn't overcharged, and the distal is still present, it indicates an emotional idealist. Such a pattern is often found in the hands of priest and monks.

The *lower minor water* refers to physical processes and responses. It indicates a physical or metabolic sensitivity towards stimulants—usually alcohol or drugs. The line occurs at the bottom third of the water quadrant and forms a direct, usually deep line reaching across the quadrant towards the major earth line. The more strongly formed the lower line, the more effective the physical responsivity. Such responses may take the form of allergic reactions—say to dental anaesthetics or ordinary medicines—and may be very complex in nature. An individual with this line must take care when choosing any medicinal substance; likewise, excessive consumption of alcohol should be avoided. Natural (that is, herbal or homeopathic) medicines are the only safe methods with such a line.

Subsidiary Water Lines

These lines are found on the edge of the water mount and come across towards the center of the palm. They are rarely long and, when found, are usually numerous. They are symptomatic of an excess of water energy—indicative of too much excitability or restlessness. In palmistry these were called *Travel Lines*, however, people who travel a great deal rarely exhibit such lines. They are common with individuals who are dissatisfied with their present circumstances—they suggest internal stress or pressure felt by the subject. The major water line usually shows the reason for this.

Scattered lines: If we visualize the major line as the tides of the ocean, and the minor water line as the ocean currents, the subsidiary water lines would be the waves. Scattering their forces around the palm, they indicate the clatter of our minds and feelings searching and striving for change and expression.

Lines that leave major earth and drive towards the water quadrant are expressive of the desire for change and all it implies: re-evaluation, emotional redirection, travel, and releasing of responsibilities. When lines are found on the water mount, at the furthermost edges of the water quadrant, they signify emotional outpourings—expressions of imbalance that have passed into consciousness, leaving their shadows within our minds as memories of disappointments and turmoils experienced. Often these lines take a fire element form, indicating the depth to which the desire for expression

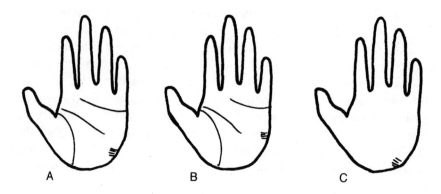

Figure 74. This formation of the subsidiary water lines is known as *scattered lines*. Here we see a) scattered lines high on the water mount; b) on the middle of the water mount; and c) low on the water mount.

was felt. The elemental quality of such lines should be noted carefully. You should observe at which height the greatest number occur, for this tells you in which area the expressive desire was felt most of all. When they are on the water mount (figure 74a) they indicated the realm of artistic and literal expression; on the middle of this mount (figure 74b), the realm of security, domestic satisfaction and family relationships. When low on the water mount (as in figure 74c), they indicate mystical, sexual and inherited experiences.

Upper rings: A partial form of the minor water line is sometimes seen on the digital mount areas and takes the form of rings which run around and toward the bases of various fingers. Ancient palmistry used to give these exotic names—such as the "ring of Jupiter" and the "hangman's ring"— however, such terms reflect an era and a social structure long gone. Rings should be thought of as conductors of energy going from one finger to another. If they connect antagonistic elements—such as earth to fire, or water to air—they indicate a disharmony in the palm. The ring is an attempt to "earth" excess or hyperactive energies safely. Rings that connect complementary elements (such as earth to water, or fire to air) accentuate or balance the creative aspects of those elements within the consciousness. In order to make such a connection, the ring must encircle or connect the bases of at least two fingers. Rings occasionally isolate the finger from the rest of the palm lines and energies. Such a ring prevents the balancing functions of energy and serves only to over-activate the energy within the digit it encircles. This is always a negative trait and usually indicates that the finger energies or qualities are, or will become, highly exaggerated. Figure 75 on page shows some examples of ring formations.

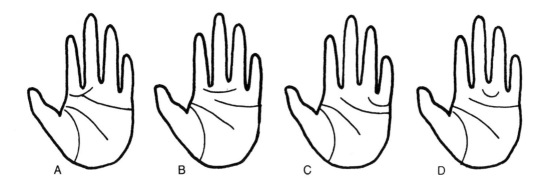

Figure 75. Element rings: a) uniting water digit and earth digit; b) uniting water and fire digits; c) uniting air and fire; and d) uniting fire and earth.

MINOR AND SUBSIDIARY FIRE LINES

When worship of the goddess finally faded, it was replaced by its opposite: worship of the gods of power, warfare and patriarchy. The fire god, in his many forms, began to take shape in Middle Eastern religions and still rules much of our present day and age. He brought order, civilization, and structure to human life. No longer did people preoccupy themselves with nature or intuition. Instead they began to build villages and wage war against each other. The patriarchal ethic brought with it many associated cultural concepts such as authority, approval, sectarianism, and retribution in law. The fire god was unusual in that he demanded priority over other, giving his devotees a special place in his favors and promising them further benefits if they perpetrated his authority. The emphasis on personal and national identity intensified; in fact, intensification became his keyword. State organized religious monopolies replaced the pleasant, pastoral rituals.

The minor fire line represents a sublimated, microcosmic form of the fire deity's wish to be acknowledged as master. Its presence indicates the image and persona we present to the world. When it is present in the palm it indicates our contemporary environment accepts and appraises us en masse. Thus it is, in palmistry, credited as being the *fame* or *success* line. Many an aspiring cheirologist has been misled by this interpretation, being convinced that his or her subject is an unrecognized genius! Unfortunately, in present times, fame is a much varying quality. We may appear on T.V. and reach millions of people simultaneously—reaching more people than any medieval monarch saw in his whole lifetime. But it does not last. We are gone as soon as the program ends, and usually forgotten. The fire line

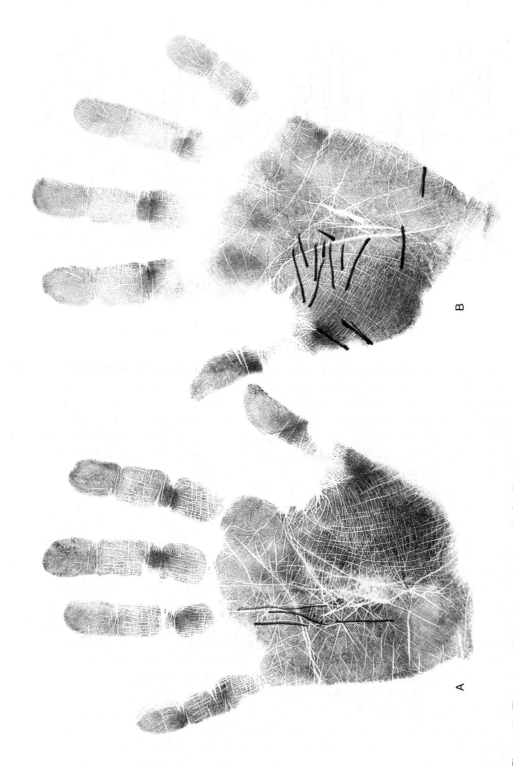

Figure 76. The minor (a) and the subsidiary (b) fire lines.

certainly does relate to mass exposure, and delineates a physio/psychologi-
cal response to social situations and influences, and vice versa. The minor
fire line is shown in figure 76.

As we have already mentioned, the minor fire line, when present,
shows that the subject's image and persona are found acceptable by society.
If found in conjunction with the minor earth line, the individual will use
this acceptance constructively. If the minor fire line is found without the
solidifying aspects of earth, it tends to indicate the attitude of Apollo (a fire
deity of a pleasanter type): a playful, happy and trusting mental state, having much in common with children and animals.

The minor fire line stems from the water quadrant and always rises up
towards the fire digit. The more well–formed its nature, the more successfully integrated is the individual's personal image and projection to others.
If the line rises deeply set in the water quadrant, it has much the same
significance as the minor earth line, namely the ability to deal with others
with sensitivity and delicacy. As these qualities are more often found in
females, such a commencement usually indicates an influence similar to
that of a mother, sister, wife or colleague. This placement indicates attitudes
especially suited for public affairs, including such Apollonian fields as fashion, the performing arts, and all vocations requiring a publicly acceptable
face. Other commencements have the same meaning as for minor earth
(see page 183).

Malformations in this line are rare: more often than not the line is
simply absent or only partially present. When interpreted chronologically,
it should be related to the minor earth line as it has the same time scale.
The quality of the line is ordinarily fire ruled, but other elements can be
seen. The air quality would tend towards literal images; water quality
towards music. There is no earth form. If the line is found in a wave-like
(water) form, it gives a vacillatory quality to the image; an individual's outer
face is subject more than usual to public whim. Islands can also show periods of emotional conflict in the private and public lives, and are often associated with scandal or infamy. All water markings are basically antagonistic
to this line. Consider these as the goddess trying to usurp the god!

When observing this line always look also at the thumbs to see if they
indicate persistence. Without this, the finest minor fire line merely shows
an interest in self-identity. Straightness of the fire digits along with a good
line indicates love of truth in the chosen art. Hyperflexibility of the fire
fingers shows versatility of expression.

Subsidiary Fire Lines

Subsidiary fire lines are found all over the palm (see figure 76b). They are
most common in the earth and water quadrants. This is because the fire

quadrant is one source of fire energy, and earth and fire "bake" each other into solidarity.

Subsidiary fire lines are rather like thunderbolts from heaven, for they signify sudden, dramatic and intense experiences in the subject's mind or body. Most bar lines on the palm will be of the fire element type and when interpreted chronologically, they are commonly viewed as signs of accidents or inflammatory illness. These subsidiary lines also show zones of demarcation within the hand, rather like "flaming walls," which prevent other forms of energy penetrating. Within the digital phalanges, they indicate the impetus to manifest or actualize the concepts they encounter.

When viewed as health indicators, the subsidiary lines tend to point towards fire organ weakness or fire symptoms (heat, fever, infection, cut, etc.) of other element ruled imbalances. Taken as a whole, fire signs should be fewer than other element lines. If they predominate they tend to show a predisposition to intense strain or stress. When fire subsidiaries cross water element lines, emotional symptoms will always appear, whatever the initial cause of such lines. Quite commonly, these lines join the major air and major water lines, where they energize both into decision making situations. So called *affection lines* may also appear as subsidiary fire lines. This indicates that strong physical or vocational activity is involved in relationships as a whole. The need to share is strong.

MINOR AND SUBSIDIARY AIR LINES

Air represents the god of knowledge in our historical overview—who knows or seeks to know, more than seeks to feel or control. The air god rules study, logic and science; the intellectual rather than physical authority. Education, propaganda, and mis-information fall under the domain of the god of knowledge. To the air god, to *know* is of prime importance, not to know is slavery. Because fire and air complement each other, their combined influence still predominates in our present world, although air is gradually increasing. World War II was probably the last big venture of the fire deity. Today's air god represents ideological, bacterial and radioactive weapons, not blood and thunder.

The minor air line descends from the air digit diagonally towards the lower earth quadrant, bypassing the fire quadrant entirely (see figure 77). Its significance relates to the finer processes of the physical organism. Endocrinal harmony, in particular, comes under its rulership as do other related actions. Air is synonymous with neural activity and influences parasympathetic responses in addition to the brain itself. The presence of the minor air line is a sign that the bodily metabolism is hyperactive and it

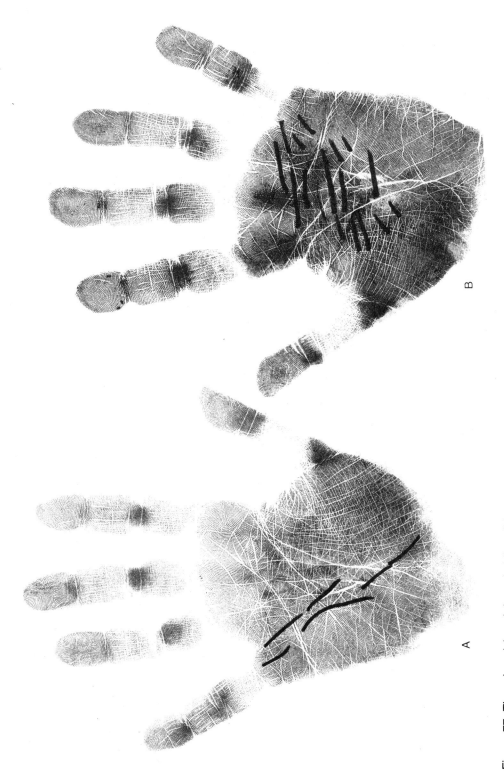

Figure 77. The minor (a) and the subsidiary (b) air lines.

usually appears only as a symptom of imbalance. Its absence has no significance. Because this line is symptomatic of so many influences within the
body, it is difficult to pin it down to specific imbalances. However, its presence can be symptomatic of two areas: the digestive system and respiratory
system. It is symptomatic of respiratory problems when the line is clearly
formed straight and of air quality (see figure 78a)—usually indicating general hypersensitivity. If the line is fragmented and formed of continuous
overlaps (see figure 78b), or has a spasmodic appearance (figure 78c), a
nervous condition of the stomach is indicated. Digestion is likely to be interrupted, as indeed is the appetite itself. Severe striation shows deficient
respiratory action, most often cause by stress (see figure 78d). All these
conditions of the line are like gusts of wind. If the line exists at all, it should
be like a firm, a continual breeze. Interruptions to this flow are caused by
the subject's hyper-receptivity and the immediate bodily responses to such
receptivity. The two are inseparable from each other. Because the actions
indicated by the minor air line belong to the parasympathetic nervous system, they are not directed by the conscious mind. Breath regulation and
control is important to all those whose hands show minor air malfunctions.

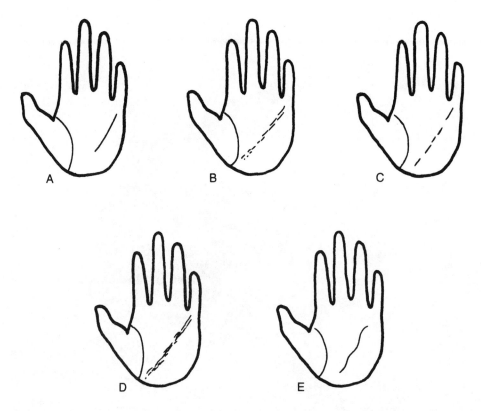

Figure 78. The varying quality of the minor air line: a) a straight line; b) overlapping fragments;
c) spasmodic fragments; d) severe striation; and e) a wave-like appearance.

Figure 79. The minor air line crossing the major earth line (a) indicates illness; the minor air line stopping at the major earth (b) indicates symptoms only. Because of its placement, we can tell that the illness or symptoms relate to the mid-body.

Because air represents various forms of bodily intercommunication, a wave-like condition of the line (figure 78e) indicates some misdirection or nullification of its normally direct impulses. The wave is associated with rheumatism and general joint weaknesses. Muscles and joints (ruled by fire and earth) require articulation and impetus to interact properly. Air activates those bodily processes that produce joint (synovial) fluids. Faults of a congenital nature in air can produce conditions that can manifest as arthritis (or related diseases) later in life.

Generally, the minor air line travels to the earth quadrant—the height at which it hits the major earth line indicates which area of the body is involved. If we visualize the beginning of the earth line as the head and its base as the feet, the remainder of the line correlates to all the bodily organs as they actually rest within the body: the top third rules the head, throat and lungs; the mid-section, the stomach, liver and kidneys; the lower section rules the intestines, bladder, knees and hips. The spine is represented by the minor earth line, and the major earth line represents the front of the body. The air line ending in one of these organic areas indicates a neural or metabolic malfunction. If the line crosses the earth line as in figure 79a, the imbalance will manifest as direct illness. If the line doesn't cross (figure 79b), there will be only minor symptoms or referred, related imbalances. Their cause is shown by the area towards which the air line points. Beside this general line and organ correlation, there are other linkings between organs represented in additional parts of the palm; this general correlation is a handy expedient only.

When the minor air line does not approach the earth line, but instead goes lower down towards the base of the palm, it loses its significance as an indicator of physical health. Rather, it transforms into a line revealing specific orientations of consciousness, and relates more to the manner in which the body picks up the sensory data it responds to. Interruption in the line can signify, for example, lack of physical coordination between sight and

Figure 80. Doubled minor air line: a) exterior line stronger; b) interior line stronger.

gesture, deafness, or poor spatial awareness. The longer or more fire-like such a line, the more active the imbalance. When the line appears only faintly and is air-like in elemental quality, it merely suggests fundamental nervousness or apprehension in dealing with life. Doubled lines increase this predisposition—you must note which line is the more powerful one. If the line on the thumb side is stronger (see figure 80a), the hypersensitivity is due to conscious attitudes. If stronger on the other side (figure 80b), it is due to emotional barriers and hyper responses.

Subsidiary Air Lines

These lines are delicate and fine as shown in figure 77b on page 199 and figure 81. They are most commonly found on the Venus or Mars mount in the earth quadrants, and stretch across the hand towards the air digit. Occasionally they will be found as auxiliaries to the other air lines. Their action is ephemeral and they are found in those prone to hyper-activity of mind. Worry and apprehension come naturally to these individuals. When found vertically on the phalanges, they show in which area (physical, practical or mental) the subject predominantly dwells, and thus what he or she sees as areas of stress. This may not necessarily be the real area, for the action of air is often parasympathetic, and the source of stress is often difficult to consciously identify. Such phalangeal lines will show how the subject resolves or affects the three areas. Clear phalanges indicate that their action is stable and harmonious; striated phalanges show that nervousness and worry are likely. If we find the top phalanges most striated, the problems are seen as being those of ideals, policy or principle. When the mid phalanges are predominantly striated, the problems are related to troublesome situations concerning others. Change of job, home and friends is likely with such a sign. Lower phalangeal striation indicates worry about

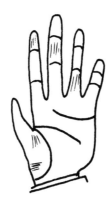

Figure 81. Subsidiary air lines.

one's body, hypochondria, physical feelings and desires, or materialistic modes of satisfaction.

All subsidiary air lines are unnecessary to the hand and are potential sources of antagonism. When you find subsidiary air lines, you should note the qualities of the finger they are found on. Note also the thumb to see if ideas are traditional or unconventional, and if the staying power is strong. These two will give you some ideas as to whether the individual will resolve worries usefully and creatively. Some worries, of course, have good cause, and a cautious but optimistic approach can help solve them to everyone's satisfaction.

CHAPTER 12

Special Analysis of Lines

Cheirology is one of the serving professions: that is, most of the time we are concerned with helping others in one way or another. This often means that the time available for private research is limited, and consequently personal discoveries become a rarity. This section introduces two subtle and advanced principles of lineal analysis that will make you a better cheirologist: the study of doubled lines; and the study of chronology, or the ways in which we arrive at an assessment of time in the hand.

Doubled lines are often a problem to interpret as they can be understood in so many ways they are easily misinterpreted by the newcomer to the art. I have outlined here some of the principles you should consider when attempting to classify a line as being doubled. There are, of course, many more factors than are mentioned here, but the purpose of this introduction is merely to give you something to think about—and hopefully to initiate further research on your part.

Chronology is a difficult subject all around. In European palmistry, there is almost no agreement as to how or when particular lines should be assessed to indicate the time of a particular event or circumstance. Cheirology doesn't suffer from this problem as the traditional method of assessing time is so flexible it can be applied to almost any lineal situation. However, I do not want to underestimate the difficulties involved. Assessing chronology takes time and practice. When you first begin, you should check you judgments of time by working on print of people you know well. Use the methods here to assess various events in their past—then ask if you're accurate! It's a good way of getting instant feedback as to your abilities. It's not uncommon for some cheirologists to find that they are consistently two or three years ahead or behind of the correct time for events. If you do tend to be ahead or behind, you will learn to adjust your findings by a couple years either way. Personally, I think that this time variation factor is dependent on your own personal balance of elements—those of us with more fire tend to be ahead of the correct time, and those of us with more earth tend to run late!

DOUBLED LINES

During your cheirological examinations, you may often find traces of lines that have doubled themselves, so that there appears to be two separate lineal formations instead of the normal single line. Usually we interpret this as giving the line a "double measure" of quantity and consider its action to be strongly active. This is often the case with the water line. In essence this principle of double measure holds reasonably true: however, the law of reflected lines elucidates the presence of double lines clearly. From basic cheirognomy we know that the quadrants deal with four basic aspects of consciousness (conscious and unconscious, active and passive), and together with the reflected principle this gives us a guideline by which to explain the double manifestation more accurately.

Each line has two aspects: its inner and outer, or a higher and lower, depending on the angle of the line involved. When we find a line that has doubled, we are observing a separation of these two aspects. No longer can they function together; they must exist independently of each other. When observing a doubled line, we have to judge which line is the strongest—this gives us the normal predominant function. The other line is thus seen as the "sister" and represents a distinctive faculty or orientation in *addition* to the normal function. The doubled line can also be a sister line in the sense that it acts as a support to the main one. If the main line shows a defect, this will always be so. In general, however, a sister line (as a distinct category of line) is always weaker than the main one it supports. When you see two lines of equal depth, color, or length, you have a true double line. Let's look at some examples of double lines and their basic psychological meanings:

Water line: When there is a strong line above the major water line, it indicates a development of the idealistic and emotional sensitivity of the individual. If the double line occurs strongly below the water line, this will indicate a tendency towards a lack of control or inhibition of emotions. The individual has an impulse to experience rather than direct situations.

Air line: When there is a strong line above the major air line, near the major water line, it indicates a wish to experience the ideal, both emotionally and mentally. When the line is strong below, near the major earth line, the individual will tend to relate to friends and the environment in a materialistic, professional or business-like way. When this formation occurs, it will run parallel to the main line, and not depart from it in any way. It should be noted that the doubled air line formation often occurs in cases of schizophrenia. Here we see a cheirological suggestion that schizophrenia itself is in fact a division between an individual's desired physical orientations or requirements and the moral or ethical values. One mind says "do this," and another mind says "don't do it." The resulting dilemma causes a condition of inner tension and mental breakdown.

Minor earth line: When there is a double line on the thumb, or radial, side (near the major earth line), the individual will tend to consciously adopt the attitude that personal success is dependent on self-understanding. Even if this isn't carried out in life, the individual will tend to recognize this value. When the double line occurs on the ulnar side, near the water quadrant, it shows the subject has developed a personal image (or wishes to develop) in dealing with the outside world. The individual depends on the goodwill of others.

Major earth line: There is no double form of this line. The nearest to this would be the major fire line. As the inner (radial) side of the fire line, lines running parallel to either fire or earth lines are often present. These indicate specific attempts to express and include the earth qualities of external factors within the personal balance of the subject. Their presence therefore reveals the wish to encompass external sources of balance and to recreate this balance within a personal frame of reference. In many subjects these balances will be found in other persons (hence the traditional rendering of such lines as "influences"). This interpretation is not valid in all cases however.

The predominant trait can always be said to be the desire to restrict oneself to specific forms of stability within one's cultural, spiritual or social environment. When many of these lines are observed the paternal/maternal instinct is heightened, for this multiple presence reveals a desire to surround oneself with many balances. With the majority of people this indicates the wish to produce offspring. It is, of course, also found on the hands of childless people who either adopt children or act as foster parents, and in those who by temperament are suited to relate with groups.

CHRONOLOGICAL ASPECTS OF LINES

The concept of time is a man-made phenomenon, and different cultures diverge both in their attitudes towards it and in their methods of calculating its passage. I am dealing here with the individual's experience of time within his or her own environment.

A serious student will become aware, at an early stage, of the difference in timing between the various elemental factors found in the hand. The factor of *timing* is very important to understand. Assuming the reader understands the principle of elements, we can see that the earth factor demonstrates the slowest chronological factors—those relating to physical growth and organic functions. Water operates at a higher speed, governing blood and other liquid flows. Fire is much faster, governing physical actions (such as reflexes, etc.). And air is as fast as thought itself. Lines belonging to each of these elements demonstrate their chronological rate accordingly. The fastest lines to change are thus those ruled by air, then fire, then water, and finally earth. These variations can be observed by any researcher over a period of time.

We can express these varied changes and their rates in many manners. Usually we relate them to a common human experience and then substitute that experience as a metaphor for the change itself. In the past this was commonly done. So much so in fact that most European students never progressed beyond the metaphors. Relating the element to bodily factors (as above) enables us at least to see a simple correlation in action. We can understand that physical growth takes place at a slow but steady pace, and that thought can be very fast and changeable.

The main palmar lineation showing consciousness is the air line. In cheirology this has the greatest number of possible variations. Each line associated with or demonstrating the effects of an elemental principle reveals a chronological statement according to that principle. We expect, and indeed find, that the portions of our existence that we choose to isolate and invest with special significance reveal that significance *in elemental sequence*. That is to say, the earliest representation of an event of personal and dynamic significance shows itself on a line of the air of fire element. The nearer we draw to that event, the more the water and earth elements begin also to show that event. By the time earth factors begin to demonstrate it, the subject is physically and metabolically prepared to experience it. *Bear this fact in mind continually.* Events shown on one set of elemental lines *only* show that a subject cannot fully understand the significance to that event at the present time.

In terms of health we also find that lines show imbalance relative to the element ruling that imbalance itself. Thus, to use the example previously given, we would find nervous imbalance shown most clearly in the line ruled by the element governing nervous imbalance itself (air). The air principle also rules digestive action, breathing, memory and personal nervous energy. These would also be affected to varying degrees by an air line imbalance. A student can do much personal research in this field by observing a collection of prints over a period of time and interpreting them with a view to uncovering the chronological elemental affinities. You can thus see that a specific set of experiences does not manifest at the same (correspondent) point on each of the major elemental lines. Experiences are shown earliest in air lines, last in earth. Not until an event or experience has passed through all the elements can it be considered as either having been fully manifest within the subject's consciousness, or as having occurred at all. This is particularly important to remember when attempting to point out the full implications of, say, an accident. If this shows on only three elements, there will be a further backlash illness to come. Not until all elements represent an event can it safely be said to have been fully experienced and accommodated within the subject's mind, body and metabolism. The elemental chronology is as much a qualitative assessment of the individual's physical and mental relationship to inner time as to that of the external, conventional time. You have to decide which is predominant when you consider your subject's hands. The qualitative judgment can show a potential or desired event as if it had already occurred. A subject's memory of childhood is often interpreted in this manner. A happy childhood, marred only by one overbearing parent, can cause a subject to recall only that parent. His or her hand pattern then appears to show that the whole childhood was one of despair. A careful examination of both hands and a balancing of their quality can reveal such tendencies to the analyst.

Metabolic time is highly significant. Some say it is the only time, and recent research shows that much of its action is geared to light cycles (photochronicity). Light is subject to the elements, or is interpreted through them, at all levels simultaneously. It is, in other words, ruled by the fifth element commonly called energy (or ether). It is a symbolic synthesis of all the elements (which is why it is the fifth element). Light by nature is energic. It moves (air), and possesses heat (fire). It causes the rhythms of nature (water), and initiates the growth of seeds (earth). It cuts through all the elements and thus symbolically was used as a symbol of spiritual understanding and presence. In Chinese, Sanskrit, Egyptian and European languages, light is associated with Wisdom or God likeness. That light affects skin growth and causes changes in it is now beyond doubt (from the suntan to the fingerprint). The significance of this correlation is of great importance to cheirology, for it reveals at least one manner in which a process or experience of timing can be affected or changed by an energy source, be it consciously, physiologically, metabolically, or religiously. That the elemental pattern confirms and explicates such a modern discovery is ample proof of the validity of the elemental system itself.

The greatest source of light is of course our sun. It gives birth to the seasons and natural phenomena of many kinds. When the ancients fixed the dates of religious ceremony, the planting of seeds or festivals, they used the cycles of the year as a guide to when these should occur. Depending on natural phenomena became so buried in the consciousness of people that it became part of their very being. Certain times were seen as more beneficial than others. No doubt this principle was drawn from the fact that seeds planted at the wrong time did not grow—starvation is a hard teacher! The art of keeping track of, and elucidating, beneficial times became the property of special classes of people, usually religious leaders. Table 14 on pages 210 and 211 shows the various forms of charting and describing the time periods used by the Orient and Occident. The first two columns on the left detail the time periods used in European astrology. These were, of course, derived from and influenced by Oriental teachings. The next column shows the Buddhist elements associated with these periods. Columns four and five show the Chinese traditional folk practice of dividing the year into periods of fortnights—their Chinese names and dates are given. The next column gives an English rendering of the name of the first week in these cycles.

Table 14. Chronological Paradigms of East and West

Astrological Sign and Period	Buddhist Element	Chinese Fortnights	Name of First Week	Taoist Tradition	
				Old Chinese Elements	Bodily Rulership and Acupuncture Meridian
Aries Mar. 21–Apr. 20	Fire	Apr. 6 KUAI 21	Brightness	Lake Heaven	*Head/Eyes* Kidney
Taurus Apr. 21–May 20	Earth	May 6 CH'IEN 22	Early Summer	Heaven Heaven	*Throat/Ears* Three-heater
Gemini May 21–Jun. 20	Air	Jun. 7 KOU 22	Grain Midsummer	Heaven Wind	*Arms* Liver
Cancer Jun. 21–Jul. 20	Water	Jul. 8 T'UN 24	Late Summer	Heaven Mountain	*Stomach/Breast* Stomach
Leo Jul. 21–Aug. 21	Fire	Aug. 8 P'I 24	Autumn	Heaven Earth	*Heart/Spine* Heart
Virgo Aug. 22–Sep. 22	Earth	Sep. 8 KUAN 24	Equinox	Wind Earth	*Intestines* Intestines

Table 14. Chronological Paradigms of East and West (*continued*)

Astrological Sign and Period	Buddhist Element	Chinese Fortnights	Name of First Week	Taoist Tradition	
				Old Chinese Elements	Bodily Rulership and Acupuncture Meridian
Libra Sep. 23–Oct. 22	Air	Oct. 9 PO 24	Cold dews	Mountain Earth	*Liver/Kidney* Circulation
Scorpio Oct. 23–Nov. 22	Water	Nov. 8 K'UN 23	Lesser Snow	Earth Earth	*Genitals* Bladder
Sagittarius Nov. 23–Dec. 20	Fire	Dec. 7 FU 22	Great Snow, Winter	Earth Thunder	*Hips, Thighs* Spleen
Capricorn Dec. 21–Jan. 19	Earth	Jan. 6 LIN 21	Lesser Cold	Earth Lake	*Bones* Gallbladder
Aquarius Jan. 20–Feb. 18	Air	Feb. 5 T'AI 20	Rains	Earth Heaven	*Ankles* Lung
Pisces Feb. 18–Mar. 20	Water	Mar. 7 TA 22	Awakening	Thunder Heaven	*Feet*

The column headed Old Chinese Elements outlines the earliest known form of the elements ruling the various periods. These were used in the *I Ching*. We can see from their names that the Taoist elemental system used in the *I Ching* bears no correspondence to the Chinese elemental system. The last column lists the organs of the body said by traditional Chinese acupuncturists to be particularly sensitive during these fortnightly periods, along with the traditional European astrological rulerships of the body. In some cases we can see a remarkable coincidence—Virgo and Scorpio for example.

Each of these different ways of gauging time relies on a different use of the element. We always judge time according to our own predominant elements and the element(s) governing our particular society. The body does the same thing. Only instead of towns, cities and borders, the body has organs, metabolisms and qualities of activity. Each reflects the other and can furnish us with information concerning the macro-microcosmic unity we personally experience. Only when we are aware of this unity can we come to understand it and its meanings. The judgment of time itself is a venture into the realm of the unity of the cosmos and ourselves. As long as you remain aware of this fact, and not be caught up in the lure of making predictions, your study and accuracy in the timing of events will prosper.

RELATIVE TIME SPANS

The different elements differ in their manifestation of the same periods. As the cyclicity of elements increases with their lack of density, so their portrayal of events is compressed into a smaller lineage formation. Elements increase their rate during seasons associated with them, reaching a peak in the middle of that period and thereafter decreasing gradually towards the form of chronology of the following elements. Figure 82 graphically illustrates the different sense of time within each elemental line. Let's say the top of the chart represents fifty years (it could represent any length of time). We can see that the earth line has the most length associated with it, the water line is shorter, and so on, although all four elemental lines represent the same fifty year span. However, lines reflect varying chronologies when related to other lines. Thus we see that the fire line on this chart is half the length of the earth line—this means that the time sense of fire is twice as fast as that of earth.

When you are analyzing a subject's personality, such a time warp wouldn't mean anything special. But if you are trying to ascertain dates or events in the subject's life (if these are shown by a line formation at all), you should note the fact that the event will occur at different places on different

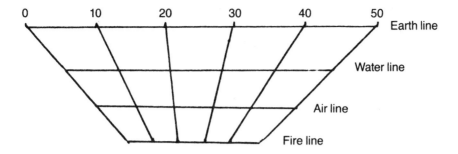

Figure 82. Time warp chart.

lines. We can deduce from this chart that the only points that coincide in years are birth, death and midlife. Traditionally, these will correspond to the years of 0, 35 and 70. Midlife is a good point at which to begin practicing event/year judgments. Practice with air and fire, and earth and water, for these pairs are closely linked in terms of length.

The Timing of Specific Events

In cheirology, time is not only a chronological system—a system of measurement—but is also viewed as a memory of actual experiences. When we observe an actual hand, we should see it as a living representation of time in both its physical and mental aspects. The ancient Chinese used several concepts of time, depending on the nature of what they wished to measure, and the purpose for which measurement was needed. There was celestial (star) time, used by astronomers, lunar time used by calendericalists and farmers, body time used by doctors based upon sun cycles, and mystical time used by shamans for oracles and divination.[1] Each of these "times" interconnected. The timing system used by diviners in India was immense, and stretched into enormous units called Kalpas and Yugas that recounted periods of trillions and trillions of years. Theirs was a notion of time unrestricted to one lifetime, and instead spread through multiple rebirths. The Wu Hsing school adopted this cyclic time and adapted it for Chinese use.

The Wu Hsing method teaches that certain cycles of life are repeated over and over again, and that such event inter-relation obeys certain ratios that are reducible to smaller amounts. We can reduce a ratio into a period coincident with our lifespan and from such a reduction develops a method

[1]Research in 1977 by several Chinese scientists in the United States reached the conclusion that the Chinese shamanists' elements of metal, wood, fire, water and earth were in fact symbols for expressing an altered time measurement rather than actual physical or symbolically physical substances or processes.

of gauging specific years of human life. Though cheirologists use differing forms of measuring time on the hand lines, all use a general system that has proven at least reasonably accurate in direct experience over many years. We can therefore take common elements of a solar chronology and blend it into the Wu Hsing system quite easily to produce a usable system.

In all judgments of years it is wisest to use lines of the four elements equally to pinpoint a period. This allows mistakes to be noticed easily, forming as it does a cross-reference of time sense in both the subject and analyst. The lines to begin with are those representing each element, major and minor. These lines reveal an inter-connectedness and continuity of experience within the life of the subject. The method to be described avoids the pitfall of making lines fit a favored and rigid chronological system, and is attuned to reality rather than hypothesis. Everyone has an individual timing and there can never be a rigid structural formula for calculating it to fit all equally accurately.

Basic Method of Determining Time Periods

The four elements provide a basis for this method by representing the periods of childhood, teenage, middle age and old age. This pattern is projected onto the chosen line, which is then subdivided into equal portions. Examples are shown in figure 83—the lines are subdivided as recommended.

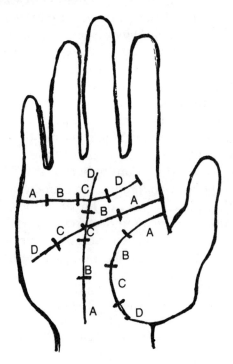

Figure 83. The four main time periods—a) childhood, b) youth, c) middle age, and d) old age—are shown on the major and minor lines.

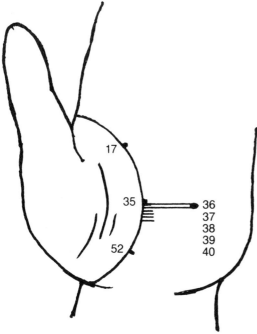

Figure 84. The width of a matchstick usually covers a portion of a line representing one year of time.

Generally speaking, use an average life expectancy of seventy years and divide all lines by half (which will represent about thirty-five years of age). Repeat this for each line. If you are practicing on a print, you will find that the period covering one year is usually about one tenth of an inch—or the width of a matchstick (see figure 84). The point where major air and minor earth meet each other, in the center of the palm, is usually thirty-five on each line (see figure 85 on page 216). Apart from the major lines and minor earth line, timings on other lines are highly erratic and unreliable for general guidance. Most of these other lines change, fade or redirect themselves every two to three years, proving unreliable to use as a "ruler" of judgment. There is no system in the Wu Hsing tradition for timing the so-called "marriage" lines, nor have I personally found any within other systems that has proven accurate.

When assessing a subject's lines, it is wise to fix one point or time of significance and to verify this by questioning. Observe this point on all the lines, noting what adjustments have to be made for the subject's personal nature—one event on the earth line at thirty-seven may show on the water line at thirty-nine, etc. With practice this becomes easier and more intuitive.

Every practitioner must develop his or her own sense of timing and be prepared to modify it as circumstances direct. The lifespan of seventy years mentioned here is only general, and other longevity periods may be substituted according to your own experience. Always remember that when you posit an occurrence within time you are only approximating physical, men-

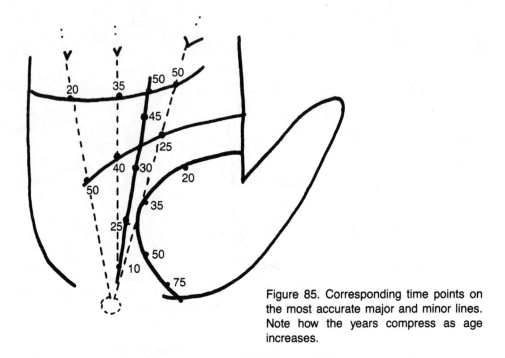

Figure 85. Corresponding time points on the most accurate major and minor lines. Note how the years compress as age increases.

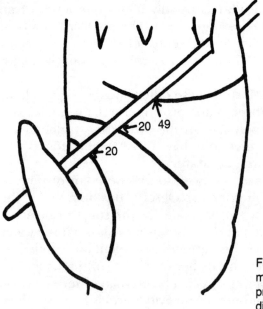

Figure 86. A traditional "rule of thumb" method, utilizing a chopstick. This is pressed down between the thumb and air digit as shown. The corresponding time points are read off the lines below.

tal, emotional and spiritual experience cycles within the mundane world. When you have understood those cycles within your own existence, you will truly be accurate in each of the time cycles themselves.

Event-Line Correlation by Chart

Often, when faced with the bewildering mass of events shown in the lineal formations, the research cheirologist may often despair at the thought of ever integrating all the occurrences. In fact, a good cheirologist becomes so by the ability to integrate simultaneously all the data. This talent comes with long practice and experience. One precise method used within the Wu Hsing school to arrive at simultaneous awareness of major lines is to construct parallel schematic charts of these lines. This enables one to see, at a glance, correspondent occurrences in each of the major lines. This often leads to a greater understanding of the inter-related causes and effects taking place within a subject's thoughts and feelings at any given point of time.

Although the idea of making a chart seems cumbersome, with practice it becomes very simple and quick to complete. Such a chart's value as a teaching aid in discussing various points in a specific print becomes abundantly obvious. Outline a chart containing four horizontal divisions of equal height (figure 87 on page 218). Each of these divisions corresponds to an element, the highest being earth and so on to air. Make perpendicular divisions onto these divisions—in this chart four are used. Each of these corresponds to ten years of life, thus this chart will show a period from birth to forty years of age. Into each element division we now draw out certain lines; for example, major earth, major water, major air and minor fire, or the minor air if present. When you draw out each line, you should try to reproduce all the actual patterns and characteristics as shown in the original handprint. Next add all subsidiary, joining, or other lines found. Place these under the main line first inserted. The main line should be placed to the top of the element division or in a bold outline to make it clear. Indicate on each line markings such as islands, corresponding in time to the vertical time divisions already drawn. If a line appears significant, indicate the direction it goes by placing a sign—usually a planetary one—at its end. These planets refer to the palmistic mount planets and are used so as not to confuse you if you add elemental signs relating to the quality of the line. For instance, you may want to show a line has fire quality and mark it so. If you then used the elemental sign to show direction, you may get confused later when you have forgotten what it was you meant to show at the time. The planet area the line commences from may also be added. If you are familiar with where these areas are you will see the direction of the line. If not use an arrow to show direction. You now should have an

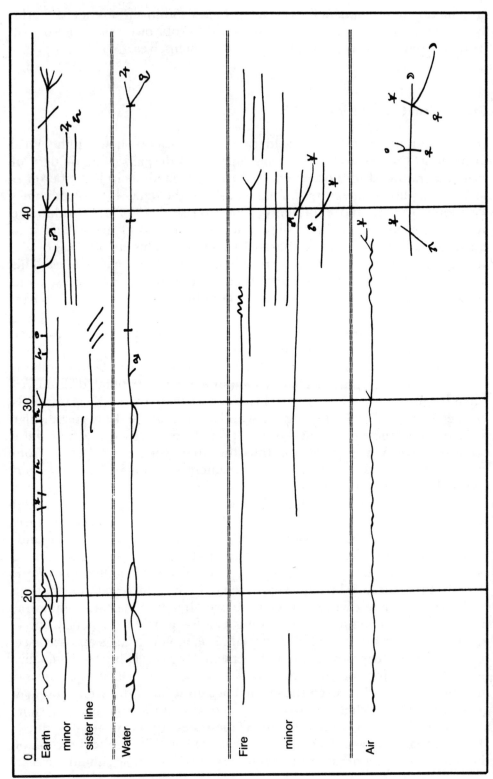

Figure 87. The basic method of event/line correlation.

accurate and visual presentation showing length and quality of all the lines reproduced. The information shown in figure 87 is based upon Master Print One, and all the important characteristics up to forty years of age are indicated in the figure.

Judging Time on the Chart

By covering the chart with a piece of paper (a ruler would do equally well), and gradually moving it across to the right, the various features and influences on all lines simultaneously reveal themselves. You can observe the beginnings of occurrences in one line that produce responses in the other element lines. For example, in our sample chart you can see that the new earth line at eighteen occurs at the same time as the island in the water line. The termination of the island in the water line at age thirty creates rising lines in the direction of the major earth and secondary earth lines and the new water line. With practice you could add much more data to this chart. It would be good practice to start on the print of a close friend—that way you can ascertain the accuracy of your analysis and chronological findings through questions.

CHAPTER 13

Health Analysis by Lineal Formation

Within Wu Hsing all health imbalance is diagnosed and analyzed in terms of the five elements. Any tendency to combine antagonistic elements must necessarily indicate an imbalance of some form; whether this is understood as physiological, psychological or spiritual is irrelevant. Health analysis is simply the observance of antagonistic features within the hands which are then interpreted purely as diagnostic features. Such analysis has its limitations but, when considered first distinctively and then in conjuction with all possible levels, a reliable view of physio/mental condition can be assessed. With practice such assessment increases in its accuracy.

From the point of view of lineal analysis, all lines connecting antagonistic quadrants either reveal or cause imbalance. Thus lines from earth to air, or water to fire, in the main are symptoms of this imbalance. Such lines can be evidence of past imbalances depending on their quality as lines. Obviously, a fire quality to such a line renders it active and descriptive of the present condition. Water, earth or air are not so active, and tend to reveal past or incipient imbalances.

You should keep in mind the following general considerations:

• Major lines of an air quality predispose to a health balance dependent upon external or social factors;

• Major lines of a water quality relate to emotionally dependent health balance;

• Major lines of earth quality are influenced by organic or dietary factors;

• Major lines of fire quality reveal health imbalances caused by accident or misuse of the bodily functions.

In general all lines should be clearly formed and free from interruptions. When such features appear they can be symptoms or presages of health imbalances either inherited or being developed by the subject's habits or attitudes at that time. The nature of the imbalance is revealed by the element line on which detrimental markings occur, i.e., earth line markings relate to earth element organs, functions or structures of the body.

The Wu Hsing school emphasizes the development of intuitive diagnostic technique. However this requires familiarity with basic physiological structures of the body. When such knowledge is acquired, the significance of imbalance in any organ, as seen via lines, becomes recognized. You should avoid symptomatic methods of analysis, although these appear more amenable to use. Think instead in elemental, non-specific terms and your knowledge of physiological processes will furnish the rest. However, at the onset of studies in diagnostic technique, the simple symptomatic technique can be used to become familiar with it and to experience the fact that health imbalance does actually manifest within the hands. However, the symptomatic method has no lasting value: It is much better to study the actual way in which we should track down the causes of health disorders. Let's turn our attention to considering how this is done. We begin with a simple method involving a study of the cross lines and take our first steps into diagnosis.

CROSS LINE DIAGNOSIS

A good place to start in an analysis of your subject's health is with something simple and clear. The fire cross lines (stress) running across the earth quadrant fit the bill. Such lines are not uncommon; you may have some like these on your own hands (see figure 88). First of all, check that the lines you are looking at are really cross lines. Make certain that the lines run from the earth mount *towards* the air mount. Remember—a line is thicker at its beginning, thinner where it ends. So in this case, the line would be thickest in the earth mount. Remember also that the line must begin within the major earth line's area. This type of line usually begins within the highest (fire) area of the quadrant (as shown in figure 89), or lower down on within the area enclosed by the major earth line as shown in figure 88.

For the purpose of our example, let's say that the line has a fire quality, it is deep and red, and begins on the middle area of the earth quadrant. The fire quality will represent the strongest type of energy disorder on whatever organ it affects. This in turn means that any illness it reflects is likely to have strong or sudden symptoms, which the individual will easily be able to recognize. Of course, this cross line could be of another elemental nature and its effects will correspond to the qualities of that element. Now, there are already traditional meanings associated with the cross line— each placement, termination, and so on, has a special significance to the

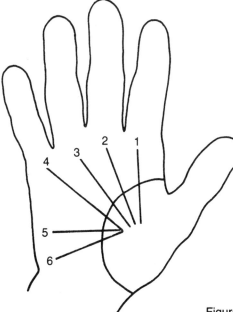

Figure 88. Fire cross lines from the earth mount.

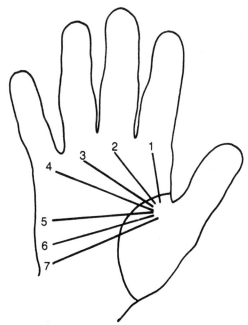

Figure 89. Fire cross lines from the fire mount.

body as a whole. There are specific dysfunctions associated with each and every ending outlined in figure 89, and we will outline these messages in the following section. However, if you simply look up the meaning of the line placement, you will never learn how the meaning has come about. In other words, it's more important that you learn how to *think*, or you will never understand the *process* of diagnosis used in cheirology. All you would be doing is employing a symptomatic reference method—in the manner palmists are prone to do. It is more important for our purposes to try to see both how and what we should *think* about such features when we encounter them, so let's consider the processes involved in making a judgment. So what do we know? We know that the cross line stems from the earth quadrant. This tells us that the disorder is concerned in some way with the fundamental activities that preoccupy earth in general—i.e., stabilization, continuity, and the capacities of the physical organism. We know that a line of fire quality represents a quality of intensity, suddenness, inflammatory conditions, high temperatures and defects in activity (if hyperactive).

When the elements of earth and fire are united in this form, they show that the imbalance is generated in earth and has a fire action or manifestation. Both these elements are strong in their effects but in different ways. Fire activates and energizes. Earth stabilizes and contains. There is a fundamental contradiction in their combination! Such a combination suggests an oscillation of energies, a stop-go situation in which each restrains the other and both realize they are being inhibited in some way. So far so good—we can see the seeds of conflict in this line. Now we must ask ourselves what is its aim or goal? We know that every line has a source quality and a goal or orientation. The nature of this goal we can tell from the line's terminal direction. Let's consider termination 4 in figure 89. Since this is the air mount, it tells us that the cross line is concerned with a function associated with an air element quality or function. What are air functions? Some obvious ones are respiration in general, neural actions and responses (both conscious and unconscious) and thought itself. This latter factor (thought), in negative manifestation, represents worries and apprehension, indecision, and mental disorientation in general. Which of these should we choose? If we examine the end of the line we can see it stops on the air mount. We know that a mount represents the earth level manifestation and processes of an element. The air mount governs the physical factors of respiration and the organic condition of the lungs (and also brain) in general.

Now we are getting closer to a diagnosis. We have an earth source line (stabilizatory function) taking on itself a fire quality (it is inflamed or hyperactivated) and pointing towards the earth level (physical base) of the air element function (respiration, thinking, metabolic inter-communication). If we turn to the list of traditional illness associated with this line, we find them to be neural disorders, psychosomatic disorders, metabolic malfunctions, and so on.

As you can see, we got this far through simple elemental deductions. All of our conclusions so far are in accord with these illnesses. Our next task would be to pinpoint precisely what our subject is suffering from—but we can't do that without reference to some other lines and features of the hand.

Looking at figures 88 and 89, the traditional diagnosis associated with the cross lines are are follows. If you study these you may be able to work out for yourself why the particular illnesses they indicate are associated with the elemental meanings of the line positionings. Health disorders associated with fire cross lines from the earth mount (figure 88) are:

Ending 1 connects earth and water elements: apoplexy, thrombosis, infections, emotional imbalances.

Ending 2 connects earth to earth: muscle cramps, mitral valve insufficiency, piles, skeletal or postural disorder, respiratory weaknesses.

Ending 3 connects earth to fire: anemia, all heart and blood disorders, mineral or hormonal imbalances, fistula, skin, nail and hair infections.

Ending 4 connects earth to air: neural disorder, psychosomatic illness, stomach and digestive weakness, metabolic malfunctions, excretory disorder, teeth and gum infections.

Ending 5 connects earth and water: emotional hyperactivity, urinary weakness, infertility, genetic disorders, diabetes, kidney and bladder weakness.

Ending 6 connects earth to water: reproductive insufficiencies, genetic disorders, diabetes, kidney and bladder weakness.

Now compare the imbalances shown in figure 85, where we see fire cross lines from the fire mount. This combination increases the tendency to sudden or inflammatory conditions caused by accident or infection:

● ● ●

Ending 1 connects fire to water: gout, infections to the circulatory systems (blood, lymph, etc.). It is also seen in some respiratory illnesses due to a reflective effect.

Ending 2 connects fire to earth: liver disorders. It is associated with moodiness and all vitamin B difficiencies.

Ending 3 connects fire to fire: heart failure, eye malfunctions, muscular injuries, sunstroke, fevers.

Ending 4 connects fire to air: neural disorders, paralysis, biliousness, dyspepsia, hyperactivity, sleeplessness.

Ending 5 connects fire to water: lymph infections, impairment of emotional receptivity, temperature regulation and respiratory stress.

Ending 6 connects fire to water: digestive and nutritional insufficiencies, rheumatism, gout.

Ending 7 connects fire to water: venereal disease, dysmenorrhea, womb infections, infertility, prostate malfunctions, gonad disorders, excessive weight or anorexia.

Other indicators are relevant to cross lines in addition to their basic position on the hand. One of the most significant is the nature or characteristic of the terminal line features. Lines may end in many different manners, but each ending tells us something about how the line is working, what it is doing where it is. If this terminal end of the line exhibits a distinctive formation, we can learn more about its activity. Some of the traditional distinguishing signs are explained in the next section.

Terminations of Cross Lines

Each of the cross lines here shown indicate the presence of an elemental hyperactivity which is being dealt with by the physical or neural organism. Other distinguishing features of such imbalances can occasionally be found by observing the pattern or form assumed by the hyperactivity line. If this does evidence a distinctive structure, more can be ascertained about the nature of the imbalance itself in addition to its basic elemental nature (which is what the hyperactivity line reveals).

Markings of cross lines are as elsewhere. Their significances are as follows:

Grille
This reveals that the imbalance is debilitating the action of organs belonging to the element of the area in which it occurs.

Island
This reveals that the purpose or flow of the organs belonging to the element of the line is at fault. If found at the very end of the line the organ itself is congenitally malformed.

Cross or Star
When a definite cross or star is found across a hyperactive line, it gives a spasmodic action to the organs ruled by the element within which the hyperactive line terminates. At the end of the line these show sudden drains upon the resource energies and possible danger of stoppage.

Striation
These reveal malfunctions of the neural stimuli required by the organs ruled by terminal zone elements.

Waviness
This feature gives a vacillatory action of the organ or process ruled by the terminal zone element.

Thickening
This earth feature occurs when fever or inflammation occurs.

Bars
These occur when the energy of the source organ deteriorates.

Each of the terminal signs can also occur on a line, and these should be interpreted according to the prevailing dominance of the elements present. For example, if there is a surfeit of fire markings or qualities, suspect fevers or infections; if there is a surfeit of earth markings, organic or nutritional insufficiency must be suspected. Water brings bad circulation, responses or resistance. Air brings over-reactions, breathing difficulty, etc. The nature of elements must be balanced with others in both hands.

OTHER HEALTH INDICATIONS

There are many other lineal markings and features that indicate health imbalances. Some of these are very easy to notice, others are more subtle. All the features mentioned above have significance when they occur on other element lines, but the precise disorders vary greatly. A marking that is easy to observe is the island—a loop formation within the line. It looks like the line has split in half and then rejoined, but has left a bubble in the middle. It can occur in any line, and always indicates a weakness or debilitating factor. What this will be depends on which line the island occurs in, how large the island is, and how long it persists. The longer the loop, the more serious the weakness—it will also be likely that the disorder will already be manifest and the subject will be aware of it. Let's survey the significance of the islands within the major element lines:

Islands in the major air line: When the appear under the water digit, islands indicate rheumatic disorders usually caused by bad diet. Under the earth digit they indicate liver disorders caused by over-indulgence. Eye weakness through weakened muscle action is indicated by islands on the major air line under the fire digit. And when islands appear under the air digit, a predisposition to lung illness due to faulty respiratory patterns is indicated.

Islands in the major water line: When they appear under the water digit, they indicate low blood pressure and a tendency to infections. Under the earth digit they indicate valvular insufficiency and/or weak systolic action of the heart. When islands appear under the fire digit on the major water line they indicate high blood pressure, anemia, and weak dyastolic action. Under the air digit they indicate congenital heart disorder, and palpitations.

Islands in the major earth line: In the upper fifth of this line, islands will generally indicate stress and general delicacy. In the second fifth, look for throat and neck symptoms of physical disorder. Islands in the third fifth will indicate chest and stomach area symptoms. In the fourth fifth, intestinal and hip bone symptoms are indicated. And in the last fifth of the earth line, look for urinary, excretive or sexual symptoms.

Islands in the major fire line: These are interpreted the same as those found on the major earth line, but are rarely found. This line describes the body's source energy rather than physical symptoms of imbalance.

HOLISTIC INDICATIONS OF LINEAL FORMATIONS

So far we have considered health disorders in a specific manner—we have concerned ourselves with those lineal features that describe distinctive disorders in special organic functions. Cheirology also utilizes another type of diagnostic practice, one which is based on an overall assessment of the hand lines. This type of analysis is not rooted in time, meaning it does not look to the distant future to see what lies ahead in terms of health. Instead, it views the here and now as the most important phase of a person's experience and attempts to portray the quality of the subject's present health. Of course, such a presentation can reveal conditions which extend in time— but the object of this form of analysis is more subtle. Its aim is to reach an understanding of the subject (or for the subject to reach self-understanding) and discover just where he or she really is in the world. This means seeing through adornments and pretenses to the physical qualities and inner forces.

This may seem strange to the newcomer to cheirology, but the principle of "body knowledge" is an ancient one in the Orient. We are so used to thinking of ourselves via our minds that the idea that our bodies can "understand" us seems absurd. Look at it this way: all our personal habits and life patterns are reflected in how we live and conduct ourselves. The foods we eat, the things we drink, all represent personal statements of the quality of our lives. It is our body that is the recipient of these personal choices—it has to bear them, balance them or neutralize them if they are harmful. Our conscience rarely answers us back. When it does, its reply takes the form of illness. To get to know our bodies in a better way, to "listen" to its speech, is a factor in self-diagnosis. The main problem we encounter is what language to use? It's not much use waiting for illness to tell us, for then it's usually too late to do much about it. We need some form of preventative principle or communication to warn us when we are going too far. The overall, here-and-now cheirological assessment is one of these. In cheirology, we term it simply holistic analysis.

A complete holistic analysis would take a long time to outline, but its principles relate to all hand features equally. For introductory purposes, let us deal here with the earth line. As it is an important significator of bodily vitality, it is the best place to start. We will first discuss the holistic principle our analysis is based upon.

When the principle of inter-reflection has been recognized, you will come to recognize this principle in other forms. By viewing the palmar lines as microcosmic forms of organic and physical activities, some assessment can be made concerning the overall physical tone and condition. This is of great use in medical diagnosis as it often reveals inherent weakness not previously suspected. You should, of course, look for confirming signs elsewhere. It is by combining several methods of physiological analysis that you attain the greatest accuracy. In order to present the essence of the holistic diagnosis of physical being via lines, I will give some examples to illustrate its principle. It is this principle that must be understood primarily. Palmar diagnostic technique should never be simply a matter of relating this line to that condition or vice versa.

Bearing in mind the principle of graduated materiality, we see that the earth line (ruling the energy of vitality) represents fundamental structures of the body and the basic framework of its existence. Earth's significance thus indicates basic functions and action at many levels according to its correspondences, as shown in Table 15. If we view the length of the earth line as indicative of the subject's holistic fundamental energies, an island at its distal end (corresponding, if chronologically viewed, to seventy years of age) represents a weakening of energy in all areas regarded as the summit of earth energy manifestations. If we apply table 15 to this diagnosis, we would come up with the following holistic view for this individual:

Body: Weakening of cervical vertebrae (the top of the spine); jaw and skull bones (air level of bones); and top or outer edges of spine (when standing this is furthest from the earth).

Chronology: Faulty metabolic interaction (timing) and memory of events in old age.

Height: Weakness of the neck and head. Tendency to slouch (kyphosis) and head injury.

Light: Restriction of visual organs (optic lens is the earth of the eye).

Season: Heightened sensitivity to illness at the end of winter (the end of earth period).

Health: Mineral deficiency, especially iron. Anemia (red blood cells are more earth).

The system of correspondence here shown can be easily extended to all other major lines. The major air line reveals disorders of consciousness; major water of emotional expression; major fire of activity. We can chart the most basic correspondences in Table 16. Of course many of these areas overlap and intermingle; a good understanding of basic anatomy and phys-

Table 15. Holistic Correspondences of the Earth Element

Physical manifestation	Skeletal structure and posture
Body chronology	Ages one through seven (fundamental years of body)
Body height	Below average
Chromatic quality	Dark
Season	Winter
Health constituent	Blood, specifically vitamins and organs that create, store or replenish the body as a whole

Table 16. Elemental Correspondence for Beginning, Middle and End of Lines

Line	Beginning	Middle	End
Air	Initiating ideas Active study Neural tissues Genetic patterns	Implementation Rhythmic presentation Translation of concepts into actions Body electricity	Ideals and aims Fulfillment Satisfaction Reflexes
Water	Emotional energy Heart as an organ Blood quality Bone marrow	Expression of love Blood vessels Values Blood circulation Antibody manufacture	Ideal fulfillment Heart mechanism Blood pressure Children/fertility
Fire	Wish for recognition Muscle tissue Joint articulation Self-esteem	Professional activity Physical labor Physical exercise Self-valuation	Public approbation Muscular power Efficiency of movement Self-progression

iology is therefore required before venturing into the study of diagnostic technique. As your ability to understand the interconnectedness of physical activity increases, so will your ability to integrate the interpretation of lines. You should develop your own chart of correspondences, and work according to the principle of graduated materiality—from fundamental conditions to the most refined—in all the levels of interpretation possible. Each line can, of course, be viewed as composed of four elemental progressions. The triple division given above is simply for purposes of explanation.

Illnesses or events due to external karmic forces are not foreseeable by line as these are ruled by ether (a non-material element).

PART FOUR

Advanced Studies

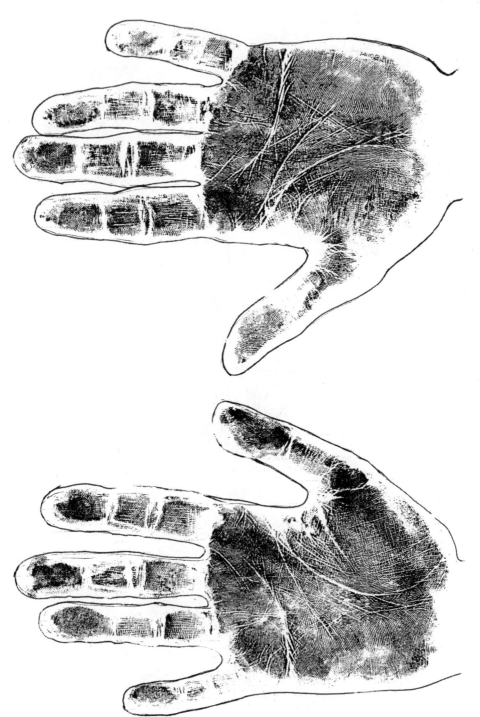

Master Print Two

CHAPTER 14

Balancing Techniques

Since these techniques require understanding of elemental combinations, you should begin by studying Table 17 on page 236. It should be remembered, however, that this is only an *aid* to the synthetic understanding which must develop primarily through personal experience and imagination.

ELEMENTAL COMBINATIONS

The interaction of elements in their major and minor predominances will give you a vital clue to the particular mode of individuality accessible to the subject's consciousness. This inter-balance reveals the energy balances and how they function within the different levels. We can interpret the compatibilities and antagonisms of elements at the levels of emotion, temperament, vocation, intellect, spiritual quest and health. These various levels of interpretation concern different aspects of the individual's being, and outline what he or she actually is and requires in order to be. The *emotional* level tells us if the subject has the ability to "connect" with others. The *temperamental* level enables us to see if the subject suffers from mental alienation. The *health* level tells us either about health in general or about a specific aspect of health. The *vocational* level tells us about the subject's work relationships and how he or she will respond to the demands of the job. It can also show what profession a person is suited for. The spiritual level can tell us what religious system or practice fits the subject—if any. It can also reveal atheistic or mystical orientations.

In each of these levels we translate the particular balance of elements present to the one specific field being considered. For example, if we observe an island in the minor earth line, about halfway up, we would interpret the levels in the following way:

Table 17. General Elemental Interactions Considered as Personality Patterns

First Element	Second Element			
	Earth	Water	Fire	Air
Earth	(Compatible) Inhibitive and dull, Reliable, Body orientated	(Compatible) Fertile and formative, Internal emphasis, Nature loving	(Antagonistic) Inhibitive, Prone to tension, Restrictive attitudes	(Antagonistic) Suspicious or skeptical orientations, Unsophisticated
Water	(Compatible) Fertile, Creative, Sensual	(Compatible) Over-responsive, Internalized, Ultra-feminine	(Antagonistic) Changeable quality, Over-reactive, Extremism	(Antagonistic) Vacillatory, Lack of flow, Destructive
Fire	(Antagonistic) Frustrative, Internalized, Lacks depth	(Antagonistic) Extremism, Spasmodic, Over-reactive	(Compatible) Destructive, Domineering, Insensitive	(Compatible) Exocentric, Highly active, Prone to stress
Air	(Antagonistic) Analytical outlook, Dispersive, Reserved	(Antagonistic) Difficult communication, Internalization, Intellectual alienation	(Compatible) Energetic, Highly sensitive, Constructive	(Compatible) Lacks solidarity or warmth, Dispersive or multifaceted

Emotional level: inability to connect with others emotionally.

Temperamental level: alienation from the present environment.

Health level: skeletal or postural effects—could be disorder of the mid-spine, or a break in the rib cage or arm bone. At the organic or metabolic level, it could indicate a mineral or liver deficiency.

Vocational level: difficult work relationships, probably over the implementation of company policy.

Spiritual level: a misunderstanding or lack of implementation of fundamental doctrines or practices relating to others.

The ability to understand what these different levels mean, and what is needed by your subject, depends on your ability to use your own imagination and intuition. The only difficulty you may experience in determining the importance of various levels for a client would be if you yourself have not succeeded in integrating your own personal elements. This is one of the great lessons of cheirology.

BALANCING FINGER AND PALM

In analyzing the infrastructure of hands, the relative harmony existing between the elements in both hands must be carefully considered. If you are working with only an imprint of the hands, certain factors cannot be ascertained, for example, the flexibility of digits, skin color, etc. You can compensate for these factors—although highly important—by using other techniques. One of the most useful methods is that of balancing the elemental powers of palm and fingers with each other. Before we describe this technique, let's review certain preliminary considerations.

1. We must remember that we use elements only as symbols of the varying cause and effect of consciousness.

2. That our use of these symbols is valid because they represent the interactions of different levels of consciousness.

3. That the levels are variable according to each individual, although universal patterns are recognizable.

4. That our understanding of elements in others is only as effective as our understanding of those same elements within ourselves.

All elemental techniques are related to an ideal, interactive structure within the hand. By evaluating given features of that ideal structure with what is actually present in the hands, actual meaning can be ascertained. How accurate that diagnosis is depends on how well we know the elements and their paradigmatic implications.

When we begin, we should work using strictly deductive methods. We see this, note that, and relate the observed with its attributed significance. As we progress in this deductive method, and gradually develop a feeling for elemental interactions in others, a correspondent understanding of those same elements in our own nature also develops. If and when this new self-understanding develops our internal harmony to such a degree that it begins to effect change within our own consciousness (and I mean *change*, not merely opinion), students will progress to the next method, namely the *inductive*. This is not intuition but rather a thorough understanding of elements at their many levels. This understanding occurs spontaneously, without hesitancy, and is almost simultaneous with the act of observation itself. The more specific our study—for example, the analysis geared toward medical diagnosis—then the more easily recognized this spontaneous induction will be. When it first happens, you should check your opinions using ordinary and methodical deductive analytical procedures. (This should *always* be done during the first few years of practice, as a safety measure and as a personal discipline.) When fully matured, the inductive analysis or judgment can appear almost magical.

Each element has a major aspect. This is the aspect or significance alluded to in fundamental analysis. It is this major form that we utilize in palm quadrant division, line type, and dermatoglyphic. In addition to this major aspect there is also a minor aspect. This usually refers to the particular and individual modification present within a subject. No subject is ever a pure type. Practically speaking we can ascribe to each major element the functions of the other three. Table 18 shows the combinations that occur. It is important to consider these minor aspects because they help us understand the subtle ways particular elements will express themselves in the subject's consciousness and body. To describe anything in terms of the general, overall element is not sufficiently accurate. It's almost like saying someone has a "fire" illness—this could mean so many different things. Each element works in different ways in each of us. Our minds and bodies interpret the elemental energies in ways that are coincident with our own experiences, wishes and knowledge. This interpretation takes place on two levels—the conscious and the unconscious. At the conscious level we make choices knowingly; at the unconscious level such choices are usually already made for us. We experience the interchange between these two forces in different ways. At the level of thought, they may make us subject to certain desires that we don't fully understand but act upon anyway. Think, for instance, of the strange dietary cravings some pregnant women experience. They may not seem "sensible" at all to the woman, but may represent something her body vitally needs. On the other hand, the mind may direct the body to do something that causes it great discomfort—even pain. It is

Table 18. Combinations of Elements and Minor Aspects

Major Elements		Minor Aspects
Fire	combines with	Air
		Earth
		Water
Air	combines with	Earth
		Water
		Fire
Earth	combines with	Water
		Fire
		Air
Water	combines with	Fire
		Air
		Earth

important for a cheirologist to be able to see such forces at work in the client's being and to offer interpretations of his or her condition which are relevant. The minor forms of the major lines go some way to explaining the infrastructural effects of the major elements on the mind and body and are an attempt to communicate with the subject's inner forces. Let's take a look at the elements in the order they are listed in Table 18 and explain them in terms of personal endeavors.

Fire: The air level of fire refers to the manner in which we motivate ourselves to perform an activity or achieve some goal. The earth level of fire refers to what makes up that goal—a situation, our own bodies, food, or the kinds of rewards we want out of life. The water level of fire refers to our kind of social environment, the way in which we enjoy or relax ourselves.

Air: The earth level of air represents what makes up our knowledge—the expertise we require to balance ourselves in the world. It indicates studies and self-improvement schemes. It also tells us what our obsessions may be. The water level of air relates to our intuitions and our manner of socially communicating with others. The fire level of air tells us what inner drives we can muster in pursuit of our goals and ambitions. It is the level that characterizes our way of thinking and expressing ourselves.

Earth: The water level of earth relates to our senses, and our domestic aspirations. It tells us what type of people we prefer to be around and the manner in which we view our family and friends and how we project ourselves. The fire level of earth tells us about our practical skills, our likes and dislikes and our particular form of aggression. The air level of earth informs us about our environment, our personal space, and our inner sense of balance, both mental and physical.

Water: The fire level of water tells us about our negative emotional values—envy, anger, and pettiness. It describes our personal form of egocentric activity and generally enables us to feel and resent the pain caused by others. The air level of water deals with our emotional self-understanding: what we know is fundamental to our well-being. It describes the things we are fascinated by, how we attract and are attracted to others. The earth level of water represents our sense of beauty and pleasure. It tells us whether (or how) we enjoy ourselves sensorially and sensually. It describes our food and beverage preferences.

So the question arises: "How do we decide at which level a particular element lies?" The easiest way of deciding this is to work from basics. Use the major elemental lines to determine a particular area you want to know about. Let's say you choose the air line (remind yourself at this point what the air line represents). Now observe the line carefully and note all its features. It is from these very features that you can determine the various qualities of the elements. If the line is short (an earth quality), then this quality will be largely present. If the line is long, this quality is lessened. Look at the way the line moves across the hand—a water feature. If it is straight, this water feature is of a fire nature; if wavy, of water nature. Observe its elemental quality (the element quality describes how the person experiences the line)—this is its fire feature. Observe the line's termination: this is an air feature, for it describes its goal. Each of these observations tells you in which element the subject experiences the qualities ruled by that line. In this air line example, we know the various features describe the nature of the subject's relationship to consciousness. If we had used the earth line, it would have described a relationship to the body, and so on. The key to remembering which means which is to create a simple mnemonic, such as: basis, feeling, actions, understanding. These represent the four elements in the correct order of material density. If the line you observe has the elemental features present in the order of water, fire, air and earth, this would tell you that (remembering that this is an air line we are observing) the subject's basis for thought is water, feelings are of fire, actions are of air and understanding is earth. Each of the minor aspects—combined with the major element—expresses how the individual experiences or orientates mental capacities or abilities. Study this example: the element infrastructure of the air line in Master Print One shows the following qualities: earth, fire, fire, water. Can you see why?

Further Analytical Procedures for Finger and Palm

Outstanding elements can be determined by a process of elimination which, when followed, leaves us with preeminent elements that will feature strongly in the subject's consciousness. These may be useful or destructive in nature but will always symbolize dominant trends governing the various facets of the subject's life outlined previously. For this analysis we place the element orders of palm and digits side by side and, in somewhat mathematical manner, proceed to cancel out complementary elements. If we use the hypothetical elemental orders, the pattern that emerges looks like this:

	Palmar Order					*Digital Order*		
1	2	3	4		1	2	3	4
Air	Earth	Water	Fire		Water	Earth	Fire	Earth

First we subject these to a basic compatibility link up using *first* and *third* elements:

A E W F W A F E
      x   x

This gives us no compatibilities. This method reveals the personal image of the self, how the subject projects and receives environmental and social experience. If this is not compatible, a withdrawal or apprehension is felt concerning these areas of consciousness.

Then we relate the *second* and *fourth* elements:

A E W F W A F E
      x   x

Again this produces antagonistic inter-balances. This method reveals external images, wishes, ideals and life orientations at present inaccessible to consciousness. If compatible, an increased preoccupation with material, mundane or physical processes is predominant. This is really due to a lack of harmonious life orientation or experience.

We now relate *first* elements in *both* categories to each other:

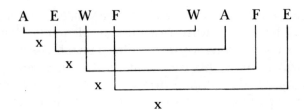

Once more only antagonisms are present. This method reveals the degree to which the subject has overcome both early family or educational influences and also how much the subject's mind and body functions harmonize. If incompatible these areas are still cogent and unresolved within the subject.

4. Lastly we relate first and second, third and fourth; and then any other fundamental, compatible, elements.

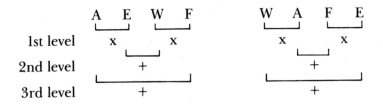

This method reveals something of the deeper motivation of the subject, particularly how to resolve basic incompatibilities of temperament and experience. In many ways it can be considered a karmic analysis. The first and second elements on the first level show where the subject should immediately turn his attention. Elements 3 and 4 on the first level indicate potential development areas. Elements 2 and 3 on the second level show motivation or impulse to act. Elements 1 and 4 on the third level reveal long term influential areas of resolve or aid. Palmar order reveals physical or bodily tasks. Digital order reveals psychological and communicatory areas of resolve.

Note that not all interbalances will work out to the third level in this method, but the print used for the original analysis here is an especially difficult one and ideal for use as an example. A fifth and spiritual interbalance is found by relating both palmar and digital areas together. This is not shown here.

In practice any comparable elements of palm and digit can be interbalanced in the manner here described, providing both categories involve the use of elemental features and criteria to decide the order of their predominance. You may use any category of evaluation involving both palm and digits. Readers may like to practice this analysis on Master Print Two.

If we bear in mind the preliminary factors described at the beginning of this section we can see that any set of representative factors describing both mind and body can be balanced or inter-related to find their harmonies and discords. In determining possible areas of weakness in health, we must use at least eight factors in both hands, there being four major and four minor forms. For best results one uses lineal and shape factors of both hands. This method should be attempted after thorough study of the lineal patterns and is described later on.

PHALANGEAL BALANCING

This method of balancing involves comparing the phalanges of the same two digits on opposite hands. Such a comparison will enable you to discern any differences that have taken place in the subject's attitudes or orientation since childhood. As we've already discussed, the passive hand tells us about the formative years; the active hand tells us what the subject made of those formative influences. Such changes will result in the gradual alteration of the shape and form of the hand. It is by noting such developments that individual changes can be interpreted.

As an example, let's consider the water digit of an individual's active and passive hands. We will be comparing the same phalanges on each finger. Begin by referring to page 81 to review the elemental qualities of phalanges by shape. Our hypothetic example has the elemental qualities of fire, water, fire in the passive (left) hand, and fire, fire, water in the active (right) hand.

This technique for balancing the phalanges involves the following steps:

1. Begin by noting the elemental qualities of the phalanges of the two corresponding digits. Always notate the left hand in the left column and the right hand in the right column. You should also list the elements in the order that they actually appear, i.e., the top phalange element on the top of the list, the mid phalange in the middle, and so on. So our two digits would look like this:

$$F \rightarrow F$$
$$W \rightarrow F$$
$$A \rightarrow W$$

2. Correlate antagonistic and complementary elements. We use the symbol + to denote complementary elements and x to denote antagonistic elements.

$$F \quad + \quad F$$
$$W \quad \times \quad F$$
$$A \quad \times \quad W$$

3. Consider the ruling element of the digit (we shall say this is water). We know that water deals with emotion, individuality and receptivity.

4. Consider the ideal elemental level (commencing from the lowest phalange) of the digit, i.e., water, fire and air.

5. Compare first the passive digit element with the ideal elements.

F	+	A	This is complementary
W	×	F	This is antagonistic
A	×	W	This is antagonistic

We can see that the early formative influences—be they parental, cultural or environmental—are only harmoniously energized at the air (conceptual) level. The other two (ideal) levels represent the creative/active. The mid level (ideally fire) is water here. This shows a background attitude of emotional relationships towards creative energies—i.e., the subject's family encouraged action on behalf of those for whom one has emotional responsibilities, but not purely for necessity's sake. This factor tends to show family exclusivity and preoccupation with its identity or image. The lower phalance (ideally water) has air quality. This shows that, while the family or early influences ideally provide nurturing and emotional support, here an intellectualization of emotion is present. The subject sees this early environment as being primarily conducive to understanding rather than comfort. Both the mid and lower phalanges represent areas of discomfort to the subject.

The top phalange (ideally air) is fire. This reveals an early preoccupation with executing ideas rather than considering their depth. It also shows a predisposition towards radical political ideologies.

6. Now we compare the active digit elements (listed on the left) with the ideal order (listed on the right):

$$F \quad + \quad A$$
$$F \quad + \quad F$$
$$W \quad + \quad W$$

These are all complementary. Their complementary feature shows that the subject has succeeded in fully cooperating with his personal pattern and has developed a strategy towards life that harmonizes the disharmonies suggested in the early environment. The top digit shows that a personal conceptual energy is engendered by the learning situation. The mid digit shows that creativity is emphasized as well as a dislike for inactivity, with those pursuits described by the water digit itself. The lower digit shows that emotional orientation and drive are both strong and, being at home in digital and phalangeal rulership, is uppermost in the subject's consciousness. How this would manifest depends largely upon the quality of the phalange, i.e., skin type, etc.

Elements which are in accord with the ideal elemental order show inherent abilities in the fields of activity symbolized by the elements. They also relate to techniques of spiritual understanding.

7. Now we must relate each digit to the other. From this comparison we could deduce information concerning the progression of the subject. First we must lay out the elements in the order observed in the actual fingers. Again, we place the right digit elements on the right and the left digit elements on the left.

$$
\begin{array}{ccc}
F & + & F \\
W & \times & F \\
A & \times & W
\end{array}
$$

The bottom two elements, air and water, tell us about the fundamental manner in which the subject senses his stabilizing forces (it usually indicates something about a person's family or early upbringing). The middle level, water and fire, tells us something of the nature of the subject's creative impulses or skills. The top level, here fire and fire, tells us about the subject's mental attitudes and interests, and how he comprehends abstract principles.

By first noting if the formative elements (in the passive finger) balance with the present attitudes (in the active finger)—or not, as the case may be—we can see something of how the subject experiences the past and present (if he has the honesty to acknowledge it!). How we choose to interpret the various antagonisms in the two columns is very much up to the analyst. There are a variety of approaches you can take, but the overall progression of analysis should always be the same—you should always try to cover those aspects that are of use to the subject.

Since we have taken our analysis of the water digit this far, let's take a look at one way of interpreting what we have found. As an example, let's look at how the subject (a male) would view his "ideal" spouse, and how his family would view her. His view would be represented by the elemental order of the phalanges in his active water finger; his family's view would be represented by the elements in the passive finger:

Top phalange—F + F: The family sees its emotional investment in their son as being conducive to the development of an affinity with a strongly creative and intellectual woman. The son agrees with this and has fully cooperated in the generation of such an attitude within himself. His appreciation of emotional responses in others is creative and expressive.

Middle phalange—W × F: The family sees the son's wife as being sensitive in her creativity and catering for his practical needs, full of expressions of emotion. The son disagrees and desires affinity with someone much stronger, with whom he can share activities, sports, travel and creative professions.

Bottom phalange—A × W: The family background is greatly in favor of a woman who understands the need for economy and who develops shrewd tactics in personal, shared pleasures. The son disagrees and wishes a pleasure loving, sensually orientated woman with whom he can frequently indulge without thought of the morrow.

DIGITAL PHALANGE BALANCING OF ACTIVE AND PASSIVE HANDS

Using the prints of both hands, it is possible to draw up a comparative chart showing progressions of elemental potentials from the passive to the active hand. By balancing these you can recognize subtle elemental inferences, deficiencies and strengths. We will use Master Print Two as our example. Using the charting system described on page 243, make a list such as the following, of the subject's phalange elements:

	Left hand					Right hand				
Digit =	A	F	E	W	Phalange element	A	F	E	W	= Digit
	W	A	W	W		W	A	W	A	
	F	W	F	F		F	F	F	F	
	F	A	W	A		A	W	A	F	

We see two areas of balance: the relationship line numbered 1 and the line numbered 2. Line 1 reveals a balance between water and air fingers. As

Table 19. Digital Phalange Balancing in Right and Left Hands

Digit	Left		Right	Meaning
Water	W		A	Mental understanding of intuition has developed
	F		F	The executive level is harmonized
	A		F	Active appreciation of innate understanding of water realm — such as cooking
Earth	W		A	Developed understanding of intuitive philosophy
	F —— X ——		F	
	W		A	Developed understanding of craft or art
Fire	A —— X ——		A	
	W		F	Activity developed from intuitive appreciation of art or beauty
	A		A	
Air	W —— X ——		W	
	F —— X ——		F	
	F		A	Consciously developed understanding of material values, etc.

air is dominant (being on the active hand), the balance is air to water in consciousness. This shows an understanding of water activities.

Line 2 shows a balance between earth on the right hand and water on the left hand. This is a complementary blending and shows that earth activity is both sensitivized and active in consciousness.

Distinctive areas of interest can be seen by canceling complementary elements out in the phalange chart of opposite fingers—that is, the water finger of the right hand and the water finger of the left hand. We show the results in Table 19. In general, elemental compatibility between passive elements or active elements—earth and water or fire and air—can be discounted. It is the discordant elements which reveal character or unusual interests.

You must consider comparisons between the right hand showing an active element, and the left a passive. This shows the subject has developed away from the family attitudes, and is suggestive of originality or independence. The opposite of this—i.e., a passive correspondent to an active in the left hand—shows the adoption of a passive, intuitive response to the area interest. This also can show originality, especially within artistic vocations. Examine the quality of lines to see if parental or domestic discord is revealed. Figure 90 on page 248 shows a typical Chinese chart for balancing the phalanges.

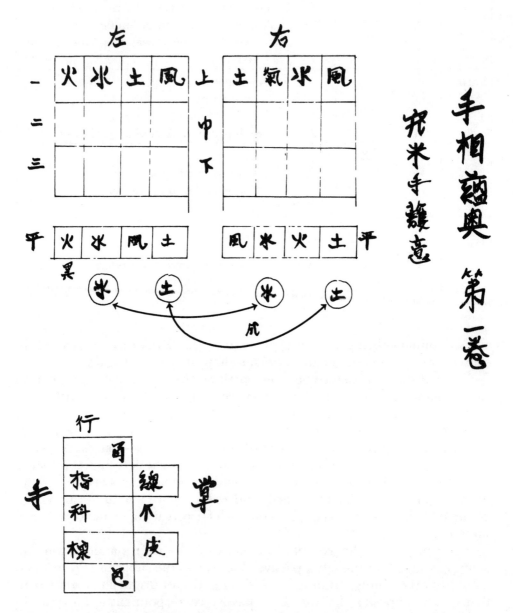

Figure 90. Balancing the phalanges, from an ancient Chinese text, the *Himitsu Teso Gaku*, by Fa Tao Meng, circa 18th century A.D. This page describes the method of analyzing phalange elements and also shows the significant factors of the hands used in balancing lines to signs, color and fingers. The whole section deals with mental well being.

PHALANGE/LINE BALANCING

Lines show, among many other things, the substantive quality and orientation of individual elements within the range of the subject's own perceptive peripheries. Each finger indicates a special area of interest and each phalange reveals a specific orientation of thought within that interest. By balancing hand shape lines, fingers and phalanges, we can reveal both their importance in the outside world in terms of the subject's conscious development, and the subject's personal responses to this. We must keep in mind these correspondences: basic elemental character is manifest in the hand shape and form; individual orientations (and conflicting features) are manifest in the finger shape and form; personal goals and patterns of achievement are seen in the directions of line or digit; and personal responses to experiences are seen in the quality of line, finger or phalange. As each new experience is assimilated within consciousness, so the inner balance and energies of the subject change and develop to accommodate further new experiences.

We can trace this basic pattern by balancing the elemental qualities of the phalanges and lines. When they are in harmony we know the individual is fully attaining understanding of his or her fundamental elemental structure; in other words, self-knowledge. When they are not in harmony we see degeneration in the subject, due perhaps to illness or social rebuffs, or to the development of new fields of interest. These show first in the lineal patterns and last in the phalange form. The correlations between line to finger shape are as follows:

1. Line commencement relates to the shape of the fingertip. This governs the beginning of emotional life, family influences and present attitudes, and any disharmony in these areas would be reflected in the commencement or tip.

2. Total line length corresponds to the top phalange. This describes the total outlook and expectations of the individual in emotional matters.

3. Quality of the line and markings in it correspond to the mid phalange. These are indicators of past experiences and encounters, and of how the individual has responded or adapted to them. They also show modifications in the individual's methods of communicating with others.

4. The angle of the line movement across the hand corresponds to the lower phalange. This relates to how the individual experiences and interprets physical responses. It reveals physical preferences and discriminations.

5. The line ending, or termination, corresponds to the mount area. These two areas will tell you how the subject chooses to relate to whatever you are considering. For instance, if you are dealing with emotional issues, it can indi-

cate when and how the individual chooses to marry, have children, etc. These two factors always relate to change—good or bad. The subject may resist it or welcome it—and how the individual relates to change is indicated here. These two features also relate to past memories and future wishes, and thus indirectly give you a clue as to his or her sense of mental continuity.

By relating all the above factors to the phalange and line balances, you can recognize both where the subject's weakness is, and where potential strengths lie. This will enable you to understand the needs of your client better. By considering the nature of phalange and line elements, you can discern whether an individual's innate pattern is being fulfilled and, therefore, whether this method of self- and other communication is at its optimum. While in many cases changes in line element are not discernible, those which are found changing are always significant. Practically speaking you should mark out the elements of a line by judging its quality as it passes over the palm. Thus, a basically fire line may evidence other elements as well—breaks, islands, etc., all show the influence of elements foreign to the root element of the line. If any of the formations in Table 20 are present within a line, their element should be added to the overall ruling element of that line, which should then be considered as possessing both qualities of its constituents. In other words, a wavy (water trait) water line bearing a sudden island has the elemental qualities of water (waviness) and water/air (island). The water element thus predominates. After the island, the line would bear an air/water quality. This is sometimes very significant in the diagnosis of illness.

In correlating line and phalange elements, you balance the order of the elements given by phalange shape with that of the line's ruler, quality and course through the palm. The finger relates to the line of the same element—i.e., the earth finger relates to the earth line, etc. If a line begins with an island it has water qualities in addition to its ruling elements. In order to explain balancing I shall use as a subject the finger element order given in the section

Table 20. Distinctive Elemental Formations

Striations	= Air	Breadth	= Earth
Thickening	= Earth	Breaks	= Fire
Thinning	= Air or Water	Straightness	= Fire
Waviness	= Water	Fine falling lines	= Air or Water
to Juptier	= Air	Fine rising lines	= Fire
to Mars	= Fire	Forking	= Fire or Water
Absence	= Earth	Bars	= Fire
Depth	= Fire	Dots	= Fire
Faintness	= Air	Fading color	= Air or Water
Island	= Water or Air	Intense color	= Fire

titled Elemental Phalangeal Analysis on page 100. This was a water finger having an order of elemental predominance of fire, air, air. If you examine the water element line and observe an island at its commencement, you would give it an element order of water, water, fire. (I am assuming here that the line is otherwise finely formed and runs in a good arc towards the water mount.) Now you balance these two elemental orders:

Phalange		Line
Fire	×	Water
Fire	×	Water
Air	+	Fire
Air	×	Water

You can see from this that the only compatibility that exists here is between air and fire at the mid phalange. Mid phalanges govern activity so you see that the subject is best emotionally fulfilled in actions of love, works of charity, giving presents, etc. However, as so many areas do not correlate properly, you can also tell that the subject has not yet developed full potential in other forms of emotional communications. You can see this from the actual phalange elements themselves, all of which tend the subject towards fast intellectual activity rather than slow emotional experiences.

The most important use of understanding the correlation between phalange and line lies in being able to advise your subjects as to the area within which they would most usefully progress. In emotional matters, understanding is needed both for yourself or others. The water digit and water line analysis is always a key factor, not only because of its connection to human love but also because of its connection to spiritual love and aspiration.

ACTIVE AND PASSIVE LINE BALANCING

The next stage in our analytical procedure lies in balancing the elements of each line with those of the other hand. This will tell us something of the progress made by the subject in modifying his early influences, be they domestic, environmental or cultural. This, in analysis, is articulated to us by means of elemental language and the interpretation of such language depends—as always—solely on the analyst's personal skill in analyzing elements. Consistent practice and thought develops this skill considerably and this method of analysis should be practiced frequently.

We shall use Master Print Two as the basis. The overall elemental power of each major line must be decided by considering all factors beforehand—commencement and termination area, element rulership of the line, quality and path of the line, plus its markings and signs. When this has been done, a summarized element is decided to represent its total quality. We shall say that the elemental quality and lineal order of predominance in this hand runs as follows:

	Left hand (passive)	Right hand (active)
1st line:	Water	Air
2nd line:	Earth	Water
3rd line:	Fire	Fire
4th line:	Fire	Fire

We can now balance these to find antagonistic (marked x) and complementary (marked +) relationships. The left hand is still in the left column:

$$W \quad x \quad A$$
$$E \quad + \quad W$$
$$A \quad x \quad E$$
$$F \quad + \quad F$$

In this analysis the predominant element relates to the manner of self-experience and response. The second relates to unconscious experience; the third to outwardly orientated actions or intercourse with others. The fourth relates to the ideal path of evolution. Here we have the first position elements in discord. Water and air show a lack of self understanding, a clash between feeling (water) and thought (air). The subject does not feel satisfied with herself. In the second position, earth and water harmonize. This indicates a wholesomeness in subconscious stimuli. The subject is not naturally prone to unrecognized depression or self-recrimination. The third elements are antagonistic. Air and earth in third position show dissatisfaction (or preoccupation) with the material needs and wants. The subject thinks she lacks material things (earth) and occupies her mind (air) with obtaining that which she thinks should be rightfully hers.

The fourth position elements are complementary. Because they are fire, they show the subject to orientate herself towards a life of useful activity and energy. Whether she recognizes it or not, her eventual happiness in life will be accomplished by learning to create, adopt or utilize the fire qualities of leadership and organization.

Practically speaking, the more intense a line, the stronger its influence in the mind. When considering both palms, the one with deeper lines predominates. If this deeper line is in the passive hand, the subject is relating to the family or childhood experiences. This is not a good sign. Length of the lines shows potential available to the subject. If the passive hand has longer lines, the subject's contemporary outlook has thwarted his or her development. The cause of this should be determined by ordinary interpretation, and again it should be pointed out and discouraged.

Psychological and Physiological Analysis of Elemental Infrastructure

All forms of interfactor analysis are refinements of fundamental cheirological observations. This type of analysis often permits us to extract information about the subject through indirect methods. By analyzing the interrelationships of certain factors we come to understand the sub-pattern or infrastructure of the elements themselves. In fact, this infrastructure is only visible by detailed analytical method.

It is a feature of both Occidental and Oriental philosophy that one observes not only the hypothesis derived from rational mental procedures but also the process or method of analysis actually employed. Infrastructural analysis of elements gives this philosophical method practical relevance and, because of the paradigmatic principles involved, places it into the realm of psychological analysis. The method is very clear and does not presuppose particular skills in either philosophy or psychology. Three major factors, determined by observation, are utilized in the basic method. These are: (1) quadrant elements; (2) line depth element, and (3) the ruling element of a line. As three factors are used, we can see that the underlying principle we are dealing with determines the personal balance of expression and impression of the subject, together with the manner in which the subject has understood and developed the personal significance of that balance. We shall use the elemental pattern shown originally in Master Print One. The three factors are drawn in columns, as shown in Table 21. By relating the ideal order of elements—i.e. earth, water, fire, air—to those factors we actually find in the palm, we can begin to elaborate on their discords. We place this "ideal" order to the left of the chart:

Ideal

E	A	W	W
W	E	A	A
F	W	E	F
A	F	F	A

In the first row, we see that the order of the elements relates to the earth sphere and level of consciousness; in the second row, to water consciousness; the third row to fire consciousness; and the fourth row to air. Now omit the ideal levels and connect the complementary and antagonistic elements:

$$A \times W + W$$
$$E \times A + A$$
$$W + E \times F$$
$$F + F + A$$

Diagnostic analysis of this elemental structure requires both knowledge of human physiology and the ability to imaginatively extend the elemental relationships onto that physiological structure and order. To interpret our example, we will look at each row relative to its ideal elemental level.

First row: Since this is the earth level, it relates to supportive functions of the body. As air is the discordant, it suggests that the neural functions associated with the earth element processes are not balanced. We can suspect that fundamental functions of the mind and/or body (impulse, consciousness or spatial awareness) are not in accord. At a personality level, it would suggest that the reasoning ability or the content of thought is not attuned to practicalities.

Second row: This is the water level, and earth is the discordant element. This shows that emotions are misaligned. The individual's receptivity to others is faulty or misapplied. At the physiological level, it suggests either a lack of minerals (earth) in the blood (water) or a vitamin deficiency of some form.

Third row: The fire level has fire as its discord. A weakness or insufficiency of enthusiasm and confidence is indicated, causing vacillation and indeci-

Table 21. The Elemental Pattern of the Air Line in Master Print One

Order of Quadrant Elements*	Order of Line Depth Element**	Ruling Element of Lines***
(Basic Consciousness)	(Individual Consciousness)	(Generative Consciousness)
Air	Water	Water
Earth	Air	Air
Water	Earth	Fire
Fire	Fire	Air

*The order of predominance in quadrant elements.

**The order of elemental predominance in the palmar lines as they appear in the palm.

***The ideal element the lines should evidence. Its variations describe the form an individual's personality assumes.

sion. It suggests a lack of emotional rapport, coldness, or even cruelty in dealings with others. Physically speaking, it suggests anemia, fatigue and low resistance to infection.

Fourth row: The air level. Here, everything is in accord. This shows that the mental attitudes and overal neural reflexes are consciously stabilized and satisfactory to the subject at this point in time. Reviewing the previous discords shown, it suggests a mental complacency, as such satisfaction could only be successfully maintained by ignoring the deeper consciousness.

Each of the columns also reveals information about the special areas of psychological influence active within the subject. This can be deduced by relating the ideal order of elements—again, earth, water, fire and air—to the predominance of quadrant elements. Therefore, we find the following correlation:

Ideal		*Actual*
E	×	A
W	+	E
F	×	W
A	+	F

We must recall here that in terms of temperament the first or ideal element is that which appears most obvious to the subject. The second element is repressed or feared most. The third is exaggerated and presented to the world at large. The fourth is the ideal field or area towards which the individual orientates in an unconscious striving for integration of mind, body and speech.

In the order shown above, the fundamental level of personality is in discord. Earth and air do not mix. Since the actual discordant element is air, it indicates that the subject is separated from the physical body, and is unwilling to accept its presence or is dissatisfied with what it looks like. Instead of basic simplicity (earth), mental confusion (air) is revealed. Physiologically, air discord also suggests faults in endocrinal timing. The second, repressed, element supports this, although earth reveals deep emotional tides not yet fully understood. Physiologically, it reveals a fertile, passive and feminine body.

The third element relates physiologically to the heart muscles, sinews and movement. As water discords on this level, it shows a surfeit of that element's qualities. Muscles will be over-soft and pliable. Flexibility rather than power is indicated. A lack of physical heat, low blood pressure or anemia is also suggested. Temperamentally, it shows a lack of drive in achieving emotional aims and an appearance or image of softness and femininity. The fire and water discord will be especially evident in menstruation, which is likely to be heavy and accompanied by hyper-emotionalism. The fourth element, showing a fire and air accord, reveals intellectual activity and a highly motivated outlook.

Health Analysis by Balancing of Major and Minor Lines (Yi Chen-Tuan Hsing Ping)

In considering areas of weakness within the hand, a practical method of determining incompatible elements may be obtained by lateral inter-balancing using the major and minor lines. As we have already mentioned, the presence of a minor line reveals a weakening of the major function. This is central to the Wu Hsing method. By lateral analysis, incompatible elements can be determined quite easily and rapidly. This method is very suitable as an on the spot aid to diagnostic procedure. Of course an analyst should, even when using this method, continue to observe the other health indications that have been given previously in order to verify suspected imbalance.

Eight factors are used in this method—these are the major and minor lines of each hand. You must list these parallel to each other across a page. Major elements are written in capitals, minor elements in lower case. The subject's palmar lines should be carefully observed and their predominant order noted along with any minor lines observed.

Lay out a hypothetical order of elements of the major and minor lines in a horizontal pattern with the left hand on the left and right hand on the right. Your layout should look like this:

1	2	3	4		1	2	3	4
F	Ww	E	Aa		E	Ff	Ww	A

This represents the major and minor lines in their order of prominence. The most prominent is number 1, next is number 2, and so on. The minor elements are the lowercase letters alongside the capitals. In the passive hand, we can see that the minor water (in position 2) is more strongly evidenced than the major earth (in position 3). Now connect, using lines, the elements that are compatible to each other. This is not done with any special regard to positionings—in other words, don't connect 1 with 1 and 2 with 2 and so on. You will now have a diagram that looks like this:

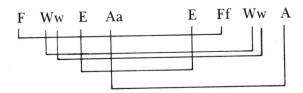

You can see that certain elements—minor fire and minor air—do not have a compatibility partner. This method will isolate those. Elemental features that are not compatible to both hands represent factors of the consciousness (or of the workings of the physical body) that are unresolved or a source of disorder. Another way of seeing this is to say that there are certain areas of experience stemming from either past memories or present psychological conditions which are, at present, causing mental or physical stress. The nature or character of the stress is symbolized by whatever elements are isolated.

The two antagonists here are minor fire and minor air. These suggest hyper-activity of their respective elemental organ rulerships. (Minors usually suggest hyper-activity, majors usually malfunction). As minor air is in the left hand, suspect an inherited or parasympathetic neural malfunction. In the fourth position it suggests (in terms of personality) the ideal function. In physiological terms this would represent bodily metabolism—endocrinal action, bodily electricity or neural activity. A minor present here suggests hyper-response. The right hand antagonist—minor fire—suggests a muscular or red blood cell imbalance. The second position relates to the repressed personality element. Physiologically, the second position symbolizes movement or flow. Since fire rules blood, suspect that blood is not reaching the muscles correctly, or if it is, not in the required quality or amount. You should then examine the water lines and nails carefully to determine heartbeat. If a disorder is present in either, suspect faulty endocrinal balance, perhaps due to hypersensitivity of mind. The reason for this must be determined by observation of both hands in the usual method.

The body is a vast and complex organism and hardly anything occurs—good or bad—without affecting some other action or process. You should develop a good working knowledge of physiology. If in your own collection of hand imprints you have sets belonging to someone who is ill, check them over using the method here shown until you are completely familiar with it. When you are skilled you will be able to diagnose imprints without having to ask about the nature of the illness. Practice until you don't make misjudgments. Until you are near the 90% accuracy level consider yourself a student. (When you are over this 90% level consider yourself a student in even greater need of practice!)

We are now going to utilize a more advanced method of analysis. For purposes of the discussion we are again going to use the chart of elemental patterns found in Master Print One, shown in Table 21 on page 258. We first analyzed the elements vertically in our discussion on page 253. What we are about to do is analyze those same elements horizontally. This is another infrastructure method, and is used to elucidate subtle aspects of personal balance.

The first row in Table 21—air, water, water—relates to the earth sphere and level of consciousness. This row is in fact an important one for health diagnosis and it is the one we shall consider as our example of this analytical method.

Each of the levels in an element layout can be interpreted vertically or horizontally. Each of the three elements relating to the earth level represents different aspects of earth activities or rulerships. Our previous vertical analysis interpreted them as dynamic forces. A horizontal analysis would take into account their nature or qualities in action. Our example in Table 21 has been erected for the air line because we were interested in a psychological diagnosis. We could assess and ascribe three elemental qualities to any part of the hand. These three elemental qualities—air, water, water—because they occur in the position that relates to the earth level, describe the way the individual's earth functions manifest and complete their alloted tasks within the body. Each element represents a special activity within the earth level—that is, the physical body. In this analytical method, lay the elements out in ascending order. This order will be decided by the activity they represent in the body: the first elemental quality is always the one concerned with the most basic function, quality, activity or nature of the element.

Table 22. Depth Order Diagnosis at the Earth Element Level

Depth	Element	Basis	Activities	Result	Realm
1	Air	Object of mental attention	Process of mental analysis	A basic opinion concerning original object	Mental
2*	Water	Emotional modes & objects of subject	Accompanying physio/mental responses to stimulation	Method of expressing or initiating emotional contact or stimulation	Emotional
3*	Water	Heart & cardiovascular system	Blood pressure & valve efficiency	Physical growth, warmth & freedom from infection	Physical

*As depths 2 and 3 are of the same element, we have included a physiological and psychological correlationship. Usually either one or the other is used, but in cases of duplicated elements as here, this double interpretation should be employed.

In Table 22, you can see the elemental quality actually representing the quadrant is the most basic one—therefore, air is the first element considered in this analysis. The next element considered should always be the one concerned with the flow, movement or communicatory nature of the feature—therefore, the next element in this ascending order would be water. The last feature is always the one that represents the ideal form or manifestation and also the goal of the activity. This often means the organ or area the feature is concerned with. In our example, this is water. Now we can see we have an order—referred to as a *depth*—in which the first element is air, the second is water and the third is water. The first element (depth 1) relates to the basic organic structure. The second element (depth 2) relates to its process or method of working. The third (depth 3) relates to the area it serves and/or the functions it is associated with. Diagrammatically, let's set it up like this:

Basic Element: earth

Elements observed: air   water   water

Depth order   1   2   3

Let's consider three areas of diagnosis. If depth 1 relates to the brain, then depth 2 would indicate its neural actions and depth 3 would indicate its physical responses. If depth 1 were the lungs, then depth 2 would be the breath, and depth 3 would relate to respiration. If depth 1 were the mind, depth 2 would relate to thought and depth 3 to expression. We can now build up a picture of the earth element and its responses at several distinct levels, and this has been presented in Table 22.

In the first analysis we did of Master Print One on page 253, we saw that both elements canceled themselves out, leaving air as the discord. In the earth element level analasis in Table 22, we can see the air discord occurs at depth 1, which governs basic organic structure. This discord suggests an air-type disharmony of one of the features or levels of activity peculiar to depth 1 itself. As air relates to ideas, breath, and nerves, this means that, depending on the level we choose to interpret, some fundamental (earth) misunderstanding (air) is present within the subject's mind or body.

When analyzing palmar elements in this manner, you should check findings with the actual elemental lines also. In the beginning, you can simply be told an elemental palmar order of quadrant and go on from there. When you have made your various findings, consult the actual print to verify them.

CHAPTER 15

Analytical Techniques

So far we have dealt with fundamental methods of analyzing fingers. A more advanced method requires that we begin to consider many more implications present within the fingers than before. By including a more subtle interplay between the various elemental energies we can become aware not only of extra data, but also of normally unseen trends existing within those elements. These trends describe more deeply the particular manner or method our body and mind use in their relationships with the world. Such analysis begins to approach or approximate the psychological diagnosis used by Western doctors. Our method offers a wider field of information and highlights aspects not covered in psychiatry in its Occidental form.

ANALYSIS OF INDIVIDUAL FINGERS

Remember that each individual finger shows a specific cornerstone of consciousness. To draw a balanced picture of what we are truly like requires that we analyze each of the four fingers and then integrate the analysis into a whole. It is this whole that presents the most real face we wear in life. Each of us needs to know this real and inner face directly for ourselves, for by understanding our own motives, fears, and wishes, we can achieve a degree of elemental stability. Only when we are stable can we begin to help others.

Since each of the phalanges can be placed into distinct patterns due to their elemental shape, we can begin to prepare refined pictures of specific modes of consciousness. General modes are shown by the finger sizes and angles. The phalange elements show the particular way the subject understands or translates the areas ruled by a finger in terms of his or her own consciousness. The predominant factor of elemental rulership in phalanges is constant—the lower phalange is ruled by water, the middle phalange by fire, the upper phalange by air. The development of individual personal interests can, however, alter their implications considerably. Thus we can often find a water ruled phalange being of the air shape. This would reveal that the intellectual or non-structural (air) aspects of the body (water) would appeal most to the subject. This is an *air* use of the *water* ruled area. This principle is applied to all phalanges. Most must analyze and balance phalange elements in both their general and ideal formations with those actually observed in the subject's fingers. There are two methods of analysis employed, the Fivefold Method (Wu-Fen Chien), and the Eightfold Method (Pa-Fen Chien).

Fivefold Method (Wu-Fen Chien)

This type of analysis is best suited when examining hand prints and when there is no opportunity to observe the live hand. The fivefold method considers the following data significant:

1. element of the fingertip shape;

2. element of the top phalange shape;

3. element of the mid phalange shape;

4. element of the lowest phalange shape;

5. element of the mount.

These must be contrasted with the ideal element rulership of the fingers as mentioned previously. By comparing each, a predominant elemental trait can be seen.

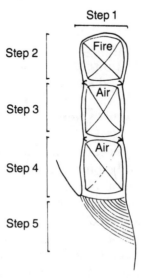

Figure 91. Analyzing the water digit according to the Fivefold Method of analysis. In steps one through five, you observe the elemental data of the finger tip, the top phalange, the mid-phalange, the lowest phalange and the mount.

Figure 91 illustrates steps one through five of this method or the five factors of consideration. We will assume that the digit is of the water element. We must keep in mind the following: all fingers are a general manifestation of air. So we are therefore considering the water expression of the air element—that is, consciousness. Looking at the digit in figure 91, we would observe the following:

1. Tip shape: the *actual element* is fire, and the *ideal element* would be fire.

2. Top phalange: the *actual element* is fire, and the *ideal element* would be air.

3. Mid phalange: the *actual element* is air, and the *ideal element* would be fire.

4. Lower phalange: the *actual element* is air, and the *ideal element* would be water.

5. Mount: the *actual element* of the mount is flat earth; the *ideal element* would be earth.

If we pair up the elements of this digit, the following balance is determined:

	Ideal element		*Actual element*
1.	Fire	+	Fire
2.	Air	+	Fire
3.	Fire	+	Air
4.	Water	×	Air
5.	Earth	+	Earth

The implications of our observations would result in the following analysis: Here we see a heightened activity of consciousness. The mental sensitivity is used energetically and creatively in areas ruled by water element: constructive criticism readily offered; mental awareness of opportunities to act; tendency to consider actions prior to their initiation; awareness of the right moment to do or say things; also the careful expression of emotions. The subject is governed strongly by principle (air) rather than expediency (fire). Good advisory ability is indicated. Personal feelings and needs are subject to thought and planning and are not therefore spontaneous in expression. The subject will feel what he thinks is best. Awareness of food and culinary art is indicated, as is careful choice of wines. The subject's mental and emotional translation of palmar (earth) energies and impulses works at the level of cohesion and creation. It is not therefore fully creative and could be

Table 23. The Eight Factors of Total Finger Analysis

Factor	Governs	Combinations
1) Nail shape	Family/social attitude	These 3 describe total mental quality and hermeneutical mode i.e., spiritual or karmic propensities. — These 4 show responses to spiritual and mental stress, and also fears or phobias likely to be created.
2) Phalange tip	Personal use of knowledge	
3) Dermatoglyph	Personal responses	
4) Skin element	Quality of intellect	These 3 describe mental attitudes, opinions and professional style — These 6 show the highest level of education accessible to subject's consciousness.
5) Top phalange	Use and area of mental concepts	
6) Middle phalange	Mode of executive action	
7) Lower phalange	Physical responses and mechanism	These 3 describe physical and professional integration — From these 5 predisposition and response towards physical imbalances or illnesses can be determined.
8) Mount height	Overall activity level and mode or orientation.	

developed more—it tends to conservatism and carefully guided intuitive responses.

Eightfold Method (Pa Fen Chien)

The next method of analysis is more complicated, subtle and characteristic of the Chinese mind. It takes into consideration eight distinct factors of an observed finger using characteristics of both the front and back of the digit. These factors are noted to the left of a page and their characteristic elements then written down. By interbalancing the various elements present information on a wide range can be determined. The cogent factors are as follows:

1. Element shape of nail

2. Phalange tip element

3. Fingerprint element (by pattern only)

4. Skin texture element (as seen)

5. Top phalange element

6. Middle phalange element

7. Lower phalange element

8. Mount element (by height only)

These are than inter-related in various combinations. For purposes of clarity I have schematized them in Table 23 together with their various inferences. The various combinations that occur need to be understood as if they are archetypal personalities. Those elements which are not present should be considered as inoperative relative to the reasons for analyzing. Thus, if air is absent there is an insufficiency in communication between various levels of activity; which level depends on the particular category begin examined. Each of the elements should be interpreted from the top one downwards. Whatever the grouping or category being considered, the top one represents the highest level available to the subject. There are several other ways of combining these eight factors, but it is most useful to practice with the categories here given. You will recognize other systems as you develop skill in the basic patterns.

FOUR METHODS OF SINGLE HAND ANALYSIS

The method of analyzing single hands is said to have originated with Master Pan-Wu (circa 17th century A.D.). Wu Hsing legend states that he had his left arm cut off during a civil battle. As Pan-Wu was reputed to be a Master of unarmed combat (Chuan Fa), the story is highly likely. Many

Masters were unafraid of armed assailants. Pan Wu is said to have concentrated on the study of single hands from that time, and to have been especially interested in analyzing the hands of children born with limb deformities.

By establishing criteria of judgment, Pan Wu solved a problem many a modern cheirologist has thought about—how to blend the attributes of both hands into one. A completely armless (or handless) person would, of course, be analyzed by body physiognomy alone. Long ago I extracted the most significant of Pan Wu's teaching principles and codified them into five methods, corresponding with the elements. Although designed for those disfigured, the methods in fact are in-depth studies of the most subtle cheirognomical implications. They can be studied and adopted by any analyst who has the time and mental intricacy to memorize them. Practically speaking, these techniques are used predominantly for difficult cases, where the data observed are minimal. A useful practice is to subject one set of prints to each of the five stages outlined here, drawing out as much information as possible. To submit even two prints to such an analysis requires ten specific stages of assessment and is not recommended for run of the mill practice! However, if you wish to really understand the elements, you will not ignore the methods of Pan-Wu!

First Method: Tan Wang P'I Hsing Ping

This method is the observation of quadrant ruling and skin elements. The quadrant (*Tan* = *fields*) element ruler should ideally contain skin texture in accord with its element. Whereas the quadrant size is generally inherited (particularly on the passive hand), the skin texture is created by the subject's individual manner of living. Diet, profession and attitudes all serve to modify skin texture from the ideal. In order to clearly discern the implications of individual attitudes, you should balance the elements in the skin pattern with the basic ruler of the quadrant. This enables you to deduce at which level the fundamental elemental consciousness can manifest. Usually there are only slight differences between them. However skin texture and dermatoglyphic patterning can reveal a fundamental imbalance which serves particularly to describe misuse or inhibition of the consciousness form or attitude genetically inherited or created by the parental domestic environment.

We will use Master Print Two as an example. We see that the quadrant order of predominance in the right hand is earth, water, fire, air. If we observe the skin texture of the palm we can see that the air and water quadrants have a fire quality, the fire quadrant an air quality and earth has both fire and air features. (We shall consider it has wholly fire.) Balancing this against the quadrant elements would look like this:

Quadrant Elements   *Quadrant Skin*

E	×	F
W	×	F
F	+	A
A	+	F

This gives first and second elements a discord relating especially to the ability of the subject to express that quadrant element. Though the passive elements dominate in this palm, they are in fact discordant. Obviously the subject's active quadrants—though minor in mental influence—are most suited for the subject to use in everyday life tasks.

If we consider dermatoglyphics, we would add other elements to this list: water to the water quadrant skin pattern (because of the loop) and water to the air (for the loop between fire and air digits). The balance now looks like this:

E	×	F
W	+	W
F	+	A
A	×	W

The second element now harmonizes but the fourth becomes discordant. From this we can see that if the subject harmonizes the water quadrant by consciously developing water-type activities or interests—thus overcoming the present (fire) tendency to act out his emotions—he will discord his fourth element. As this concerns ideals and ultimate goals, such a development is advisable only for material success. Spiritual orientation would suffer.

Our primary analysis shows us that the subject's personal and inhibited consciousness is imbalanced, but that his public image and goals are not. The second and modified balance—according to dermatoglyphic potential—shows that change would only be successful if the subject concentrates on material ends and is prepared to accept personal inabilities in self-communication and spiritual disorientation.

Second Method: Tan Chih Wang Hsing Ping

In this method we balance the palmar quadrant elements with the digital ruling elements. This tells us the manner in which the subject orientates his consciousness towards specific fields of interest. The first method showed us how he modifies his inherited root consciousness out and away from inherited cultural or environmental tracts; this second method tells us something about where he will do this. The digital order is decided simply by observing the length, straightness, quality of each digit. Again, using Master Print Two, the following comparison can be made:

Quadrant		Digit
E	+	W
W	+	E
F	+	A
A	+	F

Digit elements are listed in order of predominance on the palm. In this case accord is evident in all balances, so we know that the subject's manner of development is sound (even though his basic use of elements is not). A discord in this second chart would reveal any vocational endeavors not truly suited to the subject. For example, if the fire digit balance was weak, an active, physical or artistic career would do nothing to harmonize the subject's mind to his inner environment. He would be continually dissatisfied in his work because he was really incapable of understanding its implications at other levels of his being.

Third Method: Tan Wang Chih P'I Ping

To modify the level of usage we can introduce the skin elements of the digit and balance them to the quadrants. The fingerprint pattern element is used as the first element, then the elemental features of the next two phalanges. Lastly one adds the ruling element of the finger itself:

Quadrant Elements		Skin Elements
E	+	W (Loop)
W	×	F (Grilled lineal pattern)
F	+	F (Grilled lineal pattern)
A	+	F (Fire digit)

This shows the second (inhibited) element is discordant, revealing that the subject's fears or repressed attitudes are very powerful in his consciousness at its present stage of development. In fact his attention needs to be drawn to this factor that manifested previously. This process should be applied to all four fingers to determine the most useful and accessible form of consciousness available to the subject. It is thus one which he can adopt and nurture most successfully.

Fourth Method: Tan Chih P'I Ping

This method involves comparison and balancing of the skin elements as actually observed in both palm and digit. It reveals the accord/discord in the subject's self-image and helps us determine where he is going astray from self-understanding. Again using Master Print Two and the fire element digit, we see the following balance:

Quadrant Skin Elements		*Phalange and Digit Elements*
F	×	W
F	+	F
A	+	F
F	+	F

Discord occurs in the first position, relating to self-image as perceived by the subject. As we are using the fire digit we can deduce that the subject sees himself out of harmony with the inner and outer worlds. By realistic assessment of the subject's goals and aims, together with a change in the method used to create inner harmony with oneself and others, a good accord can be attained. This is in fact a minor, easily eradicated, discord. Analysts should remember in every case that the position of a discord—1st, 2nd, 3rd or 4th level—signifies exactly the same meaning as the quadrant orders: the 1st position relates to outer image, the 2nd to inner fears, the 3rd to how others view us, and the 4th to goal or ideal or resolve.

CHAPTER 16

Vocational Analysis Through the Fingers

Phalanges reflect individual elemental qualities, and each tier of phalangeal elements presents a specific blend of attitudes in the individual. Such attitudes are useful in suggesting professions or areas of appeal. This chapter focuses on three methods of elemental combinations, consisting of solo, binary and tertiary element consideration. These I have especially devised from both traditional Oriental teachings and direct personal experience. The professions listed are only basic and are intended to show orientation. Many more can be added to those listed. It is assumed that in these analyses the thumb and major lines are relatively well-formed in both hands. The tertiary interpretations are applied to the phalange element combinations only. All interpretations are for a right-handed person. If your subject is left-handed, reverse their import. The ether finger (thumb) is considered inoperative in this analysis.

In ascertaining particular vocational trends, you should try to work through each of the methods shown here, gradually eliminating those not suitable, and considering related occupations at each stage of the analysis. By the time you reach the tertiary method, a general field of endeavor should be manifest. The tertiary charts will give potentials for each finger. You must first deduce the ideal on the passive hand, and then on the active hand. This will show possible complementary vocations.

At this stage you should decide which of the four digits (excluding the thumb) is strongest; in other words, which is most free of negative features, largest, etc. The professions listed for that digit are those most symbolic of your subject's elemental, and thus conscious, evolution. Your subject may not, at first, like these professions, but the individual element balance shows that it is through these professions that the most useful experience will be gained. This will balance all energic disharmonies existing at the present time. The combinations shown can also be used to determine the conditions of the organs related to that digit. Balanced with the lineal indications they can prove extremely useful in health diagnosis.

The tertiary method of analysis is primarily utilized to describe vocational or professional interests only. Solo analysis is best used for the hand shape element. Binary analysis is used for either the two ruling quadrants, or hand shape element plus quadrant ruling element. Tertiary analysis is used for elements of phalanges on the most powerful digit (if none is clearly discernible use the water digit of the active hand). If a subject seems to be following a vocation found in the passive hand digit, it is a sign that he or she is still not free from the family or early environmental influence. In cases of mental depression or disorder, a reversion to the passive hand interests is often found. Using this key you can decide if this is taking place. Begin by studying Table 24 on pages 274–275. This will provide general correlations between vocational orientations and individual fingers and phalanges. You should notice that the ether digit is primarily concerned with the translation of energy impulses in the inter-personal field. It should be noted that many other traditional links are noted in interpreting this particular digit. Compare the active/passive thumb quadrants carefully to determine the development of energy translation. This indicates the form of change most desired by the subject indicating how he or she asserts personal limitations onto the external world.

KARMIC INFLUENCES

The earth level forms part of the palmar quadrants and is delineated in the traditional manner. However, Wu Hsing tradition permits the earth quadrant to be analyzed for purposes of determining karmic influences of a subject. In this method the thumb is considered without relationship to other digital phalange qualities. (See figure 92.) Through research I have determined contemporary meanings, in addition to the ancient ones. The Wu Hsing karmic indications are as follows:

Air quadrant: Incarnation as a pale-skinned person, in a cold country. One who has misled others or has to relearn lessons.

Fire quadrant: Incarnation as a dark-skinned or red-haired person in a hot or low lying country. One who has caused others to suffer pain or death. One who should study spiritual teachings assiduously.

Water quadrant: Incarnation as a light-skinned person, with long hair, in a flat country or by water. One who has been deceived by others emotionally and has to learn emotional continuity.

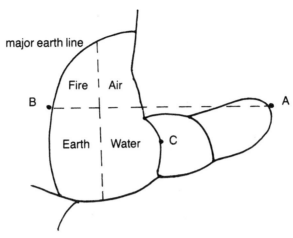

Figure 92. Determining the earth level quadranture of the ether digit (thumb). Point A is the apex of the ether digit when in its natural position. Point B is the center of the major earth line when the thumb is held in a natural, relaxed and usual manner. In forming quadrants of the ether digit at the fire and water levels, the mid point of the lower phalangeal crease of the mid phalange results in base point C. Note that the position of the fire quadrant elements is *reversed* by this method in both hands equally. This also applies to the phalanges—fire is always towards the water digit.

Earth quadrant: Incarnation as a dark-skinned person, with short hair in a desert and hot country. One who has developed ignorance and distrust of truth and needs to cultivate the religious spirit.

Positive and negative factors of karma are indicated by lineal striations. The simpler these are the more the subject is progressing.

SOLO ANALYSIS

This method uses the hand shape element only. The vocational implications of such elements are:

Fire: masseur, athlete, salesperson, police officer, revolutionary, mechanic, surgeon, traveler, arms manufacturer, bodyguard, explorer, missionary, scrap metal dealer, night club owner, dancer, criminal, physiotherapist, butcher, model, marker salesperson, driver, machinist, chiropractor.

Water: poet, author, nurse, social worker, interviewer, personnel officer, food manufacturer, musician, artist, veterinary worker, sailor, religious student, diplomat, pediatrician, swimmer, gardener, child minder, seamstress or tailor, witch, healer, model, actor.

Table 24. Vocational Orientations of Phalangeal Quadrants

Digit	Level	Quadrant	Orientation
Water			
	Air (mental)	Air	Healing or ministering to others.
		Fire	Leadership of group activities.
		Water	Religious or psychic studies.
		Earth	Property and investment.
	Fire (activity)	Air	Planning and design.
		Fire	Military matters.
		Water	Charities or nursing.
		Earth	Engineering (theoretical).
	Water (sensual)	Air	Education and teaching.
		Fire	Jewelry and art.
		Water	Wines or clothing.
		Earth	Public officer or government service.
Earth			
	Air	Air	Philosphy and ancient wisdoms or events.
		Fire	Law and justice.
		Water	Social services or diplomacy.
		Earth	Construction and creative engineering.
	Fire	Air	Accountancy, nuclear energy.
		Fire	Time and motion studies.
		Water	Chemistry, analysis and research in general.
		Earth	Domestic professions or services.
	Water	Air	Architecture.
		Fire	Craft.
		Water	Decorative arts.
		Earth	Folk arts and national sports.
Fire			
	Air	Air	Arts, opera, choreography.
		Fire	Theatre and drama.
		Water	Fashion, clothes manufacture.
		Earth	Culinary arts.
	Fire	Air	Photography (portraiture).
		Fire	Fashion modeling, jewelry production.
		Water	Furniture design, carpentry in general.
		Earth	Physics, physical arts and crafts.

Table 24. Vocational Orientations of Phalangeal Quadrants (*continued*)

Digit	Level	Quadrant	Orientation
Fire (*cont.*)	Water	Air	Photography in general, cosmetic preparation, advertising.
		Fire	Stocks and bonds, gambling.
		Water	Restaurant or club management.
		Earth	Food production or supply, public management.
Air	Air	Air	Translation, education, research into these. Psychology.
		Fire	Lecturing, teaching, neurosurgery, sales.
		Water	Psychiatric nursing, overseas travel and works computer sciences.
		Earth	Technical writing.
	Fire	Air	Writing, postal work.
		Fire	Social work and aid, finance, languages.
		Water	Sports, hobbies (teaching).
		Earth	Medicine, healing.
	Water	Air	Education, technical teaching, surveying.
		Fire	Sexual interests (general).
		Water	Domestic furnishing, children's education and welfare.
		Earth	Domestic comforts, geology, science, collecting.
Ether	Fire	Air	Desire to create, acquire or perpetuate ideologies, enclosed systems, or knowledge of the self.
		Fire	Desire to experience the external environment fully.
		Water	Desire to emotionally orientate other people or situations.
		Earth	Desire to stabilize the internal experiences produced through contact with other persons or situations.
	Water	Air	Development of diplomatic understanding with other people.
		Fire	Subtle (or shrewd) dealings with others.
		Water	Inductive responses to demands made from others.
		Earth	Development of deductive faculties.

Air: teacher, lecturer, research worker, electrician, linguist, author, energy worker, computer worker, translator, caligrapher, academic, religious leader, archaeologist, salesperson, pilot, philosopher, traveler, astrologer, designer, architect, homeopath.

Earth: merchant, retailer of natural foods, driller, jeweler, restauranteur, cook, miner, tailor, potter, herbalist, engineer, lawyer, judge, church official, laborer, osteopath, dentist, surgeon, factory worker, farmer, craftsperson, mason, slave, income tax, government official, rent collector.

BINARY ANALYSIS

In this system, the element of hand shape (1st element) and skin texture or predominant quadrant (2nd element) are combined. The second element has a diminished influence.

Fire + Air: communications, electricity, explosives, mountain climbing, steel industry, astronomy, public services, entertainment, foods, publishing, martial arts, orthopedics, psychology, teaching.

Fire + Water: medicine, printing, domestic appliances, painting, sculpture, mime/mimicry, police investigation, dancing, investment, music, collecting.

Fire + Earth: engineering, oil, mechanical servicing and production, programming, restoration, pottery, dry countries, revolutionary (political), property ownership and development, anthropology.

Air + Fire: investigative work, research, mass media, microscopy, neurology, physical training, psychiatry, mathematics, designing, surgery.

Air + Water: art, collecting, bibliophile, counseling and guidance, music, public services, cooking, philosophy.

Air + Earth: agronomy, endocrinology, dietetics, fashion design, antique collecting, investment, restaurants, social studies.

Water + Earth: gardening/flowers, collections (all types), animal breeding, overseas investment, town planning, farming, dowsing, clothing.

Water + Air: public speaking, poetry and harmony in all forms, travel and change, religious works, domestic work, reading, psychic interests, flower arranging.

Water + Fire: social services, travel agent, sponsorships, charity work, musical performance, wine and food production.

Earth + Water: children's charities and homes, supporting causes, public works, agriculture, musical appreciation, crafts and natural arts.

Earth + Fire: musical performance, merchandising of all forms, making clothes/tools, investments, garage work, processing, dancing and physical arts or skills.

Earth + Air: consultancy, selling health aids, advertising, chemistry/physics, biological research, neural surgery, solitary work, mathematics, landscape gardening.

TERTIARY ANALYSIS

This is a method of analysis which consists of classifying a finger by its elemental rulerships. To do this, each phalange of the digit is accorded its predominant elemental rulership (remember: this is done by assessing its overall area size and its qualities, such as skin textures, etc.). When this is done, the ruling elements for each phalange are listed in a vertical column. The element of the top phalange is placed at the top of the column; the mid phalange element in the middle; and the lowest phalange element at the bottom. This obviously gives you a column of elements. Elemental ascriptions can be used in a variety of ways, but the most common is for vocational analysis to determine the occupation or profession the subject is temperamentally suited for, according to his or her elemental balances. For vocational analysis, we usually use the water finger and its specific phalange elements, but this method also can apply to all fingers. Table 25 on page 278 will provide you with a complete list of vocational ascriptions for every possible elemental combination that can be found in this, and any other, digit.

To use Table 25, you must first decide which elements rule each phalange. Once you know the elemental ruler for the top phalange, look to the column on the left under that element. For example, if the top phalange were of the fire element, you would go to the section marked Fire, and follow the column across until you found combination you're looking for. Now look to the number listed under that column: this is the key number that will reference you to a vocational description on the following pages.

It's important to get the spirit of these vocations and see what they represent and symbolize rather than view them as "jobs." Each job is a manifestation of elemental energy, and it is the energy which is most important. All of the combinations shown in Table 25 have an underlying energic

Table 25. Tertiary Analysis

Top Phalange	Possible Combinations															
Fire	F	F	F	F	F	F	F	F	F	F	F	F	F	F	F	F
	F	F	F	F	W	W	W	W	A	A	A	A	E	E	E	E
	A	F	W	E	A	F	W	E	A	F	W	E	A	F	W	E
	1	2	3	4	5	6	7	8	9	10	11	12	13	14	15	16
Air	A	A	A	A	A	A	A	A	A	A	A	A	A	A	A	A
	A	A	A	A	W	W	W	W	F	F	F	F	E	E	E	E
	A	F	W	E	A	F	W	E	A	F	W	E	A	F	W	E
	17	18	19	20	21	22	23	24	25	26	27	28	29	30	31	32
Water	W	W	W	W	W	W	W	W	W	W	W	W	W	W	W	W
	W	W	W	W	F	F	F	F	E	E	E	E	A	A	A	A
	A	F	W	E	A	F	W	E	A	F	W	E	A	F	W	E
	33	34	35	36	37	38	39	40	41	42	43	44	45	46	47	48
Earth	E	E	E	E	E	E	E	E	E	E	E	E	E	E	E	E
	E	E	E	E	A	A	A	A	W	W	W	W	F	F	F	F
	A	F	W	E	A	F	W	E	A	F	W	E	A	F	W	E
	49	50	51	52	53	54	55	56	57	58	59	60	61	62	63	64

connection. Once this principle can be recognized, the vocations can be multiplied ad infinitum or analyzed into special aspects or facets of a special vocation. For example, a steel (fire) manufacturer will need sales people (fire and air), workers (earth), public relations employees (water), designers (earth, air and water) and so on.

Fire Level

Possible vocations include skills in the following areas:

1. Active fields, teachers and political leaders, inventors, organizers, choreographers.

2. Physical fields, sports, exploration, shooting.

3. Commando, sailor, social worker, gambler.

4. Building, crafts, motor racing, stocks and bonds, butcher.

5. Teachers, musicians, sports, alternative religion, conjuring, circus.

6. Jobs that demand punctuality, teacher of fine arts, jobs in wine and foods, surgeon.

7. Impatience in expression, communication difficulties in general, opera, ballet, sailing.

8. Love of wines, comfort and art, weaving, pet keeping.

9. Analysts, researcher librarian, numerologist, critic, judge, leader, cooks.

10. Cautious in plans but fast in enactments, shooting, investment, selling.

11. Social work, food preparation, interior design, movement, arts.

12. Design and construction, exploration of ideas/countries, analytical tasks.

13. Active but inhibited, assistant or aide, surveyor.

14. Self-imposed tasks, guard or protector of things.

15. Gardening and livestock, nurturing things.

16. Physical work, porter, butcher.

Air Level

Possible vocations are:

17. Philosopher, astronomer, pure science, investor.

18. Mathematics, accountancy, computer sciences.

19. Healer, psychiatry, ferryman, counselor.

20. Herbalist, osteopath, estate agent, merchant banking, nutritionist.

21. Nurse, navigation and radar, children's writer, philanthropic ventures.

22. Pediatrician, taxi driver, transport officer, comedian.

23. Poet, dancer, child nurse, religious life, announcer.

24. Horticulture, animal rearer, wine-making, public relations.

25. Construction, design, surgeon, aeronautics, economist, astrology, electrician, hypnotist, quality surveyor, linquistics.

26. Electronics, furniture design, helicopter pilot, military officer.

27. Massage, military N.C.O., salesperson, supervisor.

28. Cheirology, military sergeant, police officer, dentist, products supervisor.

29. Fine art, mathematics, measurement, paleontology, seismology.

30. Surveyor, traveler, oil driller, doctor of medicine.

31. Agronomy, civil pilot, stockbroker.

32. Livestock farmer, herbalist, engineer, roof repairer, accountant.

Water Level

Vocations could include:

33. Idealist, spiritualist, intuitive, aquarist, plumber, veterinarian, music and harmony, teacher of ideas.

34. Sublimatory nature, swimmer, natural healer, artist.

35. Devotional, psychic, inspirationalist.

36. Fertile, love of animals and nature, repairperson.

37. Children's teacher, nurse, research into lost arts and cultures and poetry, music, clothes making/sewing, anthropology.

38. Personal secretary, buyer, fashion, dancer, shop assistant.

39. Writer, poet, charity work, deep sea diver, musician, publicist, plumber, prostitute.

40. Cook, publicist, politics, group endeavors, dancer.

41. Pottery and ceramics, mechanic, signmaker.

42. Clothes maker, flower arranger, railways, fishing, choreographer.

43. Shop and factory work, fabric production, paint-making, buyer.

44. Servant, housemaid, child-minder, medium.

45. Literature, diarist, recorder, historian, music, accountancy.

46. Teacher, undersea archeology, marine research, advertising.

47. Journalist, literature, beautician.

48. Painting, embroidery, furniture making, technical writer.

Earth Level

Vocations could include:

49. Hardware dealer, mechanic, handyperson.

50. Toolmaker, traditional dancer, shepherd or crofter, nylon production.

51. Canal boat driver, gardener, oil production.

52. Farmer, horticulturist, market gardening.

53. Minerologist, government officer, legal professions, soil analyst.

54. Jeweler, church official, court official.

55. Decorator, designer.

56. Chemist (industrial and medical), landscape design.

57. Pensions official, insurance secretary, programmer, radio, veterinarian.

58. Rent collector, insurance agent, oil refining, carpentry.

59. Marine engineer, solid fuel production, dowser.

60. Chemist, mason, sculptor, policy maker.

61. Motor car design, HGV driver, physiotherapist, printer.

62. Calligrapher, sign designer, bailiff, sportsperson, investor, heating.

63. Tunnel engineer, food manufacturer, sportsperson, collector.

64. Drilling and boring (oil and water), ceramics worker, driver, bricklayer, forestry.

EXAMPLES OF ANALYSIS

If you observe the elements of Master Print One, the following indications can be seen.

- Using *Solo Analysis*, the fire element predominates.

- Using *Binary Analysis*, a fire and fire predomination is seen. This intensifies the interest of the areas indicated.

- Using *Tertiary Analysis*, each finger indicates the following:
  Water digit is phalangeally water, fire, air. See occupation 37.
  Earth digit is water, air, water. See occupation 47.
  Fire digit is water, water, water. See occupation 35.
  Air digit is water, fire, water. See occupation 39.

In combinations, these indicate interests in psychism, nursing, children, research, literature, music, plumbing, diving, beauty. The subject, in fact, is a university graduate, trained as a general and children's nurse, an excellent swimmer, a poet and keenly interested in oriental art, religion and culture. The nail (public face) is of the water element, and gives a similar temperament. In this case public and private images held by the subject coincide.

CHAPTER 17

Movement and Adornment

Gesture itself is an expression of elemental energies in a distinctive, kinetic, manner. The constituent pattern or pose of a gesture reveals the pervading or predominant elemental energy being utilized. Owing to the complexities of the human consciousness we can often use a gesture belonging to one element in a manner belonging to another! This is often seen in people forced to make unavoidable decisions. Their bodily movements reveal one thing, their gesture patterns another:

Earth energy uses the least amount of movement in gesture. This element is renowned for its lack of kinetic expression. When you observe someone who "sits tight" and moves little, earth is predominant.

Water energy moves hands and gestures in explosive circles, wide expressive interchanges of movement common especially to the Latin countries, when the hands fly around unceasingly. Water is predominant.

Fire energy uses direct, straight movements. They direct and hold movement to emphasize it. Fire moves are directional and authoritative. When you observe strongly executed movements, fire is predominant.

Air energy uses curves, a combination of fire and water. Curves are expressive and flowing. The movements of a graceful orchestral conductor typify this form. Graceful curves show self control and discrimination, the positive aspects of the controlled air element.

BODILY MOVEMENT

A subject's manner of walking also reveals the overall energy predominance. Earth walks slowly and with care. Water flows everywhere, flailing arms and hands around. Fire walks determinedly, with measured steps and speed. Air walks disjointedly, with jerks and spasms of hip and shoulder. Oriental cheirologists would assess a subject's elemental nature by observing gait long before they got around to examining the hands.

Apart from gestures used in communication with others, certain movements of the arms or body express archetypal elemental energies. These are often seen in religious dance or ritual in which one is communicating with a divinity. These may be performed with one or both arms together with the fingers placed in a Mudra. Yoga postures are a direct result of this principle being applied to bodily Mudras.

- Movements upwards, towards the sky, express *air* energy.

- Movements downwards, towards the ground, express *earth* energy.

- Movements to the right or forward express *fire* energy.

- Movements to the left or rear express *water* energy.

Chinese yoga, Egyptian dancing, martial arts, Indian temple rites and American Indian dances each express these patterns of elements superbly. They can also be noted in many Oriental sculptures and paintings.

HAND GESTURES

When we consider the various areas of the hand as energy vortices, it is not unusual to discover that certain polarities of energy develop within the hand itself. Some energies will attract, others repel. Considering this phenomenon, we can see that the flux of attraction and repulsion within the mind gives rise to distinctive gestures of the fingers reflecting this. It is an observable fact found everywhere around the world.

If we apply cheirological principles of interpretation, it is no surprise to discover we can understand specific gestures used in other fields. Not only do we develop an interpretative skill, but we realize that the interpretative meanings we discover correspond closely with those understood by the persons who perform the gestures—for example, religious or shamanistic practitioners. Certain types of gestures are almost universal and it is within these types we find the most natural or harmonious ones being communicated. Such observation validates the premise of elemental energy circulation used within our school of teaching. In Chinese Chen Yen Buddhism, hand gestures (Yin) form an important facet of ritual meditation practice and are used to convey the idea of the presence of enlightened beings. In Hinduism, gestures (Mudra) are used for a similar purpose. Indian and Thai dance is also based around gesture. The post and gesture of the hand confirms those fundamentally energic qualities which are expressions of its macrocosmic reflective ability. They also demonstrate that ancient races knew of these qualities. In ancient Buddhist religious statuary, not one can be found making a gesture which, cheirologically interpreted, conflicts with the significance given that gesture in its native religious meaning.

We should observe and recognize the poses fundamental to humanity. Many more have developed as combinations of these basic ones. Those stemming from purely social influence have little significance in holistic terms, and in fact do not correspond to the pristine elemental poses or movement patterns.

Physical or mental illness, a manifestation of energic imbalance, can be evidenced through gestures. The cause of the imbalance can often be traced by determining its ruling element and relating this to a correspondent elemental function of the body, mind or spirit. Imbalance thus enables us to determine at which level we need to readjust or grow.

ENERGIC INFLOW AND GESTURE

When we walk, the fingers point towards the ground, earthing our mental and bodily energies (which are received through the lower limbs from the earth itself), thus creating a circular cycle of flow. In prayer, we raise our fingertips to the heavens and receive energy from above. Some gestures require special positions for each fingertip, some up, some down, according to the symbolic meaning of the gesture itself. Viewed as repositories of the various forms of consciousness and awareness, ritual gestures have an increased significance beyond that of tradition. They can show specific and selective reception of natural (or supernatural) energy. Gestures or poses assumed by the hands in non-spiritual environments show clearly which forms of awareness/reception are utilized by the individuals themselves.

Let's look at some of the many gestures and poses commonly found in the Occident and Orient, with traditional and contemporary interpretations. The bold heading is the traditional meaning of the gesture. We have elaborated on the significance and interpretation from a cheirological standpoint.

Hand Poses and Gestures

Indicative Directing
The water digit extended enriches its significance as a deity of omnipotence and asserts the individuality and validity of its nature. The label "index" finger literally means *indicates*.

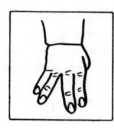

Judaic Blessing
The separation of earth and fire accentuates inner division, which is not psychologically healthy and is outwardly unspiritual! The example shown comes from a Kabbalistic work upon demonic subjugation.

Begging Pose
The air fingertips joined thus indicate the subjugation of personal pride and viewpoint.

Prayer
This pose evolved in Buddhist and Hindu teaching long before its adoption by Christianity. A beautiful gesture showing balance of inner and outer power. Clapping is a *negative* form of this gesture.

Thumbs Up
Originally a Priapan greeting. It still retains its significance as a pose indicating freedom of the will and a preference for conscious autonomy. Digits subjugated by the earth and water areas show that natural energies are being released, not concepts.

Sign of the Small Thunderbolt
Used in esoteric Buddhism and Hinduism as a symbol of power and authority. Here we see a unification of water, earth and fire energies. The opposite to the Delphic sign, this form shows rulership, subjugation and power of punishment. Communicative digits are controlled by uniting energy and air fingers.

Fist (1)
The thumb closed outside the fingertips indicates subjugation of discriminative judgment (the mind phalanges are subject to the body).

Fist (2)
Thumb held inside the fingers shows tight control or subjugation of the willpower to the mind—a mark of defeat or resignation to circumstance. Quite alien to the Northern races. Common in epileptics.

Norse Horned Fist
Buddhist Demon Fist
Used widely in the Orient as a charm against demons. The air digit carries the message, water the power of exorcism. A perfect cheirognomical communication. (The thumb is outside the fingers.)

Buddhist Teaching Pose
Water finger joined with energy finger (thumb). Water is the out-flowing of spirit, the power of wisdom. The thumb shows earth plane energy and activity. Another perfect gesture of completion.

Buddhist Gesture of Victory over Hate, Craving and Ignorance
A very ancient symbol used also by the Egyptians as a mark of royalty. Transference of each limb to its opposite side shows integration of male and female, active and passive, sun and moon. It is indicative of Divine Power and Knowledge.

Horned Hand

The thumb inserted between the water and earth fingers joins earth and water with energy. A most fertile sign of the Mother Goddess and her protection against harm. Common to many cultures, ages and spiritual systems, found in Scandinavia, Russia, China, Africa and Europe.

Meditation Gesture

An epitome of significance. All digits related to conscious action are folded away. Joined thumbs show an earthing or energy and emphasis on its circulation rather than expression.

Sign of the Delphic Oracle

Water, air and thumb reveal a perfect representation of the power of divine prophecy.

Buddhist Gesture to Beckon Ghosts

Air finger (communication) is extended and beckoning along with the other digit.

Buddhist Pose of Fearlessness

Also used by monarchs as a greeting to subjects. It means, "My life is exposed for all to see, yet I have no fear nor need you have any."

Papal Blessing

Water as beneficent power and earth as the law giver combine to epitomize the Christian concept of justice and approval.

Ritual Gestures (Mudra)

Figure 93 shows a Buddhist monk practicing the ritual arm and foot positions used in esoteric Buddhism as a means of inducing meditative states. As the monk has hair, we know that he has been in meditation retreat for at least a month (usually monks shave their heads every full moon). The blossoming trees show this is springtime, most probably the anniversary of the Buddha's Enlightenment (May/June). This picture was given to me by the monk Hyun-Ho of Korea and many similar ones exist. The crest at the top left is the one used by the Chinese monk soldiers (Seng-Ping).

Figures 94 and 95 (see pages 290 and 291) show ritual gestures found within Chen-Yen Buddhism. As a practice, you may like to interpret them according to your understanding of elemental principles.

Figure 93. Ritual gestures of a Chinese monk, circa 15th century A.D.

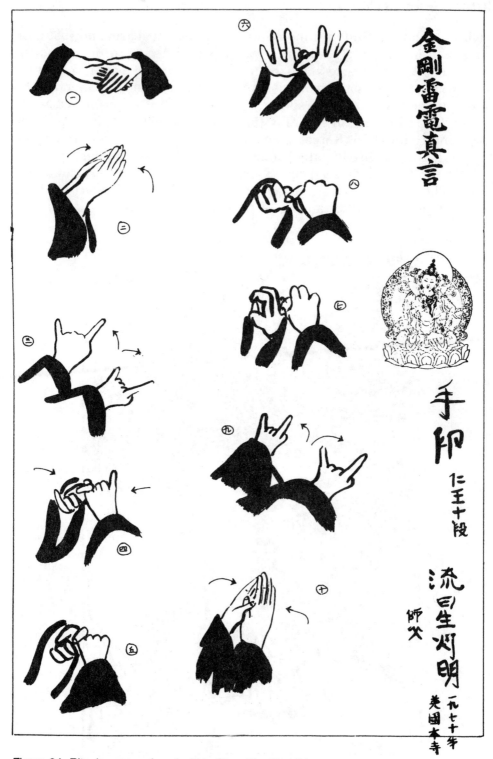

Figure 94. Ritual gestures found within Chen Yen Buddhism.

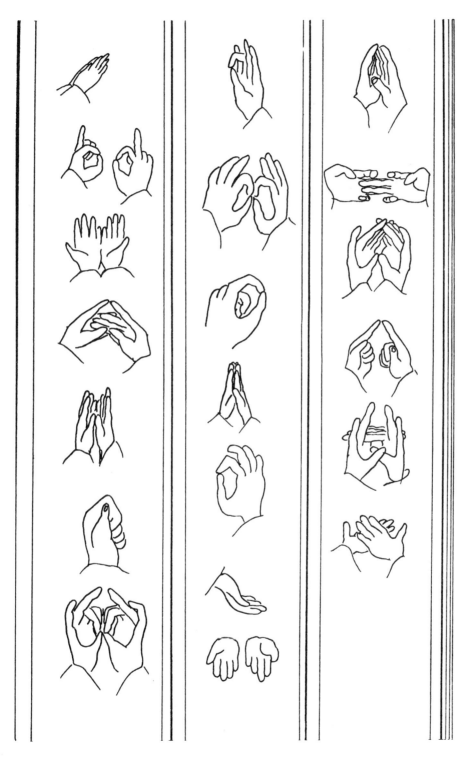

真言宗金剛雷電派

Figure 95. Ritual gestures found within Chen Yen Buddhism.

CONCEALMENT, RINGS AND JEWELRY

Hiding your hands from view in various ways is significant, as it is a gestural pattern that indicates the wish to remain mentally undiscovered. This is especially cogent in Occidental nations due to their ignorance of cheirological principle. Wringing of the hands—and all gestures akin to it—is recognized by Shakespeare and psychoanalysts alike as aberrant activities.

Rings are also notable. Often, we unconsciously feel an insufficiency in our balance, and try to give strength to the digit governing the particular area of imbalance by wearing a ring. This is a form of reinforcement of the water level phalange energy. Though much of the meaning of fire digit rings is now cheirologically insignificant due to the European marriage custom, one still sees that the ring worn on that finger is of the metal sacred to its ruling deity (gold). Even with our modern ideas regarding religion, the sacred tryst of Apollo (the ruler of the Sun's fire) is maintained! Few people realize why they wear rings on specific fingers. You invariably hear the excuse "it fits better," but the fit usually is really the feeling of the ring being "right" on that particular finger. A ring on any finger indicates a weakness or sensitivity of the phalange bearing it. Air digit rings are often seen on those whose temperament or profession utilizes the basic air energies. Henry VIII and Elizabeth I wore rings on their thumbs and forefingers. An examination of the portraits of eminent persons can reveal much information about them via their rings. Generally the larger the ring the more keenly an insufficiency is felt. Ancient races often wore rings in religious rites, but only for the duration of that rite. They were not used as decorations subsequent to the rite.

The metals associated with the various elements also indicate special orientation of their wearers, whether they be worn directly as rings, bracelets (which show total psychological influence) or jewelry. Here are some examples:

Earth is indicated by copper, iron, wood or clay on square shaped ornaments.

Water by silver or translucent stones or circular shaped ornaments.

Fire by gold, rubies or square or pointed shaped ornaments.

Air by transparent stones, glass or very small decorative jewelry and perfumes.

Energy is associated only with diamonds.

The general elemental significance of jewelry is also significant:

Rings encircle a finger to reveal a wish to completely surround or filter a particular type of elemental consciousness.

Bracelets encircle a wrist and show the desire to modify the whole physical and mental balance. The more permanent this desire the heavier or higher (an armlet) the adornment.

Necklaces encircle the neck and thus filter the consciousness at its general source. Headbands actually encircle the symbolic higher consciousness (the third eye), albeit subliminally.

In Oriental countries, particularly those which approve the doctrine of physical energy circulation (as for instance is found in China with its Meridian System of Acupuncture or India with its Marma points), jewelry or other adornments are often worn specifically for the purpose of attracting wholesome energy to the areas in which they are placed and is a common practice in Asia still. A modern day Occidental woman may not adorn herself like her Oriental sister but she often wears bright fingernail polish (to emphasize her thoughts?), lipstick (the mouth is ruled by water—emotions), and eye shadow (the eyes are ruled by fire-personal projection).

Of course there is a rational explanation of all these practices: it is for beauty. But we must remember that in most ancient countries beauty was a deity and make-up was used by priestesses for magical and energic purposed first and foremost. Beauty was inseparable from spirituality. It is only our modern day civilization which has separated the two. If we consider the inverse gestures or concealments of the above features, we have a picture of an individual who even by today's standards would seem strange if not neurotic. They would have eyes closed or lowered gaze, lowered head, fingers clenched into palms, bare lips and eyelids, no perfume, scents or adornments. The picture is one of psychological inversion. This aspect of preconsultative subject-analysis is a large one and merits some consideration, even though it is not directly related to the hands. The whole physio/psychological element balance is reflected by the holistic observation of the cheirologist.

CHAPTER 18

Sexuality Within the Hand

This subject always arouses a great deal of interest! But this chapter is not about sex but *sexuality*—which is somewhat different. Sexuality is a very difficult theme to departmentalize, as every person is different. At best we can only generalize when describing its many facets within people; at the worst, we can be inaccurate. Our own personal viewpoint on sexuality may be very different from those of others. We are also faced with the dual problem of not only describing a person's current experience of his or her sexuality but also of conveying something of its source and effect when often the person will not openly acknowledge the validity of what you are saying!

You must allow plenty of leeway in sexual interpretations and allow a subject to adjust his or her own ideas, at his or her own rate, as you progress in your analysis. At the very best, the factors you see are accurate, but you also have to relate and translate this personal accuracy into terms of the subject's experience so that he or she can utilize this information in a positive and creative manner. Interpretation and analysis should always be given in this manner, to aid and to develop the subject's inner perception.

As you analyze, you are sometimes working from very minute data, picking up a thread here, a thread there, and weaving them into some sort of recognizable fabric. Subtle factors can easily be overlooked and misinterpreted by the not-too-careful analyst. The manner in which you weave the fabric can alter the apparent pattern of each individual greatly. A small mistake here, a factor overlooked there, can result in building up a completely unrealistic picture—bearing in mind of course that a realistic picture is not always one that the subject will acknowledge.

You also have to take into account the culture of the person being analyzed. Ideas and concepts of sexuality vary considerably around the world, and you must take care to bear in mind the various viewpoints accepted in the native country of the subject, his or her age, education and religion. Each of these have some bearing on your subject's awareness and understanding of sexuality.

Sexuality itself can be described as the sum total of those characteristics which distinguish male and female organisms. There is a distinction between structural, physiological and functional sexuality. The dictionary explanation gives us a vague and somewhat general clinical definition and indicates only the area in which we are dealing, rather than something about its actual nature. We cannot define sexuality but we can give some general points which are, or were, relevant to the attitudes possessed by a subject at the time of interpretation.

By integrating findings with often scant traditions regarding sexuality in cheirology we can produce a blend of old and new data, which serves as a preliminary step on the road to knowledge. We can also see that certain archaic teachings concerning sexuality have to be laid aside. Elementally, the field of sexuality as such is ruled primarily by the earth and water elements. There are also many other factors to consider besides elemental balance, but at the onset you have to consider the quality of these elements in the subject's hand. Things like the amount of lineal formations within the hands reveal the kind of energy possessed by the subject. However, in the beginning, you must observe the earth and water quadranture and see if a natural balance of the two is present. You should also observe the major water line. In the days of ancient Greece—and even prior to that—people believed that this line related to love. They also believed that the minor fire line revealed the presence of Apollo's favor. Hence the pre-Christian saying of "cross my heart," which indicated, among other things, that the two lines of fire and water were present, thus showing the mundane and spiritual favor of Apollo in matters of affection or fortune. This also had a negative indication in that it implied that love was pre-destined. This sometimes meant that the person one loved was not the same person the gods had chosen. Thus there would be some disappointment in the fulfillment of one's ideal. One was then "crossed in love".

Modern civilization has brought with it a degeneration of moral life patterns and ambivalent sexual activity. Accordingly, the field of sexuality has progressed or rather, raced towards, the elements of fire and air. This change has great significance as it reveals the nature and power of prevalent neurosis regarding sexuality in its various forms of manifestation. Instead of the basic, natural expression of sexuality, we have a complex interchange occurring which serves to confuse and distract our energy. These days we cannot properly understand our sexuality in terms of the earth and water energies. Fire and air represent our attitude, disposition and non-physical views of sexuality; they describe various roles and functions rather than its nature.

Because the natural function of sexuality exists free of complexity, the very fact that we are a part of a civilization serves to confuse inner awareness about it. Fire and air can disturb and confound our idea of who and what others are; we do not know how to relate either to ourselves or others. This relational factor will manifest most clearly within personal sexuality.

Instead of developing a simple base of dual polarities, civilized life necessitates four polarities and enlarges the potential panorama to 180 degrees. People then feel they have to create a method for dealing with their confusion. They often project this onto others and resort to the fire and air elements in order to do this. Thus we see the slow but certain development of dualistic attitudes—the public and the private—which divorces us from real and harmonious feeling.

Fire and air are very active; they are always busy doing something. Therefore the dividing lines between what is really felt, and what must be presented to the outside world, often become less and less clear. In the end we don't even know where to begin to look. Confusion is the result and the beginning of neurotic sexuality.

In general, we can say that the four elements represent four possible polarities of sexuality, four types of extreme viewpoint along with all the intermediary exchange that such an experience produces. They form the common ground of present day sexuality, which unfortunately serves more to separate people than to bring them together and develop real communication. With elemental disharmony, people feel the need to justify what they do because they feel their attitudes will be called into question. Instead of responding to such needs in an earth or water element manner, they use fire and air. Guilt is the result.

Religious influence also plays a great part in this development, for most European religious systems are classified under fire and air elements. The mind says one thing, the physical body says another. This is the war of the elements, the battle of the gods. They also manifest in the fields of social endeavor and political ideology. Elements describe this interchange and mutual dependence accurately and clearly in a manner that can be understood and used by the cheirological practitioner.

The fire element is dynamic and active; it functions best alone. But when confronted with the other elements (especially water) it either consumes or is itself consumed. We can see that fire represents the patriarchal attitude towards life. Water represents the primordial matriarchy—it is the mystical and the unseen. Fire is obvious; it is heavily structured. Water sexuality is an inductive perception of the physiological responses and is best described by its own and earth lines. These two describe the physiological face taken by sexuality. Malformation of these two indicates that their energies are not being channeled correctly, that imbalance is both present and activated. In the major earth line you may discern physical malformation and organic deficiencies of one type or another. Through the major water line you may see whether this deficiency has been projected into relationships. The earth line also shows sexual physiology and the form of the person's body itself. It describes its energy potential. The major water line shows how much of this vital energy is being channeled into emotional fields of activity and the power of reproduction. In men the earth line serves to describe potency; in women it shows fertility.

The balance between these two is one of the first things to note in the initial observation of the cheirogrammeognomical structure of the subject. After this, examine the lesser lines—they reveal the particular manner in which imbalance will present itself to the subject and to the outside world, the image he or she will create to hide imbalance. Observe the earth and water mounts. The earth mount is important because it is also a seat of vitality and virility. A deformed, deficient or rayed earth mount is a deviation; it shows something is missing or misused in some manner, the vitality is not functioning as it should. On a woman the water mount serves this purpose. With the presence of malformation, suspect infertility or some problem connected with birth or conception in general.

Always see malformed water and earth lines in terms of reproduction and confirm this by examining the mounts. The earth and water mounts describe the type of sexuality possessed by the subject, be it feminine or masculine. If you find their powers reversed—a feminine mount strongly formed on a masculine hand or vice versa—you will know that imbalance is present and active. Coloring, of course, will give some idea of the intensity. Compare the earth mount with earth line and the moon mount with the water line. These should be equally strong in all cases. These two balances are reflections within the field of sexuality, showing the degree of communication present within the subject's psychology and body. All fire element characteristics in a woman's hand will show a repressed natural sexuality. Water elements in a man's hand also show repression. By balancing the strengths of mount and line, you can determine the manner in which a person both really understands his or her own sexuality and presents it to others. Strong fire in a woman's hand also suggests imbalance in the mechanism regulating bodily heat and digestion. Strong water in a man's hand suggests nervous weakness and excretory problems. Always look for physical malformation in cases of imbalance. Balance the strong with the weak, the active with the passive. A little deviation is natural, but a large deviation is not. It shows a reorientation away from that which should be natural to the subject, a turning back from the natural function and the adoption of an attitude which is both perpetuating and condoning of an unnatural energy imbalance.

The actual strength of the lines, their depth, coloring and terminative form, must also be considered. When the lines are weak there is insufficiency in some manner, when too strong, overactivity. Because these factors describe an inter-relationship between body and mind we can see in them the seeds for a particular orientation within a person. Personal choice or preferences are already developing from actual physiological imbalance, and can be seen from the lineal malformations. In the case of children's hands this is important to observe. An over-dominant mother will produce a correspondent weakness within her male children, and vice versa in the case of females.

Orientations towards other mounts should be observed, as should bars, crosses, etc., in the lines. In fact you must take into account everything that describes an interruption of vital energy. Grilled mounts show hypersensitivity and thus incipient neurosis. Those who are strongly opinionated regarding sexuality always have a grilled earth or water mount. Look for this yourself in your studies of hands. Many lines in general are a sign that there is too much energy. There is an overflow out into the palm surface, a discharge of some type. The elements are balancing each other out and the surfeit of lines shows how they do it. Such lines show the discharges created by mounts in order to maintain their innate balance and interharmony. To a degree this takes place all the time; however, if a particular energy gets put out of control, a sudden and sharp deviation or alteration will be observed. This is especially so in cases of emotional shock. These lines are like scars of past events; they reveal an imbalance that has taken place. Future imbalances are only suggested. These are found mainly by balancing inter-relationships, in terms of quantity and quality, during analysis.

There are two main conductors created in the hand in cases of imbalanced sexuality. These are the upper and lower minor water lines. Each works on a different level but both are *natural* in presence. Other formations always mean an additional imbalance besides that which should be discharged by these two lines.

Excessive discharge via lines is often observed on air mounts, especially in the case of dominant relationships. The air mount and air finger are highly significant in sexuality as air rules the impulse to communicate, to create, and to share experiences. In this case air can be viewed within the field of sexuality as an important functioning unit indicating *mode* of conduct with others. Sex is communication, and thus Mercury also tells us something about the nature of the sexuality mode and the level maintained. The air type of communication always includes sexuality. You must observe the air finger closely to see which phalange predominates. Does the person prefer the mental, literal (higher phalange), physical (lowest phalange) or even financial aspect of sexual communication (middle phalange)?

You should pay close attention to malformations of the finger itself as well as leans, bends, or twists. All these alter the manner in which the finger is held relative to the rest of the hand. A lean outwards reveals a more exhibitionistic nature, a lean inwards shows containment and secrecy. Bending inwards towards the palm increases the concept of gain from relationships, bending upwards shows the inability to control one's body, feelings and nervous energies. The air digit clearly describes the type of sexual sensitivity possessed by the subject and thus a malformed or over–large digit shows that the mind bears the additional weight of not only interpreting its own overactive sense impressions but that an increased awareness of the process of balance itself is present. All this serves to confuse or inhibit self communication. The bad air type rest within his lowest features; the good strives to transcend them continually. Mental sexuality, physical sexuality and the interchange between the two are all revealed in the air digit.

In general the hyper air person develops an increased sense of his or her own body; he or she is the person who feels the cold and hot most quickly. There is a direct relationship between mental and external physical phenomena which cannot be separated at will. The individual with a badly rayed or malformed air digit or mount cannot bear the have people too physically close. They are fussy about cleanliness and clothing. Malformations in the lower parts of the finger often show genetic weakness—mongolism, sterility, imbecilism, etc.

Inhibition is another important factor in sexuality that can be seen from an inspection of the major air and water line formations. If much connected they suggest inhibition. If tied around early childhood, suspect a fixation on a parent, home or social situation, hence an unfree consciousness to the world at large. A narrow space between these shows inhibition in expression, a fear of change or deviancy.

The early life period is highly significant in discovering the subject's sexuality; always observe this early part of the life on all major lines. Family inhibitions will direct the child's interest into specific fields and, at a later date, even describe the particular type of sexual deviancy he or she may adopt in order to overcome the feelings experienced as a child. When the air line is tied to the earth line always suspect a strong and active family attitude towards life. It has been strong enough to inhibit or direct the individual growth of the subject's consciousness for a number of years. The molding of consciousness always includes some form of morality. Other things, such as the thumb held close, or a general weakness of the lines in themselves, often describe early inhibitions developed by or through restrictive family environment. If the impressionability is still being maintained by the subject in later life, he or she will have great difficulty in expressing feelings and therefore some type of social contact should be advised by the analyst as a therapy. Any and everthing that encourages self expression and freedom from stress should be pursued.

CHAPTER 19

Elemental Healing and Diagnosis Through Shape

Possibly the greatest contribution cheirology made to Buddhist medicine was its system of diagnosis. In itself this is, of course, only a system of medicine that enables a healer to determine the possible causes of the condition he or she encounters in patients. After alleviating unpleasant symptoms—the first duty of all doctors—the next step is to trace the cause so as to prevent or inhibit future illness. Chinese medicine in general uses a vast panorama of different healing techniques, principles and methods to describe health disorders. It is important to note that the system of Chinese medicine most widely known in the West is based upon the Taoist system of elemental diagnosis and not the Buddhist. In this folk Taoist system, what are termed elements are not actually elements as we use them, but rather descriptions of activities attributed to bodily processes in general. It is impossible therefore to coordinate the elemental indications of the Buddhist and Taoist systems as they do not refer to the same thing. The Buddhist cheirological elements are understood as representing actual physical entities present within the body as well as accounts of their subtle interactions at other levels of existence. Therefore, in cheirology, we begin by understanding that the body and mind exist at five distinct strata, and that these strata include physiological and psychological forces relating to health.

In common with Taoism, cheirology views illness not as a distinct entity with specific causes, but as a condition of impaired interaction existing at that time. The healer's task is to stabilize the condition and aid the body to heal itself efficiently. This involves natural medicine, physical manipulations or movements, psychological harmonizations and, in the case of Buddhism, prayers and meditations of various kinds. Cheirology as an art stresses the importance of diagnostic skill and sees this as the means from which preventative healing grows. By understanding the causes of disorder we can regulate our life patterns to avoid these. One day healing may be an unnecessary art!

Monastic healing traditions also point out that the Buddha taught that only by understanding the mind fully could we truly understand the nature and genesis of illness. The Buddha's personal doctor, Jivaka, utilized the physical elemental system of diagnosis and treatment in parallel to the meditational systems of Buddhism. The Buddha taught that we primarily experience ourselves via the six senses. (*Mind* is considered a sense in Buddhism.) If we look at these sensorial experiences we can see that they are based primarily on the five organs through which we obtain basic experiences. We can apply the elemental activities to these five and develop a list of common disorders. First we must consider the elements as general principles of activity and then as sources of specific disorder.

ELEMENTAL PHYSICAL RULERSHIPS

Elements portray organic activity at the five physiological levels. Generally any malfunction of the body can be traced to either an organ (or organs) acting incorrectly and/or a level of the organ's elemental function not being performed properly. We can summarize the functions of the levels as follows:

Earth: This level relates to the presence of an organ, its physiological activity and quality; chemical and sensorial response mechanisms of balance necessary for basic functioning.

Water: Symbolizes factors of receptivity, coordinative organic systems (particularly of the liquid systems—blood and lymph).

Fire: Relates to the responsive actions, muscular condition and reflexes, immunological processes and protective functions of the body in general.

Air: Is our recognitive faculty, neural stimuli and responses; metabolic patterns and initiators.

Ether: Symbolizes innate energy. In Chinese medicine this refers to the harmonious flow of energy (chi), which acts as activator, sedative or coordinator of the organs. This category also includes spiritual possession and its therapy, exorcism, as well as carcinogenic conditions. These latter are considered to involve every element present.

These rulerships are associated with various features of the body both in ideal rulership and their actions within the body (these are often intricately complex). These two features are analyzed by examination of the hand shape and lineal balance. Shape tells us more about constitutional balances, lines tell us something of the body's *use* and action (although in some cases both are used for each line of inquiry). All cheirological health examinations occur within the framework of graduated materiality. A summary of elemental factors are shown in Table 26, whereas Table 27 on page 305 shows us distinctive personal characteristics common to either an excess or deficit of elemental energies.

Table 26. Elemental Diagnosis

Element	Rulership	Cheirological Feature	External Diagnosis
Earth	Skeletal system Nails, hair, teeth Cartilage Bone marrow, minerals, vitamins Solid organs	Major and minor earth lines Palmar mounts Hand element shape Nails, hair color of hands Skin texture	Structure, balance, posture of body Condition of nails, hair and teeth Food preferences Relationships at home, work, hobbies Dreams of mountains, large objects, animals
Water	Synovial fluid Circulatory valves and tissue Blood mineral distribution Lymph Blood Plasma Pleura	Major and minor water lines Skin texture, mount quality Flexibility of joints	Emotional relationships to people and environment Spiritual path as an experiential endeavor Flexibility of body Hobbies (art, dance, writing) Dreams of sea, fish, desert, clouds, being lost Pastel colors and shapes, enemies, flowers
Fire	Red blood cells Muscles and sinews Skin and sense organs Soft tissues Hollow organs and tissues Nerve fibers	Major and minor fire lines Hand musculature Nail moon size and quality Skin coloring Depth of lineal formations	Physical strength Movement pattern Muscle and flesh tone Body temperature Dreams of violence, pain, machines, heat Vivid colors, especially red

Table 26. Elemental Diagnosis (*continued*)

Element	Rulership	Cheirological Feature	External Diagnosis
Air	White blood cells Neural impulses, action and quality Endocrinal secretions and actions Environmental energy responses Energy meridians Mind (basic consciousness)	Major and minor air lines Subsidiary lines of hyper- and hypo-function Hand gesture and movement pattern Skin color and texture	Repiration, depth, rate and quality Body odor Voice tone and vocabulary Subject's ideals, wishes and opinions Dreams of light colors, music, buildings, promotion, rivalry and meeting famous people
Ether	Holistic physical activities Spiritual awareness and consciousness	Size, shape and angle of thumb (basic indications only) Harmonious interactive quality of shape and lines of both hands	

Table 27. Symptoms of External Elemental Imbalance in Health

Element	General Symptoms	Element Deficiency	Element Excess
Earth	Lassitude, dull pains, infection, low or gruff voice	Increased hunger, grooved nails	Lack of appetite, dull or greasy hair, slow movements
Water	Fear of change, dull and moving pain, swelling, low or soft voice	Increased thirst, desire for fruit or vegetables, rapid body temperature changes	Excessive sweating/crying, depression and emotional stress, long hair, overweight, desire to travel
Fire	Muscle contraction, sharp pains, excess anger, loud voice, inflammation	Desire for salty/strong tasting foods, stomach ache, increased desire to read, lack of energy, desire for milk or meat	Muscle aches, curly hair, dislike of study/education, high body temperature, desire for alcohol
Air	Tingling pains, stress/ fainting, loss of memory, high pitched voice	Desire for sweets, acne and skin rashes, hyperactivity	Desire for companions/ groups, back pains, insomnia, sight defects

PHYSIOLOGY OF THE HAND

We can see in figure 96 that the circulatory system of the hand corresponds closely with the division of the palm into two vertical sections—one ruling the conscious life and the other the unconscious life. The radial artery (thumb side) is found within the conscious side, the ulnar artery (air finger side) within the unconscious. The neural placements also follow this division, which suggests two distinct manners in which the brain receives sense

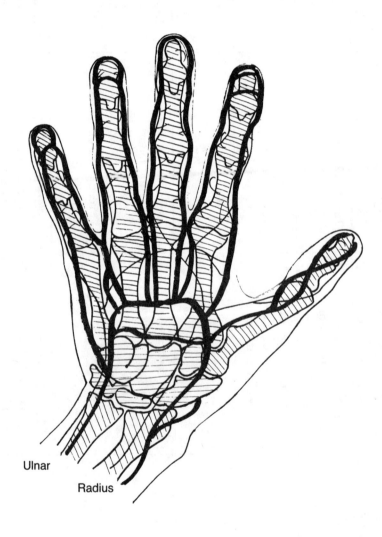

Ulnar

Radius

Figure 96. The physiology of the hand. The heavy lines trace the radial and ulnar blood vessels, and the finer lines the radial and ulnar nerves.

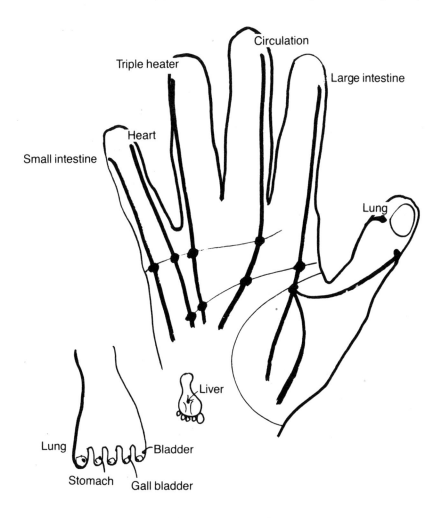

Figure 97. Acupuncture points, meridians and palm lines. The arrows denote entry or exit of energies.

data from the palmar surface. You will note a conglomeration of vessels at each fingertip. In the case of thumb, this is elongated. This suggests that the thumb receives a different form of tactile impression than do the fingertips.

There are, of course, more minor blood vessels than are shown in the diagram. Our purpose here is merely to survey the major ones. Pay attention to the cross-connections—note the linkage between conscious and unconsious vessels. These take place, cheirologically speaking, in the center of the palm and are notably absent at its basal area. The lower fire quadrant reveals four major linkages of circulatory vessels and must therefore form an area of the hand directly indicative of total circulatory power. Each of the phalanges has a double vessel system and is linked to the others by a cross vessel high on the palm—approximately in the area of the air line.

Table 28. Disorders of the Senses at Different Elemental Levels

Organ	Elemental Level	Disorder
Eye	Earth	Congenital absence of organ and/or deficiencies within it.
	Water	Insufficient blood or lubricants.
	Fire	Mucle weakness. Fertility. Inflammations.
	Air	Neural insufficiency. Lens malfunctions, etc.
Nose	Earth	Absence or congenital malformations.
	Water	Inflammatory irritations. Colds.
	Fire	Sinusitis, polyp formations.
	Air	Blockages, impaired sense of smell.
Tongue (Mouth)	Earth	Absence, malformation (i.e., harelips, etc.). Dietary abberations. Teeth or gum conditions.
	Water	Lack of saliva, excessive intake of sugar, food builk (in general), liquids and meats.
	Fire	Excessive salivation, paralysis of mouth, neuralgia. Gum inflammation.
	Air	Degenerative paralysis, inability to taste or discriminate dietary intake properly. Congenital holes in organs of mouth.
Ear	Earth	Absence, malformation or excessive size. Inner ear bone conditions. Excessive wax, lack of balance (Cochlea insufficiencies).
	Water	Eustachian tube blockages.
	Fire	Inflammations and aches of all types.
	Air	Deafness, neural insufficiencies, hearing distortions, etc.
Body	Earth	All solid organs, i.e., teeth, hair, nails, minerals and chemicals of body. Food intake.
	Water	Liquid systems (blood, lymph, urine, etc.)
	Fire	Muscle actions of all type — growth rates and fertility, immune systems and renewal processes.
	Air	Neural and respiratory activity. Hollow organs, metabolic ordering, hormal balance. Basic mind-body interactions.

The digital mounts themselves seem served only by peripheral vessels, which is interesting and suggests that their use is not directly linked with reception of sensory data (physiologically speaking) or thought processors (cheirologically speaking). The nervous system follows circulation except that the ulnar nerve crossing under the fire line links with water area and air directly. Branches link the other phalanges. Two major crossovers may be seen on the earth and water mounts. The upper connection of the ulnar nerve to water follows the approximate path of the water line.

The two most distinctive lineal correlations occur with the ulnar nerve and artery, following the minor air line closely. The radial artery and nerve follow the minor earth line closely. It is perhaps significant that the earth line does not have a correlation either arterially or neurally. Figure 97 on page 307 shows us the points of entry or exit of the body's energy (chi) according to traditional Taoist medicine. The rulerships of these flows (*meridians*) is somewhat different from that propounded in old-fashioned cheirology. However, if you think in terms of principle, there is some connection. You must not forget that Oriental and Occidental lifestyles require very different viewpoints, and that the hand rulerships show this accordingly.

Arrows show the originating or departure point of chi. A very interesting feature is shown by the large dots. These represent acupuncture points. When superimposed with the palmar lines we can see that at each point where the chi meridian crosses a line, a treatment point is found. This suggests that lineation is also a form of energy flow—or represents the same at the physiological level. Table 28 shows how physical disorders manifest at the different elemental levels. The diagnostic table shows areas of the skin upon which one commonly finds lineal disorders relating to the organs described. This should not be confused with other charts showing elemental organic rulership—which is quite different.

CHAPTER 20

The Structure of Consciousness in Buddhist Cheirology

The patterns of the human hand describe the distinctive expressions and experiences of humanity. We understand these patterns only within our individual capacity to perceive patterns at all. Such perception is both human—relative to the human world of experience and communication—and suprahuman—relative to the spiritual or transcendental reality. In ancient European monastic traditions, spiritual understanding and reality were considered as existing at three significant levels:

Cognition: thinking on a special theme or subject.

Meditation: becoming absorbed in the theme and suspending ordinary states of cognition.

Contemplation: includes cognition and meditation, but with greater loss of personal identity through absorption in the theme or subject.

The distinctive feature of this descriptive system is the degree of personal identity loss. As the ordinary personal consciousness is by-passed, the higher the spiritual—or Divine Consciousness—is developed.

Unfortunately, early Christianity lacked a long and thorough understanding of the nature of consciousness. Unlike Oriental schools—which had extensive experience and descriptions of meditative states—European monastics sought to interpret their experience within a simple dualistic teaching of good and evil. This was a distinctive feature of the European dogmatists. While some of the early Christian mystics who lived in Syria and Egypt had experiences of a similar nature to Hindu, Buddhist, Manichean, Zoroastrian and Islamic mystics, their terminology to either describe such experiences or explicate their significance was severely limited. Through no fault of their own, nor from lack of capability, they were impressed to describe their realizations in simple, ecclesiastical and dogmatic formats designed more for mass appeal than veracity. One may, of course, find rare occurrences of terms of an exalted, multi-denominational nature in their expressions; indeed the use of such an exalted and mystical language as Greek itself would guarantee this. But the writer's inferences in such terms are lost to the modern student of universal truths.

The Christian monastic understanding of *contemplation* corresponds very closely with the Sanskrit term *Samadhi* (non-differentiation), and has much the same implication. While Samadhi in Hinduism is regarded as the summit of meditative achievement, in Buddhism it is regarded as the beginning. The reason for this is that Buddhism has a vastly different understanding of the nature of the self and generally does not regard it as something to blend with another or greater self, nor as something to pass beyond, wherever that may mean. Instead it teaches that the nature of self-hood itself is illusory and that the journey towards total enlightenment con-sists not merely of overcoming but more pointedly, *not creating* this self. Although seemingly small, this distinction is in fact great, and results in a totally different understanding of the nature of wisdom.

The approach of Buddhism towards what I will term wisdom accumu-lation gave birth to widely divergent forms of practice and training in the countries to which its teachings spread. Horticulture, painting, dance, poetry, architecture, martial arts and many other seemingly contradictory practices were drawn into or created by its universal teachings. In Buddhist countries the arts associated with prognostication were also subjected to its exalted philosophy and purged of superstitious teachings. The resulting systems were vitalized, spiritually orientated and expressed in the classical Buddhist Sanskrit and Chinese languages. Both languages had similar potentials to the mystical Greek and because of this it is easy to find mutu-ally approximate translations of key terms.

Ordinary language however, is not the only (or always the best) form of communication. It is this last factor which is important. If language fails to communicate it fails completely. This is not, however, an excuse to sim-plify language into inaccuracies which do not truly represent or convey the real meaning or import of what is being communicated. Obscurity is almost as bad as inaccuracy. In order to understand the deep teachings inherent in such an art as cheirology, you must familiarize yourself with a vocabulary that does truly represent those levels or descriptions of consciousness you seek to understand. The more clearly you can describe that which you understand, the more you can develop true communication. In advising your client, appropriateness is important. You must have at your command a wide resource of available terms, even if you are called upon only to use a very narrow portion of them.

Many modern usages of language are misunderstood or even deliber-ately created to obscure precision and clarity. Ancient teachers took great care in their language and because of this they were able to describe and preserve teachings accurately for several thousands of years. We have yet to emulate them. Many modern philosophers have created language forms which have only taken them beyond the comprehension of the average per-son. As a consequence, the philosopher has ceased to have any significance to the lay person. Conversely, the ordinary person cannot describe his or her own nature in terms which are either accurate or comprehensive. Self deception or alienation are the results of this, and in turn many of societies' problems directly stem from such inarticulacy. When we begin to study cheirology we become aware that the problems of language are approached in a distinctive (and truly oriental) manner which is characterized by a universalism of expression and symbology. Cheirology utilizes a vocabulary based largely on an experiential philosophy of five elements. Such a nomenclature was used in ancient India, China, classical Greece, European alchemy and Nordic mythology. Although the interpretation of the elemental system in Europe tended to be spasmodic and often materialistic, the Orient exhibits a remarkable uniformity in its appropriation of such fundamental metaphysical concepts despite the diverse spiritual or transcendental systems it grew within.

By creating a fundamental point from which to create a measure, the Orient initiated a format which grew and developed with humanity. Because it was based on tangibles, it was ever at hand to those who sought to understand it. Unlike the astrolatrists who saw their existence or casual sources of knowledge outside of this world, the elementalists characterized themselves by an adherence to a micro- and macrocosmic world concept of interpretation in which common everyday components were used as a basis from which to explicate other, non-tangible concepts. By doing so, and observing strictly the principle that the inter-relationship of the tangible and intangible elements responded in identical manners, they innovated a self-corrective feature into their speculative philosophy which has only been equalled (possibly) by modern computer programs.

Elements and their human or spiritual counterparts form an alphabet of experience which is amenable to understanding and interpretation at many levels without mutual contradiction or lack of clarity. This alphabet could be extended to cover all levels of human endeavor and act as a hermeneutical nexus because it reliably and consistently illuminates that which actually creates endeavor—the human consciousness itself. In the Buddhist language of China, simple words such as *water* contain within them not only the noun but also composite and interrelative adjectival qualities. The word for *water* incorporates concepts such as fluidity, softness, all-embracingness, femininity, coolness and fecundity. In such linguistic environments, obtruse and mundane teachings can be readily conveyed and recognized.

What the elemental system seeks to achieve is to place language—at all its levels—within a circumscription enabling possible understandings of other modes of communication to emerge. Confining (or channeling) language to a boundary represented in nature itself insures that the constituent rhythms of human, mineral, animal, vegetable and celestial life are not ignored. Thus, the principle of inner and outer environmental harmony is emphasized. Such a condition or pre-requisite for wisdom stresses the inter-reflectiveness and inseparability of mundane and spiritual wisdom, unbounded by geographical border or custom. Whenever human life was capable of its intimation, understanding is assured. Cheirology expresses one of the significant mundane and metaphysical levels of communication. True, it is encoded, but of a cypher easily understood by those not divorced from universal life.

Hands portray the manner in which the subject understands, and expresses harmony with, the elements. They describe to what degree he or she communicates or interferes with the free flow of elements. Each hand form represents in its features (length, quality, etc.) the particular manner and degree the individual can receive, harmonize and express the quadripartite stratum of existence accessible to human consciousness. Each individual has a panorama (that range of consciousness which is readily cognized and understood), and a spectrum (the whole range potentially accessible to his or her consciousness). The degree of understanding and the quality of experience are determined by the ability to expand personal panorama to meet supra-personal spectrum. Individual features seen thus are really the sum of inaccessible experiences. The Buddha taught that, in penetrating to the true nature of individuality, we would understand the nature of existence itself. Individuality and personality stand in a direct reflexive contrast to universality.

By working within a framework of elements, we can begin to understand the full extent of the disharmony between ourselves and the universe and how this disharmony arises and incessantly proclaims itself. From within these parameters we express our energies towards ourselves (inwardly) or the world at large (outwardly). Cheirology describes and quantifies this inter-communicative faculty as it exists within our natures. An individual's ultimate understanding of his or her real nature of being (Ontology) depends on a correct understanding of the four elemental strata and of the processes involved in extending and inter-relating their mundane and supermundane implications. The necessity for such coalescence arises because individuating consciousness exists only by maintaining a separation between the physical and metaphysical through encouraging a usage of communicatory language or symbol bereft of references to both aspects. Alienation of either (or both) is the first result, an inability to understand oneself the next.

All things within the realm of experience are manifestations of the elements—not only their substances but also the qualities and properties of their being. In order to realize the ramifications of elemental nomenclatures, the ancients developed various forms of meditation. Aware of the fact that all things proceed from consciousness, the sages quite reasonably recognized that it is from that source we should begin and, until we have understood that from which all proceeds, we cannot truly understand anything. Of course we may develop partial understanding or specialized information—but these, as we have seen, are themselves regarded as prime causes of human suffering and alienation. We have to be careful that we don't maintain only those conditions to which we are personally attached and ignore other—perhaps more creative, but feared—endeavors. It is in the silent practice of meditation that we permit ourselves to become aware of mental activity and its four element nature.

Distinctive features of the hands describe the various elemental predominances in our consciousness, those we consciously encourage or not. From these we develop an understanding of individual psychology. Elements are not a form of psychology in the modern sense. To the ancients, of course, psychology meant what it literally and truly means: psyche = spirit/soul, and logos = word—spiritual language or terms. However, we must explore human thought processes in order to explicate elemental hermeneutical teachings.

Each part of the hand represents not simply the ordinary human consciousness but also a form of spiritual and apperceptive consciousness relative to the personality—a form of what could be called "that intuition which lacks dependence upon an intuitor." This apperceptive consciousness is not explicable in ordinary terms since it is not subject to conscious or unconscious controls. It acts as a substratum (or superstratum) to consciousness itself. Apperceptive consciousness is the means through which our ordinary consciousness gains access to and interpretation of the realm of experience and expression beyond that limitation created by elemental disharmony or misunderstanding.[1] It is considered one of the synonyms for the transcendental element ether.[2]

Every major line represents a particularized form of apperceptive consciousness, a form understood within certain exclusive levels. We usually translate such levels into mundane realms, such as physical being, emotional life, technical or practical expertise and intellectual ability. The activities of apperceptive consciousness commence long before we get around to becoming aware of them. The nature of consciousness is relevant to us for we have to realize its constituents in order to refine them. In cheirological terminology they are classified quite simply as earth, water, fire, air and ether consciousness. We can regard these four forms of manifestations as follows:

Earth: Consciousness within and of the physical body. Sometimes called "body wisdom."[3]

---

[1] In ancient Egypt, the activities of apperceptive consciousness were anthropomorphized as the divine being Thoth, in Greece as Hermes, and in Rome as Mercury. The Egyptian god Amun is the non-cognitive form of Thoth. This name, A-mun, means "the hidden or silent one." Compare it with Buddhist title Shakya*muni*, where Shakya means tribal name and Muni means a silent one, i.e, a sage.

[2] Ether is considered also as the consciousness exclusive to spiritual beings and is not coincident with human consciousness in general.

[3] Body wisdom means both *of* (in a physical sense) and *from* the body, i.e., an instinctive semi-divine faculty usually only manifest in times of great physical stress or trauma. Hence the religious nature of the Greek Olympics and Chinese Kempo. Each strived to attain this faculty by mastering the physical arts.

Water: Consciousness which contains concepts such as ego, identity, personality, etc.

Fire: Consciousness of individuation—that which separates us from others.

Air: Abstract consciousness—that which does not interpret itself as either personality or body. Sometimes know as "coconsciousness" or genius.[4]

Ether: Transcendentally orientated consciousness. In cheirology, this is regarded as an unmanifest mode of experience and is not ascribed human qualities as such. We have to therefore disregard this as a practical classification for purposes of analysis and work with the other four elements.

Apperceptive awareness belongs to fire but has to manifest in water to be understood, or translated. It loosely represents what we call intuition. We should not lose sight of the fact that we are dealing here with apperceptive consciousness solely as a category and object of interest. We cannot truly have experience of apperceptions as such.

In earth consciousness, physical sensation predominates and is thus related to the earth element realm. In fire consciousness the sense or concept of differentiation predominates and is therefore in the fire element realm. In water consciousness, the free flowing, non-differentiating and associative principle predominates. It is thus represented as the water element. In air consciousness, the aspiration to understand or to attain knowledge predominates. It thus falls in the realm of the air element.

Each kind of elemental consciousness forms a significant part of human psychology and cannot be omitted without drastic consequences in understanding consciousness. All possible forms of consciousness can be represented in various combinations of the above four cornerstones. When an experience presents itself to consciousness, whatever tendency predominates in it seizes and translates it into some amenable form. It is then subjected and translated to the other levels of elemental consciousness and finally cognitively expressed in its final form. The elemental nomenclature forms a reflex substratum to this process of developing experience. By examining this process we can see the elemental principles in action. (See figure 98.)

---

[4]A genius was originally an actual guardian-like spirit attached to every individual person and to whom one addressed problems of a spiritual or mundane nature. The genius could, if he wished, solve these by breathing on or speaking to the questioner; hence the term "inspiration." Compare with the Arabic *Jin*, the Sanskrit *Jina*, and the Persian *Genii*.

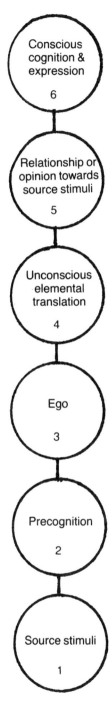

Figure 98. The growth of consciousness from distant and non-cognized stimuli (1) to a fully formed concept (6). If we reverse this order of growth and subject it to elemental comparison we can discern—by contrast—the stages and features of elemental cheirological analysis in action.

SUMMARY OF MAJOR POINTS

1. Apperception is an amorphous, multi-level awareness existing but inaccessible to ordinary consciousness.

2. It is present at all encounters with things/persons/situations.

3. Consciousness awareness, leading to formulation of judgment or limiting description, is a manifestation of apperception translated into the four elemental levels of import. This translation takes place in what could be termed unconscious areas and is always preceded by apperception.

4. The effect of humanized apperception is to render it subject to specific functional levels of ordinary individuated consciousness and thereby to form some workable relationship to it. From this relationship understanding of personal experience is formulated and expressed.

5. Personal experience is interpreted, analyzed and expressed by the four elements as is the nature of personality itself. The four elements describe the limits of our ability to experience and express consciousness.

6. Major lines represent humanized (translated) elemental energies and describe the quality, nature and extent of specific individualized consciousness in the subject.

7. Elements are expressions of the *all* within specific functional areas of conscious activity. The purpose of such expressions is to bring within the cognitive processes of a subject those experiences or impressions normally inaccessible and of relevance to his or her holistic evolution.

Any description of consciousness—which by its very nature is capable of infinite variations—seems a daunting task. Oriental tradition uses several aids to serve this end. Classification of the objects of consciousness alone does not suffice, as subjective preferences do not reveal anything about those objects. However, the spiritual tradition from within which elemental concepts arise uses the various general modes of consciousness itself as a basis from which to typify its various constituent aspects. These modes refer to both subjective and objective patterns, together with a pattern of associative mental events involved in each. From such a base we can begin to familiarize ourselves with the *feel* of consciousness.

It is very important to be able to recognize and identify consciousness fully and such recognition should not be regarded solely as either religious or psychological dogma. The Buddhist tradition is a very unique corpus of teachings based directly on personal experience. It also defies classification as an -ism or -ology, for it maintains teachings which do not fit into any other religious vocabulary. In other words, it is not theistic but does not deny theism; it is equally metaphysical–existential and practical. Westerners are quite unused to the panorama of mental and spiritual life presented by it, but such teachings, cutting as they do through mystery, dogma and authoritarianism, are much needed by the modern person. Any person who has every wondered "who am I", "what does the universe mean"? will find, after exhausting gurus and psychological systems, that the Buddhist teaching fills the gaps the other cannot. The answers to such questions are arrived at more easily if we have a vocabulary to use for this purpose. Self clarity is required if we want to aid others. It is not enough to describe their problems—we need to understand their constituent causal forces. Tradition points out that we all need to understand ourselves before we can understand others.

The nature of consciousness is represented by the five elements of earth, water, fire, air and ether. In Buddhist tradition these represent physical form, feelings, cognitive activities, mental volition and human consciousness respectively. Only a human being possesses all five and these constituents form the basis from which identity and personality develop. In Chinese Buddhism the five are described as follows:

Physical form is described as being based on the subjective five senses and their objective results: eye (sight); ear (sound); nose (odor); tongue (taste); body (touch); and mind, which is imperceptible form. Moreover, these are related to the five elements in the following way: eye relates to the element fire, ear and nose to air, tongue to water, body to earth, and the mind relates to ether.

> *Feeling* has three types—pleasant, unpleasant and neutral.

> *Cognitive activity* has two divisions—recollective cognition and absence of such recognition—these are further classified as limited, extensive or unlimited.

> *Volition* has two types—associated or disassociated from consciousness.

> *Consciousness*—in this lies the sum of the previous conditions, all connected in the senses described.

These total to what are called the eighteen elements, producing consciousness (Shi Pa Hsing Hsing). Despite the teaching of ultimate selflessness, we have to deal with consciousness as it is experienced—albeit imperfectly—by the ordinary human. For this reason cheirology attunes itself to the identity and ego as if they were ultimately real or permanent in themselves. Cheirology describes the nature of this self in elemental language, and accords it a provisional reality in order to communicate its imbalances or disorders in ways accessible to the average person. Elements have natural principles or qualities, and reviewing these will help us in our discussion of consciousness. Earth demonstrates the principle of solidarity; water demonstrates the principle of cohesion; fire demonstrates activity; air, extension; and ether is an energizing quality. We then think of each element as being permeated by an energy through the above qualities, and we come up with the following correspondences: earth is conducting; water is circulating; fire is radiating; air is convecting; and ether is generating. We can now consider the following types of elemental consciousness:

Earth consciousness is characterized by its solidarity of intent. It seeks to stabilize and preserve all it comes into contact with. It achieves this in several ways. The following are predominant:

> • Increasing awareness and attachment to the quality of sensorial experience/material objects/natural phenomena.

> • Maximizing the value of constancy, regularity, tradition and radicalism.

> • Increasing attachment to the above by seeking to expand/ increase or readjust ownership and dependency on them.

> • Rejecting, or at least regarding as highly suspicious, intellectual, theoretical or hypothetical mental activities at all levels.

Water consciousness is characterized by its faculty of multi-natured cohesion. It seeks to unite, in non-expressable manners, all forms of experience, actions, persons, emotions and intuitions. Water stresses the universality of experience and from this basis expresses its concomitants at all and every level of physical and mental being.

Fire consciousness is characterized by action being the basis for its evaluation of experiences. It seeks to extend to itself and others all forms of purposeful activity. It does so by stressing the need for order, structure, and schedule and needs to set life goals. To fire, inaction or prevarication is valueless and a prime source of what it views as nihilism. Fire uses intellectual pursuits only as a means of achieving its visualized goals. It is rational in a limited manner, and highly tactical in its outlook to persons, objects or situations.

Air consciousness is characterized by its preoccupation with motives and causal concepts. It seeks to understand or express that which lies beyond the obvious or ordinary. It relies heavily on scientific and conceptual ways of approaching life's experiences. It decries superficiality or generalism and views activity as something that should only take place after due consideration of the principles of intellectual purity involved.

Etheric consciousness is characterized by its unknowability. It is not used in the formation of identity, personality or in any other mundane preoccupation. It is considered transcendental and of use only to those who have passed beyond attachment to this world. Though ether is the synthesis of all elements—and as such under- and overlies all the other manifest elements—it has only a universal context in explanation. Though its condition

Table 29. Summaries of the Consciousness's

Element	Level of Expression	Quality
Earth	Physical mode (earth) Emotional mode (water) Activity mode (fire) Intellectual mode (air)	To manifest To simplify To persevere To preserve
Water	Physical mode (earth) Emotional mode (water) Activity mode (fire) Intellectual mode (air)	To be gentle To share feelings To care for others To share experiences
Fire	Physical mode (earth) Emotional mode (water) Activity mode (fire) Intellectual mode (air)	To refine skills To express in action To achieve goals To refine strategy
Air	Physical mode (earth) Emotional mode (water) Activity mode (fire) Intellectual mode (air)	To be indifferent or objective To be unbiased To acquire knowledge To know in reality

may become an object of aspiration by the other elements, it cannot be understood or realized by incarnate beings. Table 29 provides a quick summary of the elements, their levels of expressions, and consciousness. You should study this table until the relationship of consciousness to element is second nature to you, for this will be a crucial aspect of any cheirological reading.

APPENDIX I

HOW TO TAKE HAND PRINTS

You will need the following equipment, usually available at art supply stores:

Ink Roller
This is used to spread ink onto the base.

Ink (Lino Printing)
Water-based is best as it cleans off easily. Lipstick of a dark color can also be used where no ink is available, providing one takes care not to smudge the imprint.

Base Plate
The ink is spread out on the base plate by rolling the ink until a thin layer is formed. Using the roller, one then transfers this ink to the palms.

Magnifying Glasses
The large one is used in general examination of hand imprints. The smaller one is more powerful and used for close up work or for dermatoglyphic inspections.

Fixative and Spray
Helps prevent imprints smudging or marking themselves. Both can be obtained from art shops where they are used for fixing charcoal drawings, etc.

Pen, Pencil, Ruler
These are used to trace outlines of the hand and to record details of the subject's age.

Ring Binder
An essential and cheap way of storing hand imprints for future study or research.

PROCEDURE

1. Spread the ink smoothly onto the palm, making sure the ink is in equal depth over the palm.

2. Place the hand (allowing it to assume a natural position) onto the paper. Gently press down each digit and the palm to ensure an even pressure.

3. With a pencil, trace the outline of the fingers and palm, taking great care to reproduce the exact shape.

4. Hold the paper so it won't adhere to the hand, and raise the hand from the surface. Take care not to move the hand once the print has been made for this will result in smudging of the finer details of the print.

5. Write down the subject's name, date of birth (or age) and the date you are taking the print. Do not forget to do this.

6. Allow the print to dry in a warm, draft free place. Examine it to see if it is clear. You should be able to discern all the fine details such as fingerprints and palmar dermatoglyphs. If not, take several more prints. Re-ink the hand if the print is not clear enough.

7. When the print has dried, spray fixative over it and allow this to dry completely before storing or handling the imprint again.

8. Now repeat the process with the other hand. If both prints are satisfactory allow your subject to clean his or her hands. It's a good idea to take three or four copies of each hand imprint. One of these copies should be sent to the Cheirological Society's Research Library in Norfolk. If you ever lose your copies of the print the Society can always then supply another.

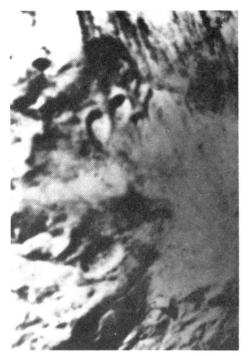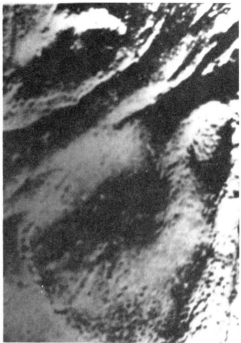

Figure 99. The oldest handprints in the world. Fossilized impressions made by children around 8,000 years ago in the caves of Niaux, France. Photograph from *Secrets of the Ice Age*, by Evan Hadingham; reproduced by permission of William Heinemann, Ltd., London.

SUGGESTED ORDER OF CHEIROMORPHOGNOMICAL OBSERVATION

1. Observe subject's walk and physical form prior to consultation.

2. Observe hand gestures.

3. Note rings, temperature of room, skin color and nail shapes.

4. Examine hand shapes and determine balance of quadrants in each hand.

5. Decide ruling elements of both hands (by hand shape) and note elemental antagonisms of features mentioned in 3 and 4 (if present).

6. Check whether skin texture element corresponds to elements of the above categories.

7. Note mounts and decide their overall quality and influences.

8. Note strengths and weakness of digits as well as spaces, leans, etc.

9. Decide how the elements predominate in body (palm) and mind (fingers)—which have developed and which are natural to the subject.

10. Examine individual digits, noticing straightness, flexibility, dermatoglyphic and phalange quality of each.

11. Observe nails, knuckles and skin on back of hand for weaknesses.

12. Compare the flexibility of each finger and phalanges on both hands.

13. Observe strength or weakness, shape, and setting of both thumbs.

14. Compare again each hand with the other, decide the predominant factors and organize your findings to show clearly the formative and present characteristics utilized by the subject.

APPENDIX II

CHINESE REFERENCE MATERIALS

There are three distinct types of reference material. By far the greatest number of these are compilations of the lore and techniques of famous teachers. These have invariably been re-written or commented on by later teachers, and it is often difficult to distinguish the original materials from later alterations. The second type of source works are manuals written by teachers especially for a select group—their own schools or immediate disciples. These are usually more accurate than the preceding type, but often unobtainable by ordinary means, even to native Chinese researchers. Allied to this difficulty is the fact that many great teachers deliberately refused to commit their knowledge to a literal record. Their disciples' accounts are often the only record we have of their instruction and methods. The last and most rare types of material are accounts or diaries kept by students within which they recorded oral teachings. The Wu Hsing school is almost exclusively of this latter type. Many masters explicitly refused to permit notes to be made of their lectures and students often had to make them in secret. Due to the fact that many Wu Hsing teachings were delivered within the framework of esoteric Buddhism, the rarity of such accounts is increased.

Indirect references to Wu Hsing methods may also be recognized in the literature of esoteric Buddhism in general, particularly its Chinese form (Chen Yen). Compilations of source material are mostly Taoist in nature. Often these are adaptations of Chen-Yen or include their principles. Traces of other teachings, as well as those based upon Buddhist esoterica, can be found within them, particularly those from the 500 to 700 A.D. period.

Both Buddhist and Taoist shamans show a tendency to add or update ancient findings in the light of their contemporary experience. Unfortunately, where an original teaching of esoteric importance has not been properly understood, it was often omitted as irrelevant from an otherwise consistent account of teachings and principles.

You should keep in mind that much of what we now term Taoism was in fact the property of the Chinese court elite, and does not reflect or reveal the general beliefs or practices of the populace at large. With the Chinese agricultural classes—who were by far the predominant strata of society—the most common means of mantikal reference lie in what we now term the shaman or wonder workers. These shamans are found in both Buddhist and Taoist source materials and were commonly called *Wu* or *Yin Yang masters*. Later historians have tended to ascribe to these all the prevalent or literally extant knowledge of their age and thus create an image of a teacher following a specific method or pattern. In the case of the Taoist this was not so. More often than not, it was the Wu who utilized the phraseology of

Figure 100. A 16th century Chinese diagram of auspicious palmar markings.

the court elite for their own prestige. Also relevant is the fact that many Wu had traditions of their own, which were not necessarily compatible with general Taoist teaching. Many Wu combined Buddhist, Taoist, local and foreign (i.e., Indian) teachings in their repertoire of arts. The teachings of the Wu were oral and usually only found in actual schools they formed and which faithfully carry on the pristine tradition nowadays. In the islands of Ryukyu which lie above Taiwan, the native Wu are called *Yu-Ta* and they coexist with their female counterparts, *No Ro*. In Ryukyu the No Ro are held to have greater power than their male equivalents. Japanese invading forces also termed the native Shaman *On-Mio Sha*, meaning "practitioner of the hidden light," or *In Yo Sha*, meaning "practitioner of yin yang techniques." Both these names are inaccurate because they are based on terms used in Japan for people practicing a native form of shamanism quite unlike the Ryukyuan or Chinese originals.

From the European students' point of view, Chinese sources are in the main inaccessible. The only places usually possessing copies of relevant texts are university libraries of Oriental faculties. If access can be gained to these, the works listed here are of most relevance and interest. Of course works containing local traditions or special studies are unlikely to be found even in the best libraries without much research.

Bibliography

The following texts contain significant cheirological principles:

Chinese

Chou-I (the *I Ching*). Wen and others, circa 12th century B.C. This work contains records of the earliest Chinese adaptions of the Indian elements and precedes the Taoist systems of wood, metal, earth, fire and water.

Ku Chin T'u Shu Cheng, by Ch'en Meng Lei, circa 1728.

Hsiang Fa Ju Men, by Lu Tung Pin, circa Tang Dynasty.

Hsiang Wu Te Plei Wu Hsiang, by Kuo Lin Tsung, circa late Han Dynasty, This is in manuscript form.

Ma-I Shen Hsiang, by Ch'en Tuan, circa 10th century A.D.

Shang Shu Shu-Ching, various contributors, traditionally dated around 2000 B.C.

Shen Hsiang Hui Pien, by Kao Wei Chang (1821-1851).

Shen Hsing Ch'uan Pien. Chang (1376-1458) version.

Shi Pa Lo Han Shu Ching, by Ta Mo, circa 6th century A.D. This is in manuscript form.

Sun Tzu Ping Fa, by San Tzu, 5th century B.C. (This author is a military tactician and expressly forbids prognostication.)

Ta Fung Fu, by Chang Hsing Chien, circa 12th century A.D.

Wu Hsing Tao Li Pien, by Tai Yu, circa 6th century A.D. This is in manuscript form.

Ryukuan

Most of the important texts were destroyed in World War II. Manuscripts preserved by my teacher, the Acaryu Fa-Tao Meng included many from China and some native ones. Among these were:

Teso-Jitsu Ongyo (Hidden Forms of Hand Analysis)
Teso Ho (The Laws of Hand Analysis)
Yu Ta Ki (The Record of the Prophets)
Ki-Ju (Precious Jewel)
Himitsu Teso Gaku (Studies in Esoteric Hand Reading)
Juhachirakan Shu-Kyo (Eighteen Hands of the Elders). This is a version of the work by Ta-Mo, *Shi Pa Lo Han Shu Ching*.
Shinden Teso Gaku (Studies in Diagnosis by Hand Form)

Modern Texts

Benham, W. *The Laws of Scientific Hand Reading*. NY: Putnams, 1900.

Cigman, R. *Practical Cheirology*. London: The Cheirological Society, 1983.
    The elements are explained in detail—ideal for beginners.

Figure 101. From an ancient book of Chinese cheirology, describing incidents in the lives of famous masters. Here we see a monk in meditative retreat.

Dukes, T. *No Nonsense Hand Reading*. London: The Cheirological Society, 1978. A good introduction for beginners.

_____. *A Sourcebook of Shingon Buddhism in the Chinese Esoteric Tradition*. London: Hakurenji Temple, 1976.

_____. *Teachings of Shingon Buddhism*. London: British Shingon Buddhist Association, 1981.

Jacquin, N. *The Theory of Metaphysical Influence*. London: The Cheirological Society, l978. All works by Jaquin are significant as preparatory studies.

Journal of the Cheirological Society. Research articles published for members of the Society each quarter since 1899. Back issues upon specific themes generally available.

Wolffe, C. *The Hand in Psychological Diagnosis*. Delhi: Sagar, 1972.

_____. *The Human Hand*. NY: Methuen, 1949. Recommended—good bibliography.

_____. *Studies in Hand Reading*. London: Chatto & Windus, 1936.

NOTABLE PERSONAGES AND PRACTITIONERS OF CHINESE PHYSIOGNOMY, CHEIROLOGY AND RELATED ARTS

The dates listed here are approximate. The abbreviations stand for Buddhist Monk (B) and Preserver of Texts (P).

B.C.	1200	Wen (Legendary)
	400	Wang Tzu, also known as *Kuei Ku*
	240	Tang Chu
	206	Hsu Fu
A.D.	200	Chu Lu-Yen
	300	Sh'e Kung (B)
		Fo T'u Ch'eng (B)
		Kuan Lo
	400	T'an Wu Ch'an
		Tan Yao
	500	Ta Mo (B) (P)
	600	Lu Tung Pin
		Ati Gupta (B) (P)
		Punyo Daya (B) (P)
		Kuo Lin Tsung (B)

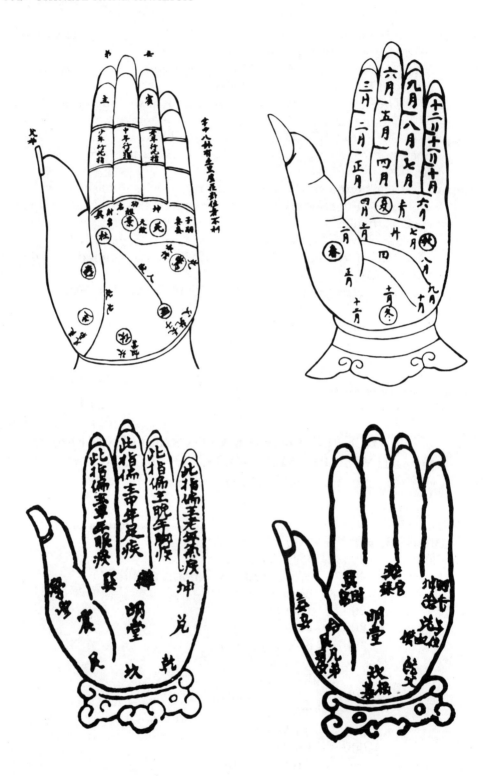

Figure 102. Ancient palm outlines from Taoist works.

700   Fu Kung Ching Kang (B) (P)
        Ching Kang Chih (B) (P)
        I-Hsing (B) (P)
        Li Fu Kuo (B)
        Lu Hsien Chung (B) (P)
900   Wen Ts'an
1000   Sung Ch'i Chin
        Chan Tuan
1100   Chang Hsing Chien
1300   Chang Chung Yuan
1400   Yuan Chung Ch'e
        Yuan Liu Chang
1500   Ni Yueh
1600   Ching Kang Li (B) (P)
1700   Ch'eng Meng Lei (P)
        Shao Lien Tzu (B)
1800   Kao Wei Ching
        Liang Seng Po (B) (P)
        Li Weng Tien (P)
        Hsu K'o
        Li T'iao Yuan (P)

WU HSING SHI: NINE PARAGRAPHS
ABOUT THE ELEMENTS

This is translated from a Chinese Buddhist training manual of the Chen Yen sect.

1. The esoterical appreciation of the human body is profound in its implications. By coming to understand its tenets a student may extend his range and awareness into many other forms besides the physical. The principle employed is universal.

2. The symbolic energies represented as the elements should not be conceived of as distinctive. Each is an inter-reflection of the other, containing the seed principle. Thus from any one element can be realized the others; this should not be forgotten.

3. We may come to know the five major elements (Wu Hsing or Wu Tai) in two manners. The first is via unstructured awareness. This means by instinct they are viewed as part of nature's creation. This is the ordinary,

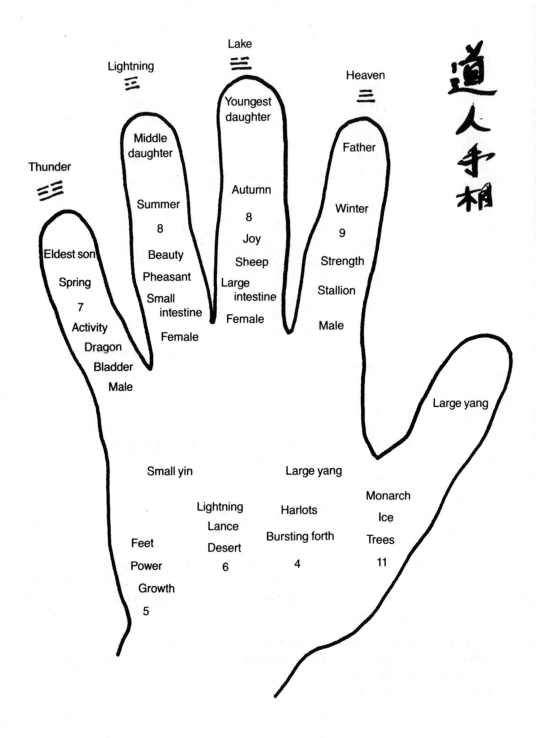

Figure 103. Taoist palmar correspondences.

exoteric viewpoint. The second is via structured understanding. This means as part of esoteric training systems. Of these systems the Chinese forms termed Chen-Yen (Shingon) have no equal.

4. Within Chen Yen the Wu Hsing are viewed as infinite replications of inner and outer life. They represent simultaneously great Wisdom and great Ignorance, forming paradigms of mind, body, speech.

5. The Wu Hsing can be represented in many manners, by color, sound, shape, movement, vowels, seasons, movement and stillness among others. Because of their multiplicity one can come to understand their presence everywhere. Because of their indivisibility one can understand all from one.

6. From the viewpoint of natural phenomena the Wu Hsing enclose earth, water, fire, air and energy/space. From the viewpoint of spiritual evolution, one extra element is introduced: earth, water, fire, air, space, consciousness. This arrangement is termed the *Six Greats*.

7. Each of the Six Greats may be understood at three levels (mind, body, speech) and four manifestations (time, matter, space, energy). All these are ultimately reducible to the one primal phenomenon of emptiness, the synonym of transcendental wisdom.

8. All activities of consciousness dwell within these three gates and four cornerstones of existence. To reach beyond consciousness necessitates passing beyond symbol, line, form and personal identity.

9. The stage attained by the esoteric practitioner is beyond description, not subject to any statement.

WANG CHUNG'S VIEW OF TIME

Wang Chung, a skeptical Chinese philosopher who lived around 25 A.D. distinguished four forms of time, which he described as follows:

時 *Shih* (Time) which indicated that during one's lifespan certain cycles or times occurred of their own accord and within which human activity could be regarded as auspicious.

遭 *Kao* (Dependent Time) In this type of time events occurred in combination, or supported by other events.

幸 *Hsing* (Good Fortune Time) Chance events which created beneficial periods or imports.

偶 *U* (Incidents) during which things occurred bereft of any apparent or purposeful plan.

These classifications are not merely a record of one's experiences or relationship to a particular moment but more an attempt to describe the interrelationship and holistic attitudes Wang Chung saw as essential to understanding the universe.

To Wang Chung, omens, signs and images (Hsiang) (in fact all that one observed) were capable of explanation and codification. His main work, the *Lun Heng*, was printed around 82 A.D. and was probably composed a little earlier. His biography is contained in the *Hou Han Shu* (chapter 79). Wang Chung's viewpoints were fundamentally determinist, and in his classification he sought to summarize and codify existent thought as he saw it. His writings also describe the classes of diviners present in his time. These classifications are:

工 伎 射 事 者 *Kung Chi She Shi Che*: Those who cast charts to find fortunate or unlucky days and hours.

占 射 事 者 *Chan She Shi Che*: The early forms of geomancers. They were also termed Kan-Yu, later Ju-Li, and finally Feng Shui Che.

候 氣 變 者 *Hou Chih Pien Che*: Diviners of the weather and utilized various arts such as oneiromancy, pyromancy, etc.

工 技 之 家 *Kung Chi Chih Pien Che*: These were pure Mantika who visited homes and predicted family events.

伎 道 之 邪 *Chi Tao Chi Chia*: Concerned with various forms of natural, physical magic such as magnets, the elements, techniques using equipment and mirrors, etc.

ENERGY FLOWS AND POINTS ON THE FACE

This illustration is a copy of an ancient Chinese chart showing the effect of correct medical treatment upon a patient. The left picture shows the illness on the seventh day. The right-hand picture shows the patient on the eighth day and after energy diagnosis and treatment (private manuscript, circa 1790 A.D.).

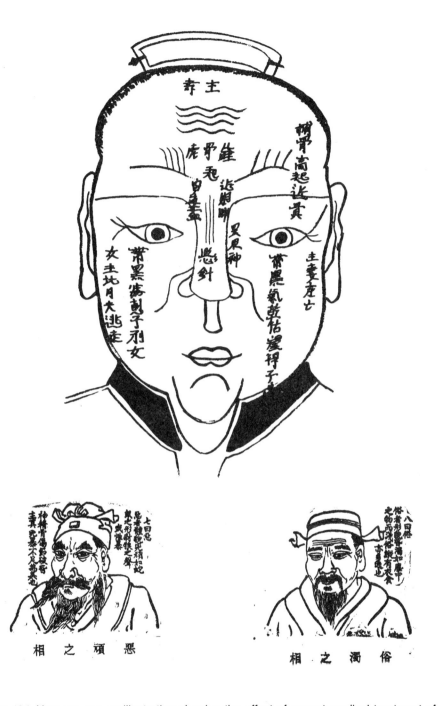

Figure 104. Here we see an illustration showing the effect of correct medical treatment of a patient. The left picture shows the illness on the seventh day. The right hand picture shows the patient on the eighth day and after energy diagnosis and treatment. From a private manuscript in the author's collection, circa 1790 A.D.

CHINESE TRANSSYMBOLISM: I-CHING AND TRIGRAMS

The earliest explicit teachings we find concerning elements are those of the Indian continent, where, earth, water, fire and air formed the object of many philosophies and pantheons. Chinese use of the elements appears rather later and in a modified form. Though many regard these as indigenous to Chinese thought, they form a body of teaching so similar to the ancient Indian that it seems highly likely that they are in fact a direct continuation, with some adjustments, of the classical Indian format. However, China did apparently innovate the concept of regarding these elements from a dual viewpoint based on both chronological change and quality. This taxonomy came to be known as Yin (passive) and Yang (active). A chain of corresponding qualities and paradigms was then attached to them. The classical elements of China used in the I Ching system evidence the earliest element forms. The later more popular Taoist variants are fire, wood, metal, water and earth. The earlier I Ching elements are more in line with the Indian. The ancients represented these elements in a lineal form to make trigrams. By interpreting these trigrams in the original elemental manner we can discover their original form and qualities.

Transposition of Elements into Trigrams and Hexagrams

It is likely that the natural elemental nomenclature preceded this Chinese classification and that the trigrams of the I-Ching developed from simplified portrayals and modifications of the elements themselves. Later knowledge of this source became lost or forgotten. Readers who have an English translation of the I-Ching will notice that the energies mentioned are not those later adapted by Taoist doctors (wood, metal, fire, earth and water). Instead they are lake, mountain, fire, thunder, wind, water, earth and heaven. These can be classified according to their two forms:

I-Ching		Buddhist Cheirology
Heaven	=	Energy
Lake	=	Still water
Water	=	Moving water
Earth	=	Still earth
Mountain	=	Moving earth
Fire	=	Moving fire
Wind	=	Moving air

Note that only the 2 basic elements—water and earth—are presented in dual aspect. These are the most ancient Chinese elements known to us, and, as can be seen, correlate closely with the Vedic and Buddhist groupings used in our Wu Hsing school of teaching.

It is possible to transpose the qualities of the original elements into a lineal structure and make a trigram—as is used in the I-Ching. In fact, transposing the qualities may reveal the original manner in which the I-Ching elements were themselves created. Here are a few examples. Many more can be discovered by personal research:

> *Fire* element is active, male and therefore is represented by a unified, definitive line
>
> *Water* is static, female and receptive
>
> *Air*, being male, is also a unified line
>
> *Earth*, being female, is broken

We can see that each trigram can be interpreted in energy terms as being of 2 possible elements:

▬▬▬▬		Fire		Air
▬▬▬▬	can be	Fire	or	Air
▬▬▬▬		Fire		Air
▬ ▬		Water		Earth
▬ ▬	can be	Water	or	Earth
▬ ▬		Water		Earth

Experience and experimentation will enable you to judge other appropriate combinations. Think of the trigrams as indicative of the three finger phalanges. The paired trigrams of the I-Ching (hexagrams) show inner and outer life structures, as if the phalanges were viewed from the back and frontal views simultaneously. Duplication of an element increases its positive qualities and all paradigms associated with them. Therefore, fire is both physical fire and the "fiery" person—those in authority, for example. Each of the combinations given in the phalange vocation list can be correlated with an I-Ching trigram. I believe that our Wu Hsing phalange format is much older than the Taoist version. Here we see the trigrams Ch'ien and K'un, and their I-Ching and cheirological meanings.

▬▬▬▬	*I-Ching meaning*: Ch'ien = heaven, active, father.
▬▬▬▬	*Element meaning*: Fire, fire, fire = the most power-
▬▬▬▬	ful (fiery) source, the threefold levels of experience.

I-Ching meaning: K'un = earth, responsive, mother.

Element meaning: Water, water, water = the most yielding water penetration of all three levels.

Trigram 1 is like a strong wall or castle barricade. Trigram 2 is like a door open in its center and allowing entry. It seems natural to give these two opposites a quality of utmost power and utmost submission. When Chien and K'un are placed together to form a hexagram, they are given the meaning of T'ai (peace):

The penetration of water above, the power of fire below. If water is placed on fire it quells and subdues it, making it controllable and useful, hence peace. If the hexagram is reversed in order, the meaning becomes P'i (stagnation).

Fire thrown on to water goes out; it makes the water dirty and undrinkable, hence the title. Interpreted phalangically, the hexagram t'ai represents the finger quality of intuition (water) over activity (fire). It is associated in the chart with the psychic qualities. The higher qualities of fire and water do blend in a powerful combination. The cheirological paradigms of fire and water clearly suggest the power of such coincidence being similar in nature to that meaning ascribed it within the I-Ching.

Bear in mind that the two base elements are capable of changing quality. Earth and water both have positions of a physical or mundane significance in addition to their higher, regenerative form. In considering activity or outer life balances, fire is more powerful than water. In considering internal activity, air is more effective than earth.

When we come to consider the balance of elements evidenced on the different finger phalanges, attention should be given to whether the phalange balance is predominately active in the air and fire fingers. Water and earth should be predominantly passive. This is the natural balance. With a little patience and imagination one's phalange balance can be transposed into a personal hexagram quite easily. There is much more than can be done in this manner—but the purpose of this section is merely to introduce the principle of transposition itself. The most interesting discoveries must be made by you, unaided, within your own personal researches.

CHINESE SHAMANISTIC CHEIROLOGY

Four Direct
Signs of fame and prosperity within life. The palm should be vividly colored and shiny. A high position in government establishments.

Learning
There are signs of scholarship and academic success during life. All examinations taken will be easily passed.

Monk Lines
These show a compassionate nature and a love for solitary livelihood. The bearer will become a successful monk in later life.

Sexuality
Lines like these indicate an obsession with sex. The subject will desire women even at the age of ninety.

Celestial Vision
Lines like this reveal that a bride will favor her husband's father. There will be unhappiness in all marriages.

GLOSSARY

C = Chinese; Gk = Greek; J = Japanese; L = Latin; Sk = Sanskrit; OHG = Old High German

Aetiology (Gk): The study of the causes or beginnings of things.

Anthropormorphic (Gk): Taking or assuming a human form or shape.

Buddha (Sk): A title meaning "one who has woken up." Most often used to represent the last historical incarnation of the sage Gautama of the Sakya class. In Chen Yen, the primordial Buddha Vairocana is signified by this title.

Cheirogrammeognomy (Gk): Study of the hand lines and their specific features and qualities.

Cheirogrammeomancy (Gk): Prognostic analysis of lines.

Cheiromorphognomy (Gk): Study of hand shape and features and the interpretation of these.

Cheiromorphomancy (Gk): Prognostic analysis made from deductive and inductive analysis of hand shape.

Cheiromancy (Gk): This is an incorrect palmistic abbreviation for cheirogrammeomancy and cheirogmorphomancy, sometimes used for the sake of simplicity in this book, as the other two are mouthfuls!

Cheirognomy (Gk): Like cheiromancy—an abbreviation for cheiromorphognomy and cheirogrammeognomy.

Chen-Yen (C): Word of reality or truth, known also as Shin Gon (J) and mantra (Sk).

Chi (C): The Chinese term used to describe the intrinsic energy of the body which regulates the physical and mental homeostasis of health. Illness is a condition of unbalanced Chi.

Chih (C): The transcendental knowledge attained by Buddha which completely understands the origins of human suffering. Knowledge developed via systematic education or study.

Deductive: Reasoning from many examples to reach a common source or meaning.

Ego (Gk): The sense of individuality permeating consciousness.

Eki (J): See *I-Ching*.

Energy (Gk): A paradigmatic term used to indicate the emerging cogency within mind, body or speech and through which change or manifestation in quality or pattern occurs unceasingly within the periphery created by time, space, matter and consciousness.

Etymology (Gk): The study of the earliest meanings, inferences or sources of words.

Evolution (L): The experience of creative association with those (karmic) forces conducive to spiritual unfoldment or emancipation.

Fate (L): The experience or occurrence caused by association with karmic forces serving to inhibit spiritual evolution or which explicitly or habitually replicate such inhibitory environments within mind, body or speech.

Feng Shui (C): Fu Sui (J). Literally, "wind and water." All methods of geomancy to determine karmic influences inherent in Lokavidya, environment, topography or country.

Geomancy (Gk): Divination by means of figure or lines or geographic features.

Gnostic (Gk): Wisdom realizable only by direct experience and not amenable to explanation or pronouncement. See also *Mystic*.

Hermeneutics (L): The study of the principle of translation. Originally appropriated by early biblical scholars to represent their translation of scripture into Greek or Latin. Now restored to its rightful position as a subtle blend of aetiology and ontology in linguistic formation.

Heterdox (Gk): Those teachings not accepted by the majority as being representative.

Holistic (Gk): Contain all parts. An attitude towards study which leads to well being and refuses to ignore the paradigms of mind, body or speech occuring within that study.

I-Ching (C): A general term describing all methods of ascertaining karmic flux, or their prior manifestations from or through the human body, mind or speech. Not to be confused with the divinatory book of the same name. See also *Eki, Mantika, Vidya*.

Identity (L): The sense of sameness which permeates mankind's consciousness.

Import (L): The essential meaning or implication of a word, phrase or situation.

Inductive (L): Reasoning from intuition (or genius) to explain external occurrences of phenomena.

Jen Hsiang (C): See *Shu Hsiang*. This form includes analysis of the whole body form. Also known as Nin-So (J), Physiognomy (Gk), Anga Vidya (Sk).

Karma (Sk): A vortex of consciousness, identity and existence habitually maintained and replicated at many levels due to ignorance of its essential causatory patterns and implications and through which is experienced separation from wisdom and compassion.

Li (C): The principle of the universe, contrasted with Chih, which is ordinary knowledge of existence.

Lokavidya (Sk): A world realm, subject to karmic influence of activity.

Macrocosm (Gk): Mankind viewed as a manifestation of the sum of all supramundane phenomena and forces.

Mandala (Gk): The periphery of a dimension of experience when viewed from another dimension of activity. A pictorial representation of this.

Mantika (Gk): The faculty or art of prophecy in general, usually by means of a technique, practice or ritual observance.

Metaphysics (Gk): The study which traditionally succeeds the study of physics. Teachings concerned with phenomena that occur beyond physical manifestation.

Metacosm (Gk): The world which is said to exist when all individual, egocentric or personality based consciousness has been completely transcended and which experiences itself beyond time, space, matter or energy.

Microcosm (Gk): All supramundane phenomena or forces viewed as manifested within mankind.

Mystic (Gk): Teachings understood only after spiritual training or Initiation and which are inaccessible to ordinary consciousness. Gnostic and mystic are not synonomous and can be used conjointly or separately from each other.

Ontology (Gk): The study which deals with the nature or essence of things or of being.

Orthodox (Gk): That which is accepted by the predominant teachers or heads of a doctrine as being representative of their collective opinion.

Paradigm (Gk): A key to phenomena which, by the nature of its manifestation, resembles another phenomena in a different order of existence. Its mode of manifestation—be it discrete or concrete—is thus ascertainable by investigation of its congruency to other mutually cogent key phenomena.

Persona (L): The mask used by ancient Roman actors to hide their faces and to project a different idea of what and who they were. Hence, personality and personal.

Resolve (L): An understanding which satisfactorily harmonizes internal or external problems or dilemmas—ideally, according to the five levels of experience. See also: *Wu Hsing*.

Shu Hsiang (C): A gnostic method of ascertaining influential patterns of karma via the holistic analysis in the structural balance of both hands. Known also as Te So (J) and Hasta Vidya (Sk) and Cheirology (Gk).

Tantric (Sk): Esoteric or integrative Buddhism.

Wu (C): Title given to those who professionally foretell the future.

Wu Hsing (C): Means "no-mindedness"—a Buddhist term indicating the supreme condition beyond suffering, ignorance, hatred and egocentricity. Also means the five elements used in Chinese Buddhist schools. These interpretations were derived from the Indian tradition and are not the same as the indigenous Taoist five elements, which are also called Wu Hsing. The five elements are used in esoteric Buddhism to represent the manifest and esoteric qualities, powers or processes of all things.

Vidya (Sk): See *I-Ching*.

THE WU HSING SCHOOL HISTORY
AND THE CHEIROLOGICAL SOCIETY

The Buddhist form of hand analysis was fortunate in that, being allied with a religious movement, it maintained a close contact with scholars and literati. This allowed its tenets to be preserved and passed from master to pupil. Because the Wu Hsing school included within it techniques of medical and psychological diagnosis, an interest was held by both monk doctors and laypersons alike. The history of Wu Hsing is told only through its spiritual environments; no secular literature exists upon it. From the 12th century A.D. a branch of the Li family came to inherit this tradition and preserve it through a lineage of master teachers. Most of their teachings were orally passed on and notebooks of lectures and other teachings were guarded by the Li clan. By the 15th century A.D., students from the island chain enclosing both Taiwan and Ryukyu (Luchu) began to be enrolled within the school and eventually brought its tradition into their own lands. By this time Li family descendants had migrated from Hopeh in the north to Kwantung and Fukien in the south where a new lineage commenced. One important reason for the migration was the arrival in Kwantung of a master teacher named Ching. He had traveled from Mongolia via western China and Tibet to the south, and founded a monastery of the Chen Yen sect. His form of Chen Yen stressed physical analysis of many types, including hands. From 1600 onwards the Li and Ching teachings intermingled, although the Ching tradition was preeminent.

During the 19th century, several Europeans began to study Buddhism and associated esoteric arts, bringing some of the teachings back to Britain. Several English tea merchants' wives, who were also esoteric students, met and taught Mrs. St. Hill—the Cheirological Society's founder. Although the Oriental teachings were kept away from the public, many devotees seem to have emerged. Many eventually blended into groups such as the emerging Theosophists, the Rosicrucians and the Freemasons, but the Wu Hsing tradition was firmly established (behind the scenes) as a motivating force in hand analysis. In 1958, fresh teachers of the Chen Yen sect, who had studied under the Ching teachers, arrived in Britain and again began to reaffirm the tradition through descendants of the 18th century students.

A branch society of the White Lotus Group was formed, entitled the Mushindokai (Society of Clear Mindedness). This initiated courses and trained students in many esoteric arts including physiognomy and various forms of Buddhist yoga. Students of MKA supported the Cheirological Society throughout this period, perserving it as the branch specifically empowered to study and research hand analysis.

By 1959 a thriving Society had re-established contact with old Cheirological Society members who had survived the second World War and many enrolled with the visiting masters. The first and youngest of these was Shifu T. Dukes, who quickly became one of the leading students. After studying under the then head tutor Henry Barr, he passed every examination possible at that time. However, Shifu then set out to study abroad and continued his researches under Chinese, Japanese, Tibetan and Indian teachers. By the time he returned (to take up a teaching position at Cambridge University), the Society had dwindled and many of its native teachers had died. Still, he carried on cheirology seminars at the university and by 1974 had a good number of student teachers. After a move to London, the Society was restored to its full activity with several tutors teaching classes in various parts of the country and with many representatives around the world. In 1976 Shifu founded the Cheirological Society of Yugoslavia at Zagreb University. Since 1979 he has been involved in creating a Cheirological Research and Seminar Center in Norfolk.

The Cheirological Society presently organizes courses and seminars for both beginners and advanced students in cheirological science, methodology and various research projects. Here the student learns to prepare written reports on a subject's health, emotional quality, vocational aptitude, personal psychology and spiritual propensities. The society was the first of its kind to be founded in Europe and was instituted in 1889 by Katherine St. Hill and Ina Oxenford in conjunction with the publisher Charles Rideal. Although at that time it was concerned with the study and propagation of Western styles of hand analysis, the founders and senior students of the society came to study the oriental form via the Chinese masters Li Wen Tien and Li Tsu Cheng.

The modern day Cheirological Society sets the syllabus for the National Diploma in Cheirology both in the United States and Great Britain. The course of study includes contemporary Western techniques and methods such as those utilzed by Noel Jacquin and Dr. C. Wolffe. The society conducts small, personal classes which usually run 6 to 8 weeks for an introductory course to quarterly terms. Some tutors accept students on a correspondence-course basis.

The society publishes its own journal, which is sent out to members. *Chinese Hand Analysis* is the standard reference work for a comprehensive understanding of cheirology. Information about society publications, and full details of membership, can be obtained by writing to:

> The Secretary
> The Cheirological Society of Great Britain
> 70 Black Lion Lane
> Hammersmith
> London, W4
> England

Please include a stamped, self-addressed envelope.

SEXUAL PALMISTRY

The Intimate Revelations of Hand Analysis

What does the colour of your nails reveal about your sex drive? How can you distinguish an honest suitor from a dishonest one? Will he/she be faithful? Is this THE relationship? Whenever anyone visits a palmist the first questions they are likely to ask are about personal relations – yet until now there has been no book which *solely* explores the extensive ramifications of a sexually orientated reading. **Nathaniel Altman** here corrects that situation. In this easy-to-read but remarkably detailed volume, he exposes – for anyone who can read the signs – the most intimate secrets of our psyche.

- Always choose the right man/woman
- Know if the relationship will be satisfactory – or not!
- Understand the hidden mysteries of your partner's mind

. . . with this, the first book *ever* to integrate scientific hand analysis with contemporary sexual psychology.

THE FEMALE HAND

Hand Analysis For Women

Behind every family there is a woman – peacemaker, advisor, confessor, mentor, confidant, counsellor, guide and friend. A woman has her finger on the very pulse of life, and, from behind the scenes, controls and influences the whole. Strengths and weaknesses, wants and needs . . . all are displayed in the palm of a woman's hand. Written by a woman, for women, **Lori Reid's** unique guide will help *all* women better understand their own characters and highlight unsuspected talents—influence more strongly those who rely upon you, and gain a new inner confidence.

FORTUNE-TELLING BY PALMISTRY

We all instinctively recognize that *facial* lines betray anger or good humour, or that the colour of skin indicates our state of health, yet somehow seem to balk at the idea of *hands* betraying the same kind of information. *But hands are active participants in the game of life whereas our faces are largely passive.* **Rodney Davies** here reveals how YOU can both foretell the future *and* gain an instant advantage in personal relationships/work situations, by learning how to recognize the tell-tale signs of character or hidden desire indelibly etched upon a person's hands. Includes full details of the secrets betrayed by the rings you wear, and the fingers you wear them on.

THE LIVING HAND

A Unique Guide To Modern Hand Analysis

Sasha Fenton and **Malcolm Wright** – both practising palmists with over 45 years of hand-reading experience between them – present a highly original, though thoroughly researched, course on this intriguing art. Includes:

- How to take a print
- Energy rhythms and sibling lines
- The language of gesture
- Giving a reading.

The combination of Malcolm's stunning illustrations and Sasha's ability to express complex ideas in a clear, easy style, make this an ideal book for both beginners and those wishing to update their technique.

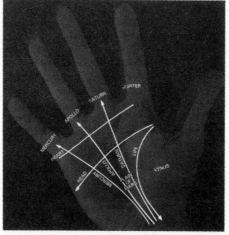

LIFE LINES

The Secrets of your Character Revealed in your Hands

In this introduction to palmistry, **Peter West** shows how to evaluate the calluses and creases that everyday life etches onto our hands. Includes: taking a hand print; evaluating hand, finger and nail shapes; mounts; lines and even gestures – in fact everything you need to know to analyse character and assess individual potential, from the clues nature has written in our hands. *'After reading just a few pages you can literally start analysing your hands and those of your friends – and it is amazingly accurate'* Foresight.

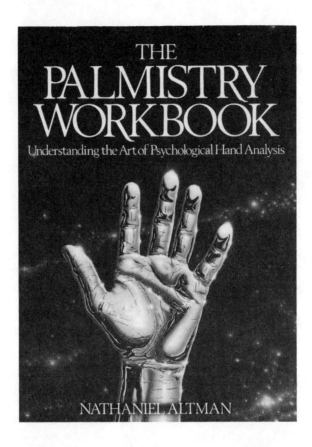

THE PALMISTRY WORKBOOK

Nathaniel Altman. Do you know your TRUE psychological nature? Do you have a tendency towards mental illness? Is your health good and will it remain good? Are you developed to your full potential emotionally, sexually and spiritually? Your hands are more expressive, more specific and can reflect the essence of your life with greater depth and accuracy than any other part of your body.

- Learn the secret language of the hands
- Discover the truth about personal relationships
- Detect potential health problems *before* they become problems
- Gain insight into the characters of those around you

An indispensible guide to psychological hand analysis. The only book you will ever need on the subject.